Second Language Creative Writers

MIX
Paper from
responsib

FSC
www.fsc.org   FSC® C

SECOND LANGUAGE ACQUISITION

Series Editor: **Professor David Singleton**, *University of Pannonia, Hungary* and Fellow Emeritus, *Trinity College, Dublin, Ireland*

This series brings together titles dealing with a variety of aspects of language acquisition and processing in situations where a language or languages other than the native language is involved. Second language is thus interpreted in its broadest possible sense. The volumes included in the series all offer in their different ways, on the one hand, exposition and discussion of empirical findings and, on the other, some degree of theoretical reflection. In this latter connection, no particular theoretical stance is privileged in the series; nor is any relevant perspective – sociolinguistic, psycholinguistic, neurolinguistic, etc. – deemed out of place. The intended readership of the series includes final-year undergraduates working on second language acquisition projects, postgraduate students involved in second language acquisition research, and researchers and teachers in general whose interests include a second language acquisition component.

Full details of all the books in this series and of all our other publications can be found on http://www.multilingual-matters.com, or by writing to Multilingual Matters, St Nicholas House, 31–34 High Street, Bristol BS1 2AW, UK.

SECOND LANGUAGE ACQUISITION: 85

Second Language Creative Writers

Identities and Writing Processes

Yan Zhao

MULTILINGUAL MATTERS
Bristol • Buffalo • Toronto

Library of Congress Cataloging in Publication Data
A catalog record for this book is available from the Library of Congress.
Zhao, Yan (Linguist)
Second Language Creative Writers: Identities and Writing Processes/Yan Zhao.
Second Language Acquisition: 85
Includes bibliographical references and index.
1. Second language acquisition—Study and teaching 2. Academic writing—Study and teaching—Foreign speakers. 3. English language—Rhetoric—Study and teaching—Foreign speakers. 4. Creative writing—Study and teaching—Foreign speakers. I. Title.
P118.2S43 2015
306.44'6–dc23 2014039831

British Library Cataloguing in Publication Data
A catalogue entry for this book is available from the British Library.

ISBN-13: 978-1-78309-300-7 (hbk)
ISBN-13: 978-1-78309-299-4 (pbk)

Multilingual Matters
UK: St Nicholas House, 31–34 High Street, Bristol BS1 2AW, UK.
USA: UTP, 2250 Military Road, Tonawanda, NY 14150, USA.
Canada: UTP, 5201 Dufferin Street, North York, Ontario M3H 5T8, Canada.

Website: www.multilingual-matters.com
Twitter: Multi_Ling_Mat
Facebook: https://www.facebook.com/multilingualmatters
Blog: www.channelviewpublications.wordpress.com

The policy of Multilingual Matters/Channel View Publications is to use papers that are natural, renewable and recyclable products, made from wood grown in sustainable forests. In the manufacturing process of our books, and to further support our policy, preference is given to printers that have FSC and PEFC Chain of Custody certification. The FSC and/or PEFC logos will appear on those books where full certification has been granted to the printer concerned.

Typeset by Deanta Global Publishing Services Limited.
Printed and bound in Great Britain by Short Run Press Ltd.

Contents

Tables and Figures

Tables

Figures

Acknowledgements

I would like to express my sincere gratitude to my supervisors Drs. Ema Ushioda and Richard Smith, both of whom gave me invaluable advice and support throughout the writing of my PhD thesis which this book has derived from. My gratitude is also due to Peter Brown, who has given me great encouragement always. I would also like to thank Professor David Morley, who kindly put me in touch with several participants in the study. I am indebted to all of the 15 Creative Writer participants who shared their writing and narratives with me. Their engagement and enthusiasm went far beyond my expectations. I am also deeply indebted to Professor Tope Omoniyi, Dr Malcolm MacDonald and Professor David Singleton for their support, without which, this book would not have been possible. Of course, I should like to acknowledge the constant encouragement of my parents, to whom this book is dedicated.

1 Introduction

Many canonical writers such as Conrad, Beckett and Rushdie have constructed creative identities and discovered stylistic liberation through writing outside their mother tongue (Pousada, 1994). Conrad rejected his first language (L1) as a medium of artistic expression in favour of English during the heyday of the British Empire (Sherry, 1972). Among a number of contemporary Chinese writers, Ha Jin made the same decision post-Tiananmen Square (Moore, 2002). Such choices raise a variety of socio-political and socio-stylistic issues concerning the relationships between language, creativity, power, repression and identity.

At less rarefied levels, second language creative writing offers a potentially fruitful area of research in the fields of identity studies, second language acquisition (SLA) and pedagogy. The increasing number of non-native English speaking writers who choose to practice or even publish forms of creative writing in English constitute a salient and legitimate social group which is ripe for investigation. Second language (L2) creative writers who 'invest' (Norton, 1995, 2000) in creative writing in English for particular purposes (e.g. linguistic, literary, professional or self-empowerment) are making their voices heard in widespread social settings, such as language classrooms, creative writing courses and interest groups, publishing and, notably, in virtual contemporary media such as social networks. Recently, along with the development of digital technology, we have witnessed the emergence and advancement of creative 'new literacies' (such as multimodal or multimedia story writing, e.g. Skinner & Hagood, 2008) and out-of-school literary practices (e.g. Yi, 2007, 2010).

Creative writing has long been an element in L2 pedagogy. Bate (2008) records that one of the activities in a standard Latin textbook used during Shakespeare's time (Erasmus's *De conscribendis epistolis*) invited learners to write imaginatively in the roles of characters from classical literature in particular situations. The rubric, quoted by Baldwin (1944: 240), goes:

> Write a letter as if you were Antenor persuading Priam that he should return the stolen Helen to her Menelaus because it would be a very foolish ruler who caused many brave men to enter battle on account of the most shameful love of such an effeminate youth as Paris.

Perhaps with tongue in cheek, Bate (2008) exclaims: 'Write that Master William and you're on the road to inventing dramatic character, to composing "Troilus and Cressida"' (93). At less exalted levels, current

ESL/EFL creative writing activities are not radically different. They focus on the opportunities offered for writing improvement, language play and an escape from the pseudo-narratives of the textbook. While fully agreeing that L2 creative writing allows learners to engage with what McRae (1994) has termed imaginative 'representational' expression (i.e. multifaceted, involving both cognitive and emotional faculties) in addition to the more instrumental 'referential' functions (i.e. communicative, informational) of typical ELT classroom activities, I would like to go further. I shall suggest that L2 creative writers can undertake creative writing not only for the purposes of language or literacy acquisition, but also simultaneously for the achievements of certain self-identification and hence self-esteem, which in turn feeds into positive motivation for language learning.

This book is centrally concerned with the relationship between L2 creative writers' socioculturally sedimented perceptions of their previous life histories and their present, emergent psychological activities while writing in the target language. The discussion inevitably involves consideration of the nature of creative writing, why writers are drawn to express themselves imaginatively, where their 'inspiration' comes from and the processes involved in transmuting ideas into creative expression. Whilst acknowledging that the ultimate wellsprings of creativity might not be available for analysis, this book rejects the typically romantic notion that L2 creative writers and L2 creative writing practices are primarily controlled by inspiration and emotion. Through interviews and think-aloud story writing sessions, the central inquiry investigates how *writer voices* reflected in the L2 creative writers' instantaneous movements of thoughts while creating short stories are mediated by the writers' *autobiographical identities* (Clark & Ivanič, 1997), namely, their sense of selves formulated in their previous language learning and literacy experiences. In what immediately follows, I shall review the current research on L2 creative writing.

Research on L2 Creative Writing

L2 creative writers have attracted attention among a variety of academic fields, including sociolinguistic identity studies, SLA discussions and, recently, literature on academic discourses.

In the field of identity studies, Omoniyi (2010) has studied postcolonial writers' 'code choices' (including his own) and their relation to writers' negotiations of cultural and linguistic identities. Similarly, through looking at the interactions between writer identity and certain aspects of the creative literacy products (discoursal, semantic, syntactic or thematic), poststructuralist L2 scholars such as Pavlenko (2006) have examined the discursive construction of emotions among bilingual writers and questioned whether the L1 always remains 'the voice of the heart' (also see Pavlenko & Lantolf, 2000; Pavlenko, 2004; Ros i Solé, 2004). Adopting a sociocultural perspective, the principal focus of such writer identity studies examines how creative writing practices serve as an empowering tool through which L2 speakers may actively construct and perform their social or ethnic identities, negotiate authorial stance, improve cultural understandings and develop their social participation and presence (e.g. Vasudevan *et al.*, 2010; Skinner & Hagood, 2008; Burkhalter & Pisciotta, 1999; Yi, 2007, 2010; Maguire & Graves, 2001). In addition, given creative writing's capacity to capture affective dimensions and draw on the L2 learners' sociocultural heritage and personal knowledge, poetry and autobiographical writing have been utilised to gain an insight into L2 individuals' personal and emotional responses to dramatic incidents or to their lived experiences (e.g. Hanauer, 2010; Chamcharatsri, 2009). In the above studies, 'writers' voices' are principally traced through examining the L2 writers' creative literacy products. In addition, although such L2 creative writing studies scrutinise the mediational values of creative writing for identity construction, they are influenced by a sociohistorical perspective. They show a strong predilection for studying conspicuous bilingual/multilingual writer groups, such as postcolonial writers (e.g. Omoniyi, 2010) or immigrants living in an English-speaking context (e.g. Maguire & Graves, 2001; Skinner & Hagood, 2008; Yi, 2007, 2010; Vasudevan *et al.*, 2010).

Secondly, led by the work of Alan Maley, ESL/EFL pedagogy has shown a growing interest in the use of creative writing activities (e.g. see *Teaching English – British Council & BBC*, 2013). Such activities, it is argued, encourage learners to engage playfully with the target language and develop a writerly identity in the new code (e.g. Maley & Duff, 1994, 2005; Duff & Maley, 2007; Maley & Moulding, 1985; Maley, 2009; for computer-based EFL creative writing projects also see Ensslin, 2006; Tsou *et al.*, 2006). Similarly, Cook (2000) has vigorously pointed out the value of language play and the authenticity of creative fictional discourse in language learning (also see Elgar, 2002; and Belz, 2002). Indeed, EFL/ESL teachers themselves have sought to enhance their creative practice through poetry and short story writing workshops (Maley & Mukundan, 2011a, 2011b; Mukundan, 2006; Tin, 2004, 2007). The initiatives suggested in current L2 creative writing literature reflect a distinct pedagogical interest and, understandably, tend only to scratch the surface of some significant writer identity issues. Most noticeably, although it is recognised that creative writing is executed through an intricate orchestration of choices and actions, its well-springs are most often located in rhapsodies of capricious creation processes, especially when compared with the ratiocination of argumentative or persuasive writing composition (see Duff & Maley, 2007; Maley & Duff, 2005; Maley, 2012; Tin, 2012). This assumption will be interrogated in what follows in this book.

Finally, it is worth noting here that some L2 writing research has included persuasive rationales for the connection of creative writing to the development of writing for academic purposes. For example, Tickoo (2001) has demonstrated that the 'attention-getting power' of his ESL students' expository writing could be noticeably reinforced by equipping them with the 'narrative art' of developing the crisis of a story. Similarly, at the University of Warwick, Professor David Morley, director of the Warwick Writing Programme, has suggested that 'all writing is creative writing' and introduced 'creative writing across the curriculum' (Morley, 2007: 244). The initiative is 'predicated on the need to help new scientists and businesspeople write more clearly and engagingly' (Morley, 2007: 243). It takes the form of interdisciplinary creative writing projects in which creative writing tutors and students work with students from a variety of non-English departments, including medicine, business, biology, computing, engineering and physics.

The projects have been well received across the disciplines and have even successfully convinced some tutors to incorporate creative writing elements into their assessed coursework (Nesi & Gardner, 2005; Morley, 2007, 2012). For example, in one Sociology module the tutor provided the students with the option of producing 'a piece of crime fiction' to illustrate particular sociological theories (Nesi & Gardner, 2005: 110). Likewise, in a current law module, students are asked to construct a fictional court scene not only to demonstrate their interpretation and practical use of certain law models, but also to encourage their empathetic understanding of the complex social and emotional points of view involved (Morley, 2007: 244). Finally, some science students have been invited to engage in 'creative nonfiction' (Morley, 2007: 242–243; 2012) or 'empathy writing' (Nesi & Gardner, 2005: 110). The rationale is that if students have thoroughly grasped and engaged with their subject, they should be able to explain even rather abstruse science theories to the general public, such as 'school children, friends, museums, or newspapers' (Nesi & Gardner, 2005: 110), with interesting and lucid storytelling.

The above review shows that the motivational and mediational values of creative writing for language learning, for identity construction, for emotion-expressing and for academic literacy have been empirically investigated, and that L2 writers' creative literacy products and their sociocultural presence have been examined. Such work has focused on the creative product of the writers; what this discussion hopes to add to the debate is a consideration of the processes involved in L2 creative writing. The essence of creativity may be essentially enigmatic, but its processes are open to investigation. Therefore, this inquiry adopts the position that L2 writers' implementation of specific forms, language or content represents identifiable choices. It is argued that L2 creative writing research might delve beneath the linguistic or writing innovations manifested in the *texts* of the language learners and look into the L2 writers' self-representational actions, especially as revealed in the movements of the writers' emerging *thoughts* in the writing process. This insight could benefit language teachers and writing instructors in understanding how learners distinctively readjust their self-identity through performing creative writing activities – e.g. integrating new perceptions of the self as an imaginative writer or as a perceptive or empowered commentator – which, in specific ways, develop individual thinking, authorial stance and artistic engagement with the language. This is a process of identity formation which enhances self-esteem, a positive characteristic of the motivated language learner, as shown by Rubio (2007).

To sum up, research on L2 creative writing practices has not sufficiently investigated the following three issues: (a) the nature of L2 creative writers' cognitive writing processes and accordingly the performance of identities as reflected in the writers' mental activities; (b) how L2 creative writing practices intersect with the L2 individuals' identity negotiations and how such literacy practices mediate the writers' social relationships with the world; and ultimately (c) how a more in-depth understanding of the above dialectic (in point b) could inform L2 and writing teachers' execution of creative writing activities.

Focusing on the notion of *identities*, the central enquiry in this book: (1) elicits 15 L2 creative writers' own perceptions of their life histories through the form of interviews and (2) investigates the writers' emerging writing processes under particular short-story writing tasks through think-aloud protocols. The 15 L2 writer participants are all advanced adult English L2 speakers who were undertaking either undergraduate or postgraduate studies at a UK university (except for one). In the next section, the distinctive perspectives of this L2 creative writing inquiry are further clarified.

New Perspectives on Tracing L2 Creative Writer Identity

It is widely believed that creative expression, identity and language are intrinsically bound together. The key question to be asked here is the one posed by Pavlenko (2005): is the first language always the language of the heart? Driven by this question, the inquiry seeks to understand L2 creative writers' own needs and self-perceptions from the perspectives of their (1) reflective 'autobiographical identities' and their (2) performative 'writers' voices'.

I am in fundamental agreement with the position that the manner in which L2 writers idiosyncratically engage in a present creative writing activity is importantly mediated by the writers' own understanding of their particular life histories – in other words, their autobiographical identities (also referred to as self-identities in this book). However, it can be argued that this mediation has not been adequately investigated in the current ESL/EFL literature. When reading through the L2 pedagogical discussions on various creative writing activities (reviewed earlier), I cannot help asking to what extent the teacher–researchers' perceptions match the L2 creative writers' actual instantiations of personal knowledge and language use in the process of creative writing. That is, based on the tangible evidence of the L2 writers' cognitive actions, do L2 creative writing tasks indeed motivate the writers to make meaningful self-declarations and demonstrate inventiveness in the aspects of language, discourse or ideas? If the answer is 'yes', how do different types of creative writing tasks or stimuli facilitate the liberating possibilities attributed to this genre in characteristic ways? In what immediately follows, I will introduce the first innovative angle of this inquiry, namely an emphasis on the significance of L2 writers' own interpretations of their socioculturally shaped motives behind why and how they engage in specific types of creative literacy activities.

L2 creative writers' sociocultural life histories

As previously indicated, current discussions of L2 creative writing activities tend to be projected from researchers' analyses of particular features of student texts and their interpretations of the student writers' retrospective comments (e.g. Creme & Hunt, 2002; Severino *et al.*, 2010; Jacobs, 2008; Maley, 2009; Chamcharatsri, 2009; Hanauer, 2010). In such discussions, the L2 students were often portrayed as relatively new to L2 creative writing practices, willingly following the activity procedures set up by the teacher. Consequently, it is frequently claimed that creative writing activities provide an instrument which enables the L2 learners to experience a sense of empowerment in their L2 linguistic and literary identity. However, I would argue that L2 creative literary activities, especially the various forms of story-telling, are not uncommon among L2 learners outside the classroom. As mentioned at the beginning of this chapter, L2 creative writers are making their voices heard in various social settings outside educational contexts, such as creative writing interest groups, and, increasingly, in the virtual worlds of social networks (one example is 'Fandom' which has contributed to the growth of various online fanfiction communities) and blogs. In other words, our student writers in the classroom might already possess a concept of themselves as creative writers based on prior experience – at the very least some self-perception as creative writers in their L1 if not so palpably in their L2.

As stated earlier, the inquiry does not merely situate its participants as L2 learners/writers who have been initiated into L2 creative writing activities for language or literacy acquisition purposes; crucially, it also sees them as social agents who engage in creative writing to negotiate particular identities and achieve certain social positioning. In addition, this creative writing inquiry does not target mainly immigrant or published L2 creative writers, but representatives of a wider group of non-native English speakers, i.e. advanced language learners.

Two sociocultural theoretical frameworks have essentially facilitated this inquiry's consideration of the L2 creative writers' life histories, namely, the 'Community of Practice' (CoP) theory (Lave & Wenger, 1991; Wenger, 1998) and the poststructuralist perspective (e.g. Bourdieu, 1991; Norton, 1995, 2000; Pavlenko & Lantolf, 2000). In Chapter 2, I will discuss the social constructionist acuity of the CoP theory in explaining the effect of L2 creative writers' social localities, in particular, the constructing role of prototypical social relations and community conventions; meanwhile, Chapter 2 also looks at how poststructuralism serves to illustrate the significant role played by agency and intentionality in creative writing practices. Consequently, Chapter 2 explains the conceptualisation of the 'discursive construction of identities', a mix of the two sociocultural theories above. This theoretical approach is adopted for unravelling the individuals' social constructive powers reflected through their discursive accounts of life histories, i.e. focusing on the mediating role of language in the speakers' agentive interpretation and presentation of their experiences.

Below, I will move onto introducing the second innovative angle, i.e. tracing 'writers' voices' in their cognitive writing processes.

'Writer voice' residing in the cognitive writing process

Previous studies on L2 creative writing practice have managed to tease out 'writer voice' from the writers' sociohistorical or sociopolitical upbringing, and/or from the texts that have been produced (discussed in more detail in Chapter 2). So far, I have not found any writer identity study (on any type of L2 writing) which looks at manifestations of *voices* in the writers' emergent cognitive writing processes. The cognitivist process-oriented L2 writing studies (later discussed in Chapter 2) tend to normalise patterns of writing strategies with the ultimate aim of promoting teachers' understanding and consequent modelling of the expert writing strategies in L2 writing classrooms. In contrast, this inquiry aims to show that L2 creative writers' cognitive writing activities are *idiosyncratic* performances of the writers' voices rather than *normative* indications of the writers' language proficiency or writing expertise. Consequently, I hope to demonstrate that examining the L2 writers' cognitive writing activities does not automatically turn L2 writing research into a mentalistic study which perceives writing as a series of cognitive routines, oblivious to the notion of writing as a social act. This inquiry explores how L2 creative writers' cognitive writing processes, e.g. their engagements in specific language play, adoptions of particular discourses, ideologies or writing procedures in their story creation processes, are simultaneously the writers' emerging self-representational acts (also referred to as writers' 'emergent identities' or 'voices' later in this book).

Before outlining the pedagogical reasons for considering this notion of task-situated writer voice, it is worth commenting here that I can detect two predominant types of creative writing task rubric for creative writing activities in ESL/EFL contexts. First of all, there are relatively unrestricted and often autobiographical writing projects which aim to induce spontaneity and confidence in the writers to produce expressive, personal work (e.g. Chamcharatsri, 2009; Hanauer, 2010; Creme & Hunt, 2002; Tarnopolsky, 2005). Next, there are creative writing tasks which embrace some evident constraints for the purpose of pushing the L2 writers out of their comfort zone and eliciting the learners' nonconformist use of language and form, compared to their staple writing practices (e.g. Elgar, 2002; Maley, 2012; Tin, 2011, 2012). The question worth asking here is if L2 teachers' implementation of either of the above two approaches (relatively free or constrained creative writing tasks) in the whole class could accommodate everyone's need for particular self-identities to be performed in L2 creative writing, especially when each student brings his/her own unique writing history.

Hence, this inquiry examines the L2 writers' simultaneous thoughts while creating short stories under the above two types of task rubric. It hopes to show that L2 creative writing pedagogy might be enhanced if it were predicated not only on the conviction that L2 creative writing activities stimulate L2 learners/writers to make authentic meanings or claim an authorship of the language (see Creative Writing, n.d.). Indeed, it should also be predicated on the considerations of how the processes in which the L2 learners/writers make such linguistic, discoursal and ideological choices and expressions of emotions signal the development of their identity negotiations. By doing so, L2 teacher researchers could better hear and appreciate their students' 'voices' expressed in a creative writing activity so as to create and support the writing contexts which are likely to foster the students' meaningful L2 practices.

To sum up, 'writer voice' is not simply a product, a static mark left in written texts for linguists, literature scholars, historians or, indeed, teachers to scrutinise; rather, 'writer voice' could permeate everything involved in creating a piece of work, an important part of which is the movements of the writers' thoughts, their discursive knowledge and strategies (Matsuda, 2001). Such writers' 'voices' reflected in the L2 creative writers' cognitive writing processes are the improvisational enactments of the writers' perceptions of their own identities rooted in their previous sociocultural experiences. In addition, such writers' voices also serve particular intentions in the writers' constant reformulations of their identities in their on-going life histories.

The two above-mentioned perspectives foreground the overall theoretical framework of this inquiry, which attempts to integrate the issues of 'writer' and 'writing' into one, thus embodying a combination of sociocultural writer identity studies and cognitivist process-oriented L2 writing research. I believe the integration of these two fields of L2 studies to be a key contribution of this study of L2 creative writers and writing.

In the following section, I will briefly introduce the research project which informs the discussion and outline the methodological approach (detailed discussions in Chapter 3).

The Inquiry

The project, undertaken at a UK university, is an interview and think-aloud protocol-based case study of 15 L2 creative writers, 7 males and 8 females, who speak English as their second language. They are all motivated and experienced adult L2 creative writers. The data collection procedures consist primarily of one semi-structured interview exploring the L2 creative writers' sociocultural life histories and two think-aloud story writing sessions, all conducted on an individual basis. The inquiry procedures, which will be elaborated upon in Chapter 3, are presented in Table 1.1 below.

Table 1.1 Procedures of the inquiry

Task procedures	The purpose	Collection of the data
1. A semi-structured, face-to-face, in-depth interview eliciting each participant's sociocultural life history (lasting one to two hours; a basic question list for the in-depth interview is displayed in Appendix A).	Investigating the L2 creative writers' *autobiographical identities* as reflected in their retrospective accounts of their writing, language, educational, professional and reading experiences.	The interviews were audio-taped and transcribed verbatim.
2. Two think-aloud story writing sessions which were conducted separately: (1) An Autobiographical writing task (400 words min.) (2) A Story-continuation writing task (400 words min.) In each session, the writer composed on the computer provided, in my presence and within a one-hour time constraint.	Exploring the L2 creative writers' construc-tions of their *writer' voices* in the individuals' cognitive story writing processes under differ-ent types of tasks.	The think-aloud speeches were audio-taped and transcribed verbatim. In addition, a keystroke-logging tool (Inputlog) was used throughout each participant's think-aloud writing process. The gen-erated keystroke logging files assist the transcrib-ing of the audio-taped think-aloud verbalisation.

Analytical frameworks

A combination of comprehensive and trend-seeking quantitative coding with selective, highly descriptive and focused qualitative interpretations of tangible utterances is employed to investigate the participants' creative writing practices. The analytical frameworks of the inquiry, which will also be discussed in Chapter 3, are introduced in Table 1.2 below.

Organisation of the Book

Chapter 2 explains and justifies the particular socioculturalist approaches adopted in this inquiry to examine the identities of L2 creative writers from a variety of sociocultural backgrounds. Chapter 2 mainly consists of four sections which concentrate respectively on (1) a critical review of recent research directions on the relationship between L1 and L2 writing (and language use in general); (2) the sociocultural movements in L2 writing

Table 1.2 The analytical frameworks

Autobiographical identities		Sociocultural approach	Writers' voices	
Investigated through in-depth interviews			Investigated through think-aloud story writing sessions	
Theoretical basis: CoP and poststructuralist theories, and discursive construction of identity (see Chapter 2)			Theoretical basis: sociocognitive interpretation – writers' voices as embedded in their cognitive writing processes (Chapter 2)	
Quantitative analysis of the 15 participants' *autobiographical identities* (Chapter 4)	Qualitative descriptions of the five focal participants' perceived L2 speaker and creative writer identities formulated against particular social milieus (Chapter 6)		Quantitative analysis of the 15 participants' cognitive writing processes (Chapters 4 and 5)	Qualitative discussions on the sociocultural personalities of the five focal writers' cognitive writing behaviours (Chapter 7)
↑	↑		↑	↑
I-statement analysis	Textual and discursive examinations of particular interview comments		Think-aloud protocol coding	Intertextuality and interdiscursivity as evidenced in tangible think-aloud verbalisations

and L2 identity studies, with special attention given to the CoP theory and poststructuralist theory's different approaches to the agency–structure debate; (3) the discursive construction of identities which unravels the participants' reflexive constitution of their autobiographical identities; and finally (4) current conceptualisations in literature for scrutinising writers' voices.

Chapter 3 provides a meticulous explanation of the methodology of the inquiry, venturing forth the rationale for and limitations of the methods employed. This inquiry adopts a sociocognitive perspective on writer identity research. The overarching methodological principle asserts that L2 creative writers' literacy practices and identity issues can be systematically investigated by the innovative qualitative and quantitative instruments used in this inquiry. More specifically, Chapter 3 illustrates the specific ontological and epistemological stances embodied in the methodology. The ontological stance of this inquiry is a relational, sociocultural view of 'identities'. Meanwhile, the epistemological stance is a sociolinguistic approach as well as a 'Sociocultural Psycholinguistics' (Roebuck, 2000: 80) approach to identity constructions.

The next two chapters deal with the quantitative examination of the 15 participants.

Chapter 4 illustrates how the *autobiographical identities* textured by the L2 creative writers through I-statements in their self-recounts of life histories are related to the writers' *emergent identities* (also referred to as 'writer voices') which are enacted through their characteristic writing behaviours when writing on the spot under particular story writing tasks in English. To be more specific, four strands of writer voices are identified based on the coding results of the 15 participants' think-aloud protocols. When these four strands of writers' I-statement coding results are compared with each other, a pattern starts to emerge.

Chapter 5 displays how the switch of story writing task type from the Autobiographical writing task to the Story-continuation task influences the L2 creative writers' cognitive writing processes. Firstly, this chapter shows how the two different story writing tasks exert some universal influences on the L2 creative writers' cognitive writing processes. Then, it discusses how the L2 creative writers, who have constructed different autobiographical identities, react in characteristic ways to the two story writing tasks.

Chapters 6 and 7 move on to the qualitative examinations of the five selected L2 creative writers. They display how identities are manifested through varied, idiosyncratic forms, through concentrating on the sociohistorical particularities of the L2 creative writers' autobiographical identities and their actually value-laden psychological activities in the story writing processes. In particular, these two chapters postulate that what underlies the seemingly common-sense or personalistic categories of improvisational vs. methodical writers, imaginative vs. expressive writers, fantastical vs. journalistic writers or orthodox vs. experimental writers are not isolated products of expertise or knowledge, emotion or subjectivity. Rather, an active consideration of the ideological and dialogic meaning of the person's creative writing engagement is needed. For example, based on the results of We- and You-statement analysis, Chapter 6 shows how the five selected individuals position themselves in specific creative-writing-related social milieus. It also portrays the five writers' general creative writing and English language learning histories. It illustrates how we can examine the ways in which the writers reproduce the social identities of 'L2/L3 learner/ speaker' and 'creative writer' through personalising them with their own primary concerns and needs in specific social circumstances.

Chapter 8 is the conclusion of this book. In light of the findings, this chapter discusses how the inquiry might offer some contribution to two fields of L2 studies, i.e. L2 creative writing research and L2 writer identity research. Chapter 8 then reflects on this inquiry's identity-centred relational methodology and the research's limitations. Finally, this monograph ventures forth a future direction reinforced by the findings of this inquiry for another genre of L2 writing: creative pedagogical approaches to L2 disciplinary writing. Relevant literature shall be referred to; in addition, an example from my own ESL classroom in the UK will be tentatively offered.

2 Towards a Cross-Sociocultural Analysis of Creative Writer Identities

This chapter explains and justifies the particular socioculturalist approaches adopted in this inquiry to examine the identities of L2 creative writers from a variety of sociocultural backgrounds. The review aims to reach beyond conceptual debates confined to L2 writer identity studies and to encompass philosophies in L2 identity research overall.

Firstly, I will look at recent research directions on the relationship between L1 and L2 writing (or more broadly, L1 and L2 language use). Then, I will briefly examine the ideological shifts that have taken place in L2 writing and identity research which have led both fields towards an era of 'social turn' (Matsuda, 2003). Notably, part of this study investigates the L2 creative writers' interpretation, at a particular moment, of their previous literacy experience and sociocultural roots. The investigative purpose is to understand the 'whys' and 'hows', through the eyes of the participants, behind this rising social phenomenon where people voluntarily engage in forms of L2 creative writing for certain self-empowering causes. I will particularly discuss the implications for studying L2 creative writer identities offered by two established sociocultural theories: the 'Community of Practice' (CoP) theory (Lave & Wenger, 1991; Wenger, 1998) and the poststructuralist perspective (e.g. Bourdieu, 1991; Norton, 1995, 2000; Pavlenko & Lantolf, 2000). To be more specific, I will discuss the conceptual acuity of the CoP theory in explaining the effect of L2 creative writers' own understanding of their social localities, and how poststructuralism's power-centred view serves to illustrate the significant role played by agency and intentionality in writing practices and hence the writers' self-positioning in the world. Consequently, I will discuss the agency–structure debate as suggested by the concepts of 'community' and 'habitus'.

Drawing from the above theoretical models, I will then go on to describe the conceptualisations employed for investigating the two aspects of creative writer identities focused on in this inquiry, i.e. L2 creative writers' retrospective 'autobiographical selves' and their emergent 'writer voices'. I hope to explain how looking into the writers' discursive constructions of 'autobiographical selves' allows us to focus on the reflexive constitution of identity construction and to some extent reconcile the continuing debate concerning the relationships between *structure* and *agency* in identity formation – how the two relate sequentially or which regulates which. I shall go on to address the issue of 'writer voice', which has attracted significant attention in L2 pedagogies. I will comment on two general dichotomies that I have observed in the exploration of writer voices in recent studies and discuss how they have informed the present analysis.

Comparative Studies on L1 and L2 Writing

Comparative studies on L1 and L2 writing investigate the differences between L1 and L2 textual features and/or L1 and L2 composing behaviours or, on a more aesthetic or sociopolitical level, between L1 and L2 writer identities. L2 (creative) writers' emotion, experience and cognition in particular social milieu all influence the individuals' literary practices and their identity formation. In other words, literacy and identity are inseparable, each constituting the other (Pavlenko, 2008; Cox *et al.*, 2010). From what I observed in the L1–L2 comparative writing research, literacy or writing tends to be treated as a normative undertaking in an academic or professional context; and identities are often suggested as heavily relating to formative values, such as language proficiency, writing expertise, educational level, L1 rhetoric conventions or length of residence in the target country. On the other hand, people might instinctively say that individual identities cannot be carved out of stereotypical moulds. This enigma is illustrated in my following review of L1 and L2 writing studies.

Comparative studies on L1 and L2 writing have investigated the following major themes: (1) how L2 writers' texts are different from their L1 counterparts in a particular discourse community; (2) regarding bilingual writers, how the L1 and L2 are related to the writers' disparate evocation of emotion and cognitive mechanism; and finally (3) how L2 writers' text needs to conform to certain values endorsed by a specific L2 institution and how the writers accordingly balance their L1 and L2 rhetorical values in view of their identity construction. The above themes will be discussed in some detail below.

L2 texts and their counterparts produced by L1 writers

Native and non-native speakers have been meticulously compared for their dissimilar patterns in language processing or formulation concerning a range of discourses (see the established and evolving field of studies of Contrastive Rhetoric, for example, Belcher, 2014; Connor *et al.*, 2008; Kubota & Lehner, 2004). To name a few, there are: the 'subjectivity markers' produced in narrative and argumentative discourses in L1 French, L2 French and L1 English (Wolf, 2006); the different ways Greeks and Americans conduct spoken and written narratives in their respective L1 (Tannen, 1984);

L2 German speakers' sentence processing preferences for decoding particular morphosyntactic features, as compared to the native speakers' (Jackson & Dussias, 2009); or rhetorical differences in research articles written by English L1, L2 and Spanish L1 scholars (Sheldon, 2011). Such linguistic differences are perceived as holding pedagogical values in terms of providing informed suggestions to teachers on reducing the effect of L1 transfer in their students' L2 production.

This is especially the case when we compare features of the academic texts written by an ESL student group from a particular culture with those of an L1 counterpart writer group (e.g. Grant & Ginther, 2000; Hinkel, 2002; Kang, 2005; Okamura & Shaw, 2000). Compared side by side with English-native-speaker students' writing, ESL students' texts are often portrayed as possessing a less authorial or sharp 'voice' (the conceptualisation behind 'voice' will be discussed later), viewed by the researchers as owing to the students' lack of English proficiency, sociocultural ideology and knowledge of specific discourse conventions in a Western academic world. The underlying message is that conformity with standard discoursal features espoused in the target-language context is a paramount mission of the L2 students concerned.

In my opinion, this alleged feebler 'voice' in ESL writers' texts partly derives from a deterministic approach towards analysing features in discourses (in contrast, see Ouellette, 2008; Schultz, 2006). Such an approach may analyse ESL writers' discursive repertoire in establishing authorial and disciplinarily appropriate voices, and sometimes go even further to correlate the projection of voice with the 'perceived quality of writing' (Stapleton, 2002: 186). It overlooks the circumstance that even behind the seemingly 'voiceless' or 'odd' words there still exist crucial ideological struggles which are related to ESL individual writers' unique life histories and agentive evaluations of their experience *vis-à-vis* the present writing (Ivanič & Camps, 2001; Prior, 2001).

Western discourse conventions still dominate academic speeches and writing in English (despite the language's lingua franca status), given the educational supremacy exhibited by certain Anglophone countries that speak English as a native language. However, are normative language patterns prevalent in creative writing in English, a genre which most likely expresses personal style, one's sociopolitical origin and creative freedom? Is an L2 flavour or taste welcomed or frowned upon, especially when the question of who owns English for legitimate self-expression is highly contested today.

Bilingual writers

With bilingual (including multilingual) speakers outnumbering monolingual speakers in the world's population today, the phenomenon of bilingualism has proved worthy of elaborate linguistic and psychological examination. A primary investigative focus is how cross-linguistic differences – on semantic, rhetorical and literary levels – are related to bilingual speakers' disparate evocations of emotion or cognitive mechanism (Pavlenko, 2006, 2008, 2011; Cenoz *et al.*, 2003; de Guerrero, 2005; Sommer, 2003; Fussell, 2002). For example, Ayçiçeği and Harris (2004), through their study on adult Turkish speakers studying or working in Boston, identified that emotion played a stronger positive role in the bilinguals' recall and recognition of emotionally charged words in their L2 (English) than in their L1. In a similar vein, Clachar (1999) asked Puerto Rican undergraduate students to write on an emotional and a non-emotional topic respectively in English. Her analysis of the think-aloud protocols documenting the students' writing processes, along with their study of the written texts, seems to show that an emotional topic leads to more focus on 'lexical appropriateness and morphosyntactic correctness in L2 written discourse during planning and composing' (56).

The other investigative focus is how the L1 and L2 (or L3) are differently *perceived* by bilingual individuals themselves in terms of the distinct persona enacted by each language. In relation to this, cross-linguistic differences can be tactically deployed by agentive bilinguals to strike up advantageous images of themselves in goal-oriented social interactions and practices. The bilinguals' insightful perceptions of the interrelation between language and emotion enable them to strategically make 'emotional investment' (Pavlenko, 2006: 43) on social levels.

Nonetheless, bi-directional cross-linguistic transfers in bilingual speakers should be expected; otherwise, clear-cut L1–L2 differences would have endowed bilinguals with schizophrenic symptoms. L2 creative writers might not establish a completely different 'self' in their L2 work from the one enacted by the writers' L1 writing. Pavlenko (2008) emphasises that discussions on cross-linguistic differences need to be contextualised within bilingual writers' positioning in the sociopolitical contexts meaningful to their lives (347). We need to problematise the connection between language use and emotion by examining, for example, bilingual individuals'/writers' proficiency in and allegiance to particular languages during certain phases of their lives, the political system and turbulence they find themselves in, bilingual writers' power and legitimacy in society, their family relationships or even (if relevant) their sexuality and how it is positioned against the mainstream values of a specific culture or regime (Firmat, 2003; also see Burck, 2005).

Cross-linguistic influence and identity constructions

This theme echoes the previously raised question of whether an L2 'aura' in text or speech is a quality emanating individuality or an oddness to be frowned upon. Fundamental questions, which problematise the monolingual-superior or -centred view, have been raised: how do bilingual writers balance the respective forces of their L1 and the target-language literacy conventions and cultural/institutional values; and by what means does such equilibrium impact on the writers' educational, professional and economic advancement and restructuring of identities (Besemeres, 2002; Cox et al., 2010; Firmat, 2003; Menard-Warwick, 2006; Piller, 2002; Starks, 2006)?

Sommer's collection (2003) tells the stories of how bilingualism becomes a form of art beautifully played out in literary work – precisely against the background of multicultural fluidity and asymmetry – by 'the displaced and culturally overloaded artists' (1). In such cases, 'schizoglossia' (Pavlenko, 2006: 27) is replaced by the suppleness of the multilingual, multicultural identities which are empowered with the writers' tolerance for loss and a vulnerability-inspired innovation.

L2 creative writing is no longer exclusive to the geniuses and talented; it becomes a socialisation practice that flourishes in various sites outside the classroom, e.g. virtual spaces. Doing creative writing in one's L2 provides the medium for the performance of certain personas which could surpass the roles for the L2 individuals as language learner, student or just writer. This research sets out to capture and analyse an integrated picture of the L2 creative writers' own representation of their previous experience of negotiating their way into L2 creative writing while assuming a range of social roles. The issue of 'if the first language remains the language of heart' might not be the pressing concern here, rather 'if *creative writing* remains the language of the heart'. Furthermore, what space in the heart does L2 creative writing occupy for those bilingual writers?

This inquiry has 15 L2 creative writer participants; and given this sample size, it chose not to be a longitudinal study following each writer's ongoing social interactions. The sociocultural conceptualisation behind this inquiry will be discussed next.

L2 Creative Writer Identities – A Sociocultural Approach

As indicated in Chapter One, L2 creative writer identity is not a well-charted discrete domain. Therefore, the present inquiry is positioned against and draws conceptual vigour from two relevant fields of L2 studies: namely, L2 writing studies and L2 identity studies. Roughly speaking, each of the above two fields of L2 studies has experienced a three-stage paradigm shift in research and pedagogies and arrived at the 'social turn' (Matsuda, 2003) or 'sociocognitive situatedness' (Atkinson, 2003: 10). Indeed, sociocultural theories represent a dominant paradigm for L2 research at present.

Conceptual movements in L2 writing studies

In the early 1960s, the principal ideology underlying L2 writing studies was the initial *product-oriented* research approach (as opposed to the present-day product approach), also known as the 'current-traditional rhetoric' (Matsuda, 2003), influenced by the audiolingual approach in language teaching overall, with a monolithic focus on form, e.g. prescriptive grammar, syntax, spelling or textual devices (Matsuda, 2003). Then, partly as a reaction against this teacher-centred ideology, L2 writing research progressed to the later widely prevalent *process-oriented* approach which, as suggested by its name, investigated writers' cognitive activities and writing strategies. Such writing studies have stressed the characterisation of writing as a self-regulated information-processing, problem-solving and decision-making process where L2 writers constantly juggle competing linguistic, pragmatic, discoursal or ideational constraints (Flower & Hayes, 1980; Swain & Lapkin, 1995; Cumming, 1989, 1990). However, the process-oriented approach tended to idealistically heighten an individualist realisation of 'authentic' thoughts and emotions, encouraging rather nebulous concepts such as the development of writers' 'inner self'. Some researchers began to ask what L2 writers actually do with, or intend to achieve through, their writing practices, given their specific circumstances. Traditional views of writing practices as subject areas or as vehicles for self-expression were increasingly conceptually merged with concerns about language diversity and writer identity (see Black, 2005; Skinner & Hagood, 2008; Ouellette, 2008; Vasudevan *et al.*, 2010). L2 writing studies have thus entered *socioculturalism* (see Matsuda *et al.*, 2003; Hyland, 2003; Atkinson, 2003; Harklau, 2002), which advocates the 'multifocal nature' (Atkinson, 2003: 12) of writing and is concerned with issues such as power relations and politics as well as the complexities of individuality. Some avid socioculturalist writing theorists have critiqued pedagogically sanctified terms such as 'writing skills', 'writing techniques', 'writing strategies' or 'procedures' and 'tasks' as smacking of prescriptivism (e.g. Clark & Ivanič, 1997).

It can be seen above that during the first two stages of the L2 writing studies, the issue of 'writer identity' was either of little explicit concern to writing researchers or restricted to the domain of relatively asocial cognitivist or expressivist entities. Both the *product* and the *process* approaches have been criticised for exerting a normative influence on the investigation of writing issues, i.e. prescribing what the written product or the writing process *should* be like, without seeing writing as a social act, a site of conflicting ideologies and social/power relations. It is worth noting here that a writing study which examines L2 texts or L2 writing processes does not necessarily become methodologically monolithic; nor need it fail to recognise the L2 writers' socioculturally constituted reasons for the particular shapes of their texts or writing processes. Indeed, the crux lies in how writing researchers interpret or deal with the so-called 'expert' or 'novice' written products or writing processes. In other words, the conceptual nature of the study is reflected in the extent to which it primarily treats the 'products' or 'processes' as physical objects waiting to be analysed (Johns, 1990) and hence privileges the indisputable authority of 'authorities' (notably teachers) who evaluate students' texts or ratify the expert writing behaviours in L2 writing classrooms.

A socioculturalist awareness of writing practices encourages a non-deficit stance towards the writer and the writing. Thus equipped, teachers and researchers may realise that a writing task triggers diversified forms of written texts and writing processes which do not necessarily manifest problems to be unvaryingly corrected according to some sample answers. Socioculturalist writing researchers reflect on such multiplicities and see them as resulting from the unique interplays between the L2 individual writers' agency and the many nested contexts. Clark and Ivanič (1997) argued that contexts, either 'immediate environment[s]' or 'whole historical and socio-political contexts' (60) 'must be incorporated into any theoretical account of the writing process and of written language' (58). This conceptual movement in L2 writing studies is described by Hyland (Matsuda *et al.*, 2003) in terms of the social and agentive roles of the writers:

> Current conceptions of discourse shift attention from correctness to the resourcefulness of writers as *social actors* who bring *personal* and *cultural* histories to their writing and particular understandings of the texts they are asked to write. (My italics: 167)

For example, recent product-oriented writing research generally accepts that discoursal features, such as lexical richness, error occurrences, textual structure, thematic/rhetorical moves or frequency and distribution of metadiscourse features (Hyland, 2005b), are influenced by the conventions of specific discourse communities in which the texts are embedded. Also, regarding the L2 writing processes, Clark and Ivanič (1997) insist that 'there is no right "route" through the physical procedures and *mental processes* involved in writing ... but that the routes and practices selected are affected by the context in which the writer is operating ... as well as the individual writer's *ideologies and preferences*' (my italics: 81). Their argument suggests that writing processes are highly contextualised and idiosyncratic.

Conceptual movements in L2 identity studies

The recent vigour manifested in L2 *identity* studies visibly derives from the long-standing investigative initiatives witnessed in L2 *motivation* studies, especially among L2 teacher practitioners. As suggested by the slightly different connotations of 'motivation' and 'identities', 'motivation' seems to lean towards factors of individual differences (be they variables of abilities or circumstances, psychological states or varieties of actions), while 'identities' accentuates the negotiated and emergent aspects of motivation. Several SLA scholars have noted that L2 identity studies have tended to neglect consideration of L2 *writers'* mind, emotion or social relations. For example, Hidi and Boscolo (2006) consider that 'it is intriguing that relatively few research studies have been conducted in the area [of writing motivation]' (144). Meanwhile, Sasaki (2000, 2004) has expressed more than once the need to integrate issues of motivation into L2 writing research. Hence, the following review briefly addresses the three-stage paradigm shift in L2 motivation and identity research overall, which is deemed essential to the conceptualisation and interpretation of L2 creative writer identities in the present inquiry.

The three-phase movement in L2 motivation and identity research was propelled by three different ideological stances in terms of the conceptualisation of what characterises the *L2 learners* who hold such motivation or identities, what constitutes the surrounding *context* where such motivation or identities happen and what the relationship is between these two. Consequently, the three stages are different in their interpretations of the connection between L2 individuals' motivation and their language learning.

Early studies adopted the traditional *social-psychological* approach (Gardner & Lambert, 1959, 1972) which componentised L2 motivation as part of the psychological make-up of L2 learner groups who live in specific prevailing sociopolitical milieux. Under the social-psychological approach, large surveys were widely conducted in numerous geographic and social contexts to investigate the causative strength of L2 learners' attitudes and motives (Gardner, 2000, 2001; Gardner *et al.*, 2004; Dörnyei *et al.*, 2006; Chen *et al.*, 2005; Warden & Lin, 2000; Mori & Gobel, 2006; Shedivy, 2004; Lamb, 2004). However, given its usual psychometric measurement of L2 motivation, the social-psychological approach has been critiqued as seeing human internal factors, e.g. attributes and attitudes, as fixed and stable and as treating L2 learners 'as theoretical abstractions' (Ushioda, 2009: 220), whose macro traits are the focus of research to the neglect of enquiry into the complexity of individual views, interpretations and experience. In relation to this, the traditional social-psychological approach is seen as aligning itself with traditional social science in terms of its 'truth-seeking aims'; that is, it treats individual variables as something 'given' rather than dynamically evolving through the 'creation and production' of significant personalised voices in societies (Widdicombe, 1998: 200). In addition, due to its focus on the macro sociopolitical context (e.g. in Gardner's studies on Canada as a bilingual country), the original social-psychological construct was said to have minimal pedagogical or theoretical value in local, micro contexts (Dörnyei, 1994, 1996, 1998). The shift of focus onto the individual learner's mind and actions in a situated context has called forth an increasing attention to the cognitive and dynamic view of L2 motivation.

Similar to the swell of the process-oriented trend witnessed in L2 writing research, the second stage of L2 motivation research also advocates a cognitive, dynamic and individualistic view. It hypothesises that individuals make decisions about their own actions and that they critically reflect upon and take responsibility for the amount of effort put into a task (Williams & Burden, 1997: 119; Dickinson, 1995). However, the restricted scope of cognitive psychological approaches to L2 motivation gradually became apparent. Cognitive approaches were criticised for their inadequacy in exploring the social dimension of language learning, for their predominant focus on learners' individualistic, mental functioning and for treating motivation as context-independent (Ushioda, 2006, 2009). Once again, we sense that such criticism echoes that directed at process-oriented L2 writing research, especially regarding its asocial concern with cognitive routines. A new conceptualisation of L2 motivation was called for, one encompassing the dynamic construction of individuals' self-identities throughout their interactions in multiple sociocultural contexts.

Hence, under the sociocultural approach, motivation is re-conceptualised in terms of identities which are constructed in one's life experience but also embodied in one's interpretations of such experience (this research investigates the writers' such perceptions). The emphasis on a 'whole-person perspective' (Dörnyei, 2009: 9) of L2 learners' interacting with various social elements in local and global contexts is manifested in the frequent employment of qualitative research methods, e.g. interview, online correspondence, observation or narrative analysis, in sociocultural enquiry (see Lantolf, 2000). Two such sociocultural theoretical frameworks, which approach L2 identity from slightly different angles, will be discussed in the following two sections. One is Lave and Wenger's situated learning theory, which focuses on ideas of community and membership; the other is poststructuralist theory, which emphasises the L2 learner's agency in power negotiation and self-positioning, especially when facing unequal and disadvantageous situations.

Lave and Wenger's situated learning theory: Creative writers' social localities

Lave and Wenger's (1991) 'situated learning theory' argues that learning consists of people participating in an ongoing 'community of practice' (CoP). The process of apprentices learning from more knowledgeable others and progressing from novice status to that of fully participating experts taking multiple roles in the CoP is termed 'legitimate peripheral participation'.

This inquiry looks into the L2 creative writers' retrospective and personal representation of their various memberships. It did not set out to observe the writers' real-time participation in various communities. Nonetheless, the conceptualising power and subtlety of the CoP theory, especially the boundary and the distinctiveness of a community of practice as opposed to other social groups, is relevant to this research which considers the L2 creative writers' self-perceived social locality. Hence, the applicability of the CoP theory and the contention surrounding it deserve some further discussion below.

In the field of sociocultural SLA studies, CoP theory is an influential theoretical model in the interpretation of L2 learners' socialisation experience, acquisition of language and/or literacy competence and identity formation in a variety of learning situations (e.g. see Morita, 2004; Bazerman & Russell, 2003; Haneda, 1997, 2005; Toohey, 1996, 1998, 2000; Leki, 2001; Lamb, 2009; Belcher, 1994). To name but a few, applications of CoP theory have included studies concerning group projects or academic courses in Western universities (Leki, 2001; Morita, 2004); immigrant women's English language learning experiences in Canada (Norton, 2000); the discourse communities of scholarly writing and publishing (Flowerdew, 2000; Englander, 2009); and actual language classrooms (e.g. Norton, 2001; Toohey, 1998).

However, my reading of such studies suggests that, although L2 researchers have actively tapped into the explanatory power of the CoP perspective in elucidating the social constructionist nature of knowing and doing, their perceptions as regards the exact scope of relevance of a CoP entity are rather mixed.

To begin with, Wenger, the original architect of the CoP concept, emphasised the need to understand 'to what degree, in which ways, and to what purpose it is (or is not) useful to view a social configuration as a community of practice' (1998: 122). He cautioned that 'calling every imaginable social configuration a community of practice would render the concept meaningless' and yet also warned that 'encumbering the [CoP] concept with too restrictive a definition would only make it less useful' (1998: 122). Wenger (1998) meticulously theorised the notion of *locality* personifying a CoP where a shared enterprise is locally negotiated and a historically constructed practice has been locally fashioned and jointly engaged in by the members.

Nonetheless, some L2 social theorists assert that Lave and Wenger's (1991) CoP concept is somewhat restricted as it focuses primarily on a directly engaged or face-to-face CoP. It has been suggested that CoP could be expanded to interpret the particularities of 'more global communities – such as academic fields, religions, or professions – whose size and dispersion means both that face-to-face interactions never link all the members, and that their focal "practices" are somewhat diffuse' (Eckert & McConnell-Ginet, 1999: 189; also see Haneda, 2005; Lamb, 2009). For example, Flowerdew (2000) and Englander (2009), in their respective case studies of non-native-English-speaking scholars'/postgraduate students' social practices of publishing in refereed English-language journals, and hence participation in the international CoPs of particular research disciplines, stretched the scope of CoP to disciplinary discourse communities.

I would argue that the L2 creative writer community is exactly such a CoP whose practice is of an innately diffuse nature. As more than one novelist has expressed (e.g. Paul Auster, Jessamyn West), creative writing is essentially a solitary pursuit and L2 creative writers might similarly demonstrate a tendency for participating in this practice in solitude (except for those engaged in creative writer teams or creative writing workshops). Thus, there may be limited day-to-day, immediate mutual engagement with other creative writers in a particular locality, physical or virtual, and thus limited relevance or permeability regarding the idea that a rather closely bound community of creative writers in a certain intimate 'locality of engagement ...continually creat[e] locally shared histories' (Wenger, 1998: 125). In addition, creative writing practice, compared with professional practices such as that of insurance-claim processing focused on in Wenger's study (1998), allows more space for idiosyncrasy and thus 'discontinuities' (125) among individual members where a diversity of practices take place; and it also allows for higher probabilities of mobility or ephemerality for its members, travelling across/among various creative writing genres, modes, media or venues.

Based on the above rationale, this inquiry adopts the stance that the communities of practice could involve both 'narrow' and 'concrete communities' (Lantolf & Pavlenko, 2001: 148) or 'global' and 'diffuse' communities (Eckert & McConnell-Ginet, 1999: 189). Also, in contrast to the face-to-face and more tangible CoPs, there are imagined CoPs whose norms participants partly align with through imagination. For example, Lamb's (2004) case study of Indonesian pupils' L2 motivation identified one participant who envisioned her future as involving membership of a community of professional middle-class English speaking Indonesians working in international settings. How her imagined CoP was internalised and mentally depicted is closely linked to her imagined identity, e.g. that of a businesswoman or expatriate living in western countries. This imagined identity further stimulated her motivation to engage in particular activities, e.g. attending an English private school, which would be essential to the realisation of her envisioned future identity.

In the following section, I will discuss the other sociocultural framework significant to the present research, i.e. poststructuralist theory. Essentially, what distinguishes poststructuralist theory from CoP theory is that poststructuralist scholars accentuate, to a higher extent, individuals' agentive stance in shaping their own identities and striving for their own destiny against power relations and tension. For example, Pavlenko and Lantolf (2000) go to the extent of arguing that 'ultimate attainment in second language learning relies on one's agency' (169) and suggest that people who fail to 'attain "ultimately" in a second language … never set out to translate themselves in the first place' (170).

Poststructuralist perspective: Creative writing as a self-empowering tool

Poststructuralist L2 identity studies highlight the 'center stage' taken by an individual's 'agency and intentionality' (Pavlenko & Lantolf, 2000: 170) in *assuming* and *performing* an identity (Block, 2006a: 36; Omoniyi, 2006: 16). By foregrounding self-agency, poststructuralist L2 identity studies tend to reflect critically on the political, economic and power issues impacting on L2 individuals' language learning and identity construction processes and outcomes, usually in ESL contexts (as opposed to EFL), and adult migrant contexts in particular (e.g. Pavlenko & Blackledge, 2004; Pavlenko & Lantolf, 2000; Block, 2007; Norton, 1995, 2000; Norton & Toohey, 2001; Lamb, 2002, 2004, 2007; Lyon, 2009). They propose that L2 learners can either resist or accept 'the positions those [particular] contexts offer them' (Norton & Toohey, 2001: 310). As discussed previously, Lave and Wenger's CoP theory represents the social constructionist view, i.e. language learning and language using are socially constructed and situated activities; while the *poststructuralist approach* sees language and sociocultural knowledge (i.e. the 'cultural capital') as semiotic and symbolic tools employed by the agentive individuals to resist sociopolitical injustice.

Some key poststructuralist concepts are 'investment' (Norton, 1995, 2000), 'capital' and 'habitus' (Bourdieu, 1991). L2 learners, discontented with their sometimes marginalised social identities, 'invest' (Norton, 1995, 2000) in learning the L2 with the anticipation of gaining a larger amount of 'linguistic capital', i.e. 'the capacity to produce expressions' for a particular social site (Bourdieu, 1991: 18). This will help increase their 'cultural capital', i.e. 'the knowledge and modes of thought that characterize different classes and groups in relation to specific sets of social forms' (Bourdieu & Passeron, 1977, cited in Norton, 1995: 17), and their 'economic capital' and ultimately enhance their social identities and future desires. Throughout their writing-related 'socialization and experience', each L2 individual has formed his or her unique writing habitus, i.e. the 'embodied dispositions to … write in certain ways' (Fairclough, 2003: 29). However, habitus does not equal competence or skills. Norton (1995) points out that even achieving Canale and Swain's (1980) communicative competence (i.e. grammatical, sociolinguistic, discourse and strategic competence) could not guarantee L2 learners what Bourdieu calls 'the power to impose reception' (Bourdieu, 1977: 75). Such power could only be constructed through L2 learners' understanding of their own identities and positions in the social web.

The implications held by poststructuralist theories for L2 creative writing appear to be at least twofold.

Firstly, L2 creative writing could be employed by L2 learners as an empowering symbolic tool or 'counterdiscourse' that provides the opportunities, perhaps denied in many L2 learning activities, to construct and perform agentive and authoritative subjectivities through imaginative, creative, personal or aesthetic self-articulations. Some L2 creative writers actively 'invest' their time and effort in particular forms of L2 creative writing because they feel empowered or emancipated through this social act. That is, through such an 'investment', L2 learners manage to construct particular L2 creative writer identities, e.g. as perceptive story-teller, which effectively compensate for the L2 learners' sense of loss in their agentive power or their somehow marginalised membership status in other social sites, e.g. the language/writing classroom or English native speaking country. This 'investment' in creative writing practices may also help transform L2 individuals' social relations in specific communities (e.g. a classroom, a creative writing workshop or a virtual forum), thus strengthening L2 writers' sense of social existence and presence, along with the motivational acquisition of certain cultural, social and symbolic 'capital'.

The second implication is that L2 teachers need to realise that L2 creative writing practices demand more than L2 writers' 'objectified linguistic resources' (Bourdieu, 1991: 57), literary knowledge or ingenious ideas (which we may also call 'creativity'). Admittedly, these elements play an important role in positioning L2 creative writers advantageously in a particular writing activity in a particular context; however, they cannot guarantee that the creative writers will be confident, comfortable or successful in delivering their work or in encouraging effective response and reception among the audience. L2 creative writers' agentive stance is demonstrated through aligning their social identities – previously constructed throughout their life trajectories – with the kind of identity they see as appropriate, empowering or convenient or that they are driven to negotiate in the immediate creative writing context (e.g. either an L2 creative writing task set by the teacher or a self-initiated writing activity for participation in a certain creative writer community).

The agency–structure debate in identity construction

'Community of practice' and 'habitus' theories reach a consensus that identity formation results from, in a non-deterministic way, the dynamic and ongoing interplay between individual agency and the surrounding social contexts in which particular 'determinate situation[s]' (Bourdieu, 1991: 37), 'markets' (38) or 'reifications' prevail (Wenger, 1998: 57–62). However, if we look at these two concepts individually, I would argue that they illustrate this socialisation process with different foregrounding. The CoP theory highlights communities, particularly those bounded by certain enterprises and functions, emphasising that power negotiation and identity formation are 'propert[ies] of social communities' (Wenger, 1998: 189). It resonates palpably with the social constructionist view that 'reality, knowledge, thought, facts, texts, selves, and so on' are 'community generated and community maintained ... entities' (Bruffee, 1986: 771, cited in Ivanič, 1998: 12). In comparison, 'habitus' foregrounds the individual's embodied and habitual way of perceiving and acting formed through his/her accumulation of various 'capital' – in other words, his/her socially constructed ability for 'practical engagement with the world' (Fairclough, 2003: 160).

In writer identity research, the issue of balancing the social definition of identities with individuals' agentive actions on self-positioning in society attracts debate. As addressed by Block (2006a), how shall we 'reconcile structure and agency' (46); to what extent is identity 'a self-conscious, reflexive project of individual agency' (36)?

For example, in one writer identity study conducted by Ivanič and Camps (2001), a social constructionist view was embraced as the researchers aimed to provide 'a social dimension' to L2 writers' decision-making. They formulated three types of emergent self-representations engaged in by writers in each act of writing: 'ideational positioning', 'interpersonal positioning' and 'textual positioning'. Through focusing on specific 'lexical, syntactic, and rhetorical choices' in the ESL students' writing, Ivanič and Camps investigated how the writers selected 'available voice types' (6) to argue *'about something'*, to position themselves *'between interlocutors'* and to *'shape the text'* (original italics, 11). Their accentuation of the formative role played by social construction in writers' voices is shown in their statement that the above three aspects of self-representations 'construct socioculturally recognisable' identities for the writers – as beheld by the often more socially seasoned reader (e.g. their teachers) – which the writers may or may not be critically aware of or in control of (6). Despite Ivanič and Camps' explanatory and 'sustained empirical analysis of student texts', their above conceptual framework was criticised by Atkinson (2001) for attributing 'limited' 'freedom and agency' to the writers and thus for being 'monolithically social' (116). As argued by Atkinson (2001), Ivanič and Camps' framework perceived L2 writers as merely adopting, choosing, combining or opposing existing social 'voice-types' (116), rather than having their own individual voices.

Views on Ivanič and Camps' above interpretation of writer identities would be mixed among identity scholars. For example, Bakhtinian scholars might tend to accept the above approach, as they consider one's language, a sociocultural, sociohistorical artefact (Bakhtin, 1986), as 'always embedded in the language of others from previous contexts' (Maguire & Graves, 2001: 566). In contrast, Fairclough (2003) might share Atkinson's view, as he accentuated the role played by people's 'sense of the self' in identity formation, termed by him as 'personal identity' or 'personality', which is formed even before children learn to speak and which continues throughout the rest of people's lives (160; a similar notion was brought up by Block [2006a] as the 'stable deep inside': 46). Subsequently, Fairclough argued that identity is not entirely 'an effect of [social] discourse, constructed in [social] discourse', but rather, identity is significantly preconditioned by people's 'self-consciousness', 'a continuous sense of the self' (Fairclough, 2003: 160). However, giving this forceful argument does not necessarily mean that Fairclough took the position that agency deserves more emphasis than social structure. Instead, he stated that these two notions both 'have "causal powers" ... and that the relationship between the two is dialectical' (225).

Despite the seeming tension between structure and self-agency in identity formation, these two different perspectives are not necessarily exclusive of each other in the theoretical outlining of sociocultural writer identity studies. They are two sides of the same coin. I would argue that exactly which perspective is attributed more value to by writer identity scholars depends on the specific background of their participant writers (i.e. general ESL/EFL speakers in disciplinary communities or the often marginalised immigrant adult ESL speakers) and the purpose and goals behind the particular research (i.e. to demonstrate how writing is used as a semiotic mediation for social interactions or to uncover how writing has been employed to challenge patterns of privileging or to liberate one's agentive self). As mentioned previously, this study chooses to focus on the participants' personal representation of certain previous experience – to be more specific, how the L2 creative writers interpret their previous socialisation trajectories where certain contextualised learning happens and how such interpretation is related to the participants' writing tendency revealed in their present cognitive writing processes. The purpose and priority of the research decides that, here, the agency–structure interaction for each L2 creative writer is approached from the angle of self-agency.

As stated in Chapter 1, in this inquiry, in-depth interviews were used to explore the L2 creative writers' life trajectories encompassing various social sites at different times. The theoretical framework which has been used to analyse the L2 creative writers' autobiographical selves (one of the two aspects of writer identities in this inquiry) as conveyed in the writers' retrospective accounts is a mix of the *social constructionist* and the *poststructuralist* perspectives, appealing to the former's focus on the constructing role of prototypical social relations and community conventions and the latter's emphasis on individual agency in terms of how the participants make sense of, and represent to the interviewer, their experience of facing disadvantageous and unfavourable positioning in communities. This particular framework used in the inquiry is the 'discursive construction of identities'. In the next section, I will explain how this theoretical construct enables a rather micro and emergent angle from which to examine how the construction and representation of 'the autobiographical selves' are mediated through the meaningful manipulation of language in the L2 creative writers' recounts of their sociocultural lives in particular communities.

The Life-Historical Autobiographical Selves: Discursive Construction of Identities

The reflexive constitution of self

The notion of autobiographical selves in this inquiry into L2 creative writer identities is influenced by Clark and Ivanič's (1997) theorisation of the Autobiographical Self, part of their widely quoted tripartite writer identity system, which refers to the aspect of writer identity constructed through writers' sociocultural life histories. Methodologically different from their focus, this inquiry investigates the self-identities by adopting the framework of the discursive construction of identity. It conceptualises that the act of a person narrating his/her experiences and expressing his/her thoughts and feelings to others, in an interview, for example, constructs his/her self-identities which are 'to a large extent determined by the sociocultural history of the person and the discourses to which [he] or she has access' (Roebuck, 2000: 82). By adopting this term 'self-identity', a concept that has been brought up by social theorists such as Giddens (1991), Block (2006: 42), Pavlenko and Blackledge (2004) and Ivanič (1998; or for the alternative term 'self-representation' see Clark & Ivanič, 1997), I aim to foreground the 'reflexive project of the self' (Giddens, 1991: 5) or the 'reflexive constitution' (86) of individuals' identity construction, relative to the socially defined, experiential aspect of identity lying in 'the full, lived experience of engagement in practice' (Wenger, 1998: 151). This distinction is alternatively noted by Pavlenko and Blackledge (2004) as the interplay between 'reflective positioning' and 'interactive positioning' (20).

The term self-identity, along with several other terms prefixed by self-, such as self-fashioning, self-positioning or self-representation, is used throughout this book with the aim of underscoring this reflective aspect of identity construction demonstrated in the L2 creative writers' narratives of their life histories recounted in the in-depth interviews. Thus, the participants' self-identity, as explored by this study, to a great extent consists:

> not of a person's life history, but of the *interpretation* they are currently putting on their life history. The self is in this way doubly socially con-structed: both by the socially constrained nature of the life experience itself, and by the social shaping of the interpretation. (Original italics, Ivanič, 1998: 16).

That is to say, what matters is the L2 creative writers' own sense of their and others' identities, reflected through their 'discursive accounts, such as descriptions, explanations, exonerations, corrections, and reformulations', not the 'transcendental realism of identity' (Mckinlay & Dunnett, 1998: 49) which stands beyond 'the individual's social constructive powers' (48).

The above approach towards the discursive construction of identities is central to this inquiry's establishment of workable schemes to systematically yet sensitively analyse and compare the autobiographical selves constructed by the 15 L2 creative writers from a diversity of cultures and social backgrounds. The writers' autobiographical selves are discursively fashioned through the linguistic features of their self-constructed recounts as well as the 'power-knowledge' or ideology (Widdicombe, 1998) instantiated by such talk. As pointed out by Ushioda (2009) and Gu (2009), the mediating role of *language* in motivation and identity construction in a particular context, e.g. spontaneous L2 classroom- or task-based conversation, or interviews probing L2 learner's experiences and goals, has not yet been given sufficient attention in L2 motivation or identity research. In the following section, I will briefly discuss Gu's (2009, 2010) and Gee's (1999) work to illustrate the possibilities opened up by such a theoretical approach towards discursive identity.

Gu's and Gee's works and the implication for a hermeneutic model of analysis

Gu's work (2009, 2010) has persuasively demonstrated how L2 motivation and social identity could be discursively constructed by EFL Chinese learners at different levels of social contexts, e.g. within the specific learning community, the surrounding social environment and an imagined global community (Gu, 2010). Gu (2009) analysed interview transcripts and learner diaries by using Fairclough's (2003) framework of critical discourse analysis from three dimensions, i.e. text, discursive practice and social practice (304). *Discursive* strategies for establishing 'legitimation' and 'oppositions and differences', accentuated through the *textual* features of specific pronouns, modality, conjunctions and rhetorical devices, were adopted in the participants' recounting of and reflection on their English learning experiences. Participants' values, belief and knowledge systems, and their social relations revealed in their discursive comments ultimately mirror historical processes and *'social practices'*, such as globalisation, the marketisation of China's economy or Confucian altruism (Gu, 2009).

Another example of how identity could be powerfully teased out through analysing the situated meanings in verbal discourse is Gee's (1999) interview-based study which explored 'how socially significant identities are mutually constructed in language' (138) on the spot by the researcher and people from different social classes, i.e. 'middle-class teens' and 'working-class teens', or from different professional classes, i.e. 'college professor' and 'middle-school teacher' (Chapter 9). Through looking into the particular lexical items, syntax complexity, rhetorical moves and how the interviewees' 'refer to themselves by speaking in the first person as "I"' (i.e. 'I-statement', 141), Gee achieved a nuanced picture of how the socially situated identities were built though the interviewees' use of distinctive 'social languages' (e.g. 'global and abstract' language or concrete language directly situated in local experience), 'Discourse models' (e.g. rational argumentation or personal narrative) and 'Discourses' (e.g. 'academic discourse', 'teacher discourse', discourse of everyday social interaction or discourse of 'personal biological trajectories' and achievement) (138–141).

Both Gu's and Gee's work demonstrate the possibility of 'the investigation of mind' through looking to individuals' 'linguistically constructed social discourse' (Roebuck, 2000: 80). Therefore, they both adopted a hermeneutic model of analysis, rather than relying entirely on 'a preexisting, underlying system of abstract representations' (81) of culture or social identities. I see this as a particularly constructive response to the caution, expressed by some L2 motivation scholars, of the intervening influence of culture on the representation of self-identities to others. For example, MacIntyre *et al.* (2009) argued that the 'various culture-bound definitions of self', e.g. the stereotypical independent, distinct and confident Western self and the interdependent collective Eastern self, 'may impact on the motivational properties of self' (54–55). There is some truth in that, yet it is also problematic to me, mainly because MacIntyre *et al.* are reserved about the significance of specific contexts surrounding the L2 learners, within one culture or another, and the L2 learners' agency to personalise such experience, especially given the fusion of various cultural dynamics surrounding today's global citizens. Selecting a cultural lens through which to observe and interpret data about the *L2 selves* runs the risk of the researcher adopting a stereotyped or all-encompassing view of culture while losing sight of the individuals' self-identities.

For example, Taguchi *et al.* (2009) set out to validate Dörnyei's (2009) tripartite L2 Motivational Self System, i.e. Ideal L2 self, Ought-to L2 self and L2 learning experiences, in Asian contexts through large-scale well-grounded survey-based research comparing EFL motivation in Japan, Iran and China. Despite the variant internal composition of each of the three participant groups (i.e. middle school students, English and non-English major university students and working professionals), it seems that the researchers tend to attribute the differences in results among the three countries to cultural differences, rather than, for example, the participants' L1 educational background or socioeconomic background. As a Chinese native speaker, I cannot help feeling that some of their statements about Chinese culture express a received view of culture, for example the following statement by the authors (Taguchi *et al.*, 2009):

Ever since the one child policy was enforced in 1978, young people have had a heavy burden placed on their shoulders to support their ageing parents. People retire at a relatively early age in China, usually with extremely low pensions, so their children have the responsibility and obligation to take care of them as they become the sole breadwinners of the family. (80)

The above depiction of social and cultural issues in China has some value of truth. However I wonder how many of the Chinese middle school students, who constituted about one-sixth of the Chinese participants who filled out their questionnaire, were mature enough to fully apprehend this distant yet harsh reality that their ageing and retired parents will have to rely on them as 'the sole breadwinners'. Also, exactly because of this value put on family by 'Chinese Culture', parents see their children's survival and financial welfare as their own responsibility. Therefore, another trend coexisting with the one described above is that parents frequently continue to subsidise their children after they have reached maturity, for example by paying for their overseas education or providing the down payment for an apartment or car. The relationship between culture and L2 individuals' identities needs to be treated in a non-deterministic way. Therefore, I see the hermeneutic, inductive approach of attending to the individuals' discursive constructions of identities in their retrospective accounts of life experiences as subtle and fruitful.

As mentioned above, the agency–structure (or –culture) relationship is non-deterministic. It should be clarified that the approach of discursive identities does not lean towards either side of the agency–structure debate concerning identity constructions. The particular stance adopted by the discourse analysts should depend on the genre and purpose of the particular speeches under examination. For example, in public speech, self-identity might be disguised by political rhetoric and institutional agenda. In the current study, compared to the above, self-identities have the potential to become more visible and continuous when the speech genre is personal narrative and expected to be reflective and subjective. In relation to the above, there indeed are different stances among discourse analysts of speeches. Some tend to equate discursive identities with social identities (e.g. Antaki & Widdicombe, 1998). Identity is accentuated as a major player in, and product of, the societal and political discourse.

The significance of social identities in discourses

Discourse is socially established. Hence, it is anticipated that social constructionist and poststructuralist scholars, despite their somewhat different approaches to the agency–structure debate illustrated earlier, have both contributed to the ratification of the significance of social identities in discourses.

For example, embodying a social constructionist perspective, Clark and Ivanič's (1997) formulation of writers' 'autobiographical selves', constructed in the writers' personal narratives as elicited in interviews, highlights the mediating role played by 'socially constructed resources' (140). They state that writers' 'autobiographical selves' are constructed 'by possibilities for self-hood that have been made available to them by discourse conventions and literacy practices' that writers have encountered (140). Clark and Ivanič (1997) maintain that 'the practices people enter into position them in particular ways, and to some extent everyone is at the mercy of these possibilities' (138). The individuals' discursive identities are the results of the instantiations and maintenance of the 'prototypical identities' (140) in the discourse communities.

Meanwhile, as observed by Fairclough (2003: 160) and Widdicombe (1998), recent poststructuralist and postmodern views also distinctly foreground social identities, in particular how such identities are put into practice in public arenas, and hence assert the 'thoroughly political' nature of identities (Widdicombe, 1998: 201). The idea is that discourses 'form the raw materials and manufacturing processes' (200) through which the 'splits and fissures' in identities are continuously challenged and legitimised by 'oppressed and subjugated groups and individuals' so that 'new identity options' could be created (Pavlenko & Blackledge, 2004: 13; also see Widdicombe, 1998). Theoretically, poststructuralist theorists have not always reserved 'discourse' for the exclusive construction of social identity. For example, Weedon (1987) suggests that language is the place where 'actual and possible forms of social organization' as well as 'our sense of ourselves' are constructed and contested (21). However, understandably, poststructuralists' attention to power relations and explicit political agendas orientate the discourse analysts towards the speeches with relatively high levels of public exposure and social significance.

Nonetheless, some other discourse analysts associate discursive identities essentially with properties of mind which critically interact with people's social processes of identification. Firstly, Fairclough (2003) warned that we need to recognise that self-identity, i.e. people's reflexivity, serves as a prerequisite for 'people's full development as social agents' (160–161). This need to investigate the reflexive constitution of discursive identities could not have been more forcefully articulated than in the statement by discursive psycholinguist Roebuck (2000) that '[s]ociocultural theory is a theory of mind' (80), as mind is a 'discursive process' (81). Self-consciousness implies, if not determines, language use in society.

The types of interview speeches and the speech content focused on by the present study underscore the need to look at how the reflexive project of individual agency is constructed in and through language in the interviews. Hence, what this inquiry intends to unravel through 'the discursive construction of identities' is the individuals' social constructive powers, their agentive interpretation of their autobiographical identities. I am interested in how the L2 creative writers discoursally position themselves when referring to themselves as the first-person 'I', e.g. as someone taking concrete actions, as someone capably engaging in thinking and opinion-giving, as someone not timid to declare their ability or achievement, as someone not shy to reveal their weakness or constraints, or as someone bravely showing their feelings and emotions. That is to say, the discursive analytical tool 'I-statement analysis' (i.e. how people talk about themselves when speaking in the first person as 'I'), formulated and used in Gee (1999, Chapter 9), is adapted by the present inquiry (I-statement analysis will be discussed in the next chapter). In addition, to find out the various communities of practice which the L2 creative writers, in their recounting of their experience, simultaneously position themselves as members of, 'We-statement and You-statement analysis' is also employed. Its purpose is to investigate the L2 creative writers' sense of social localities when speaking in the first-person plural as 'We' or second person plural as 'You'.

In the next section, the discussion will move on to this 'emergent writer identity' negotiated in a particular writing activity, often referred to as *writer voice*. From a sociocultural perspective, Prior (2006), in a rather purple passage, comments that 'the trajectories of a particular text trace delicate paths through overgrown sociohistoric landscapes' (64). Here, with regard to the relationship between writer's *self-perceptions* of their previous experience and the task-situated, emergent *writer voice*, I would venture to say that the trajectories of an L2 story writer's cognitive writing process in a particular task, where their writer voice is instantiated, also trace delicate paths but through social and motivational landscapes. Writers cannot avoid enacting voices in what they write (Clark & Ivanič, 1997: 143; also see Ivanič & Camps, 2001). Each act of writing then is inevitably a 'process of their [writers'] own on-going identity construction' (Clark & Ivanič, 1997: 159), which further contributes to the shaping of the writers' self-perceptions, i.e. their autobiographical selves.

The Task-Situated Writer's Voice

This emergent writer identity, i.e. writer's voice (the two terms are used interchangeably in this book), has received the biggest share of attention in the field of writer identity studies, both theoretically and empirically. The following sections will critically discuss writer voice in terms of two dichotomies I have observed in the conceptualisation and investigation of this subject in recent studies. These two dichotomies are: (1) the romantic notions of voice versus the social and discursive notions of voice, also metaphorically referred to by Atkinson (2001) as the 'voice in the heart versus the voice in the head'; (2) writer's voice marked permanently in written texts versus writer's voice dynamically displayed in writing processes. The purpose of this review is to illustrate how my approach to writer voice fits in with and also complements the existing research.

Romantic voice vs. social voice

In the 18th century, Bufon claimed that 'The style is the man himself' ('Le style c'est l'homme même', Fellows & Milliken, 1972: 149–54). The debate continues about what exactly constitutes a writer's voice. There are, quoting from Prior (2001), the 'romantic notions of voice as the expression of an autonomous individual', and also the 'social voice' which the individuals have to appropriate and project for success in particular social contexts (62).

Atkinson (2001) called the first type of voice the 'individualist voice', which is associated with a range of qualities such as being ideological, romantic, personal, authentic, assertive, literary and stylish (117). Advocates of the individualistic notions of 'voice' are regarded as espousing the world views of Expressivism, Romanticism or Individualism. For example, the following definition of 'voice' given by Bowden (1999) highlights the literary, idiosyncratic and stylish qualities of 'voice': 'voice as a metaphor has to do with feeling-hearing-sensing a person behind the written words, even if that person is just a persona created for a particular text or a certain reading' (97–98, cited in Hirvela & Belcher, 2001). Foregrounding distinctiveness at aesthetic and ideational levels, such a 'personal expressive' voice could be searched for in *written texts* through 'relatively more novel means of expression' and/or 'more novel kinds of content' (Atkinson, 2001: 120).

In contrast, Matsuda (2001), who attends to the social, cultural and discursive aspects of 'voice', defines it as 'the process of negotiating my socially and discursively constructed identity with the expectation of the reader as I perceive it' (39). What is central to this social discursive notion is that the writer's voice primarily comes from outside in. That is to say, writers' voices constructed in a particular writing activity are sensitive to a variety of social factors, such as writers' positioning in power relations both inside and outside the immediate writing task, writers' social identities in various communities and the range of symbolic and semiotic mediators that have been socioculturally made accessible to the writers.

One key theoretical underpinning of this social notion of voice is Bakhtin's (1986) concept of 'dialogism' which explains how language, as a dynamic sociocultural artefact, defines its user in situated contexts. Bakhtin's view of language practice as dialogic states that 'the production of utterances involves the speakers' appropriating, accenting, and reaccenting the voices of others, thereby entering into a dialogic encounter with them' (Maguire & Graves, 2001: 589). Defined by the Bakhtinian concept of dialogism, to be in a dialogue with the reproductive power of social discourse on the formation of writer's voice, there also exists writers' own agentive power manifested in the intertextuality and interdiscursivity the writers are able to establish in a specific act of writing (e.g. Maguire & Graves, 2001). Maguire and Graves (2001), in their investigation of the writer's voice in immigrant children's creative writing in English, indicate a connection between this dialogic perspective on writing and writer cognition. They state that 'a dialogic perspective on knowledge-in-action views knowledge not as the grade or levels of a child's knowing but rather as the social space for a child's voice and participation in the activity of knowing' (566). To extrapolate from their statement on the 'dialogic perspective on knowledge-in-action', I would argue that a dialogic perspective on writers' mental activities displayed in the writing processes (i.e. where this inquiry searches for evidence of writers' voices, as discussed in the next dichotomy) should view such activities not as indicators of the writers' knowledge of writing strategies but as manifestations of the writers' negotiation of voices through their participation in knowing how to fulfil the present writing task within the social space conceivable to them.

I need to clarify that by using the term dichotomy I am not drawing some kind of artificial distinction here (or in the latter case) between the romantic and the social voices. Rather, these two types of voice stand at opposite ends of a continuum; and it is often the case that writer identity scholars' varying interpretations of 'voice' lie somewhere in between these two ends, intermingling threads from both types of voice. For example, as shown in the *Journal of Second Language Writing*'s special issue on writer's voice (2001, Volume 10), each research project variously weaves together these two strands of voices into one integrated conceptualisation. Writing researchers themselves, also members and products of society throughout their life trajectories, uphold specific world views and ideologies (often subconsciously), e.g. Individualism, Conformism, Confucianism or Eclecticism. Such ideologies, ingrained in the researchers, will influence how they perceive and determine the interplay of literary and social discursive forces behind voice construction. For example, Ivanič (1998) theorised writer's voice as 'an articulation of socially available possibilities for selfhood' (331). We can see that Ivanič's conceptualisation of writer's voice reveals a strong trace of the social notion and is very much influenced by the Bakhtinian theory of dialogism. However, if we look closer into Clark and Ivanič's (1997) widely quoted tripartite writer identity system, especially into their theoretic division between 'the discoursal self' and 'the self as author', we can see that their approach towards the above mentioned two notions of writer's voice is actually mixed. My reasons are as follows.

Clark and Ivanič (1997) managed to 'differentiate two meanings of the writer's "voice"' – 'voice as *form*' and 'voice as *content*' (original italics, 151) – which are respectively crystallised in their concepts of 'the discoursal self' and 'the self as author'. On the one hand, with regards to 'the discoursal self', they asserted that this meaning of writer's voice (i.e. voice as *form*) is constructed by 'the combination and range of discourse conventions with which the writer is comfortable' and so that '[t]here is no such thing as personal "voice" in this respect: just an affiliation to or unique selection among existing discourse conventions' (151). In the above statement, their thumping declaration of the social notion of 'voice' is hard to miss. On the other hand, in sharp contrast, Clark and Ivanič seem to purposefully allocate the romantic, philosophical voice to their concept of 'the self as author' by stating that this meaning of 'voice' (i.e. voice as *content*) is about 'writers' expression of their own ideas and beliefs' (152). Clark and Ivanič's belief that the establishment of 'the self as author' depends on writers' demonstrating an individualistic, expressive and assertive voice in the texts actually might have divulged their own (possibly subconscious) ideology of Individualism.

With regard to one study conducted by Ivanič and another colleague of hers (Ivanič & Camps, 2001), their justification of their sense of writers' authorial stance and authoritativeness (similar to 'the self as author') was critiqued by Atkinson (2001) as displaying 'residual traces of individualist voice' (118). In particular, Atkinson was critical towards Ivanič and Camps' assertion that authorial stance is *primarily* evidenced by whether and how the first person pronoun 'I' is used in the written text and by how writers position their own *personal experience* in relation to other authorities. As argued by Atkinson (2001), the frequency and the rhetorical effect of writers' usage of 'I' or their utilisation of personal experiences in their texts does not necessarily attest to their agentive endeavour in constructing an authorial stance or authoritativeness, as Ivanič and Camps have claimed. Such usages might also be influenced by the accidental availability and relevance of the writer's particular experience with regard to the topic of the writing assignment, or simply by the writer's personality. That is to say, 'the individual, as well as assertive displays of individuality' (Atkinson, 2001: 119) are not always the only or best way for writers to negotiate an authorial stance and presence in an act of writing. Writers' authorial presence could also be constructed through 'other possible ways of thinking about humans and their actions' (119), e.g. showing masterful comprehension and adaptions of the disciplinary culture as an analytical person.

My own understanding of this dichotomy between the romantic and the social notions of 'voice' is that to theorise and subsequently tease out writer voice in a particular act of writing purely from either of these two perspectives is neither realistic – due to the researcher's subjectivity in data interpretation – nor effective, as it risks the danger of a monolithic observation. It is not uncommon for people to think that the free, romantic, literary and personal notion of 'voice' is more naturally associated with creative writing than with academic writing. Similarly, academic writers are generally perceived as abiding by certain disciplinary genre conventions to a higher extent than creative writers are. For non-professional L2 tertiary students (i.e. the participants of the present inquiry), the romantic voices might be more palpable in their voluntary creative writing practices, especially as an escapist means to shake off the shackles of the obligations and pressures of daily life and to relax; while the social voices dominate L2 students' academic writing so as to enable them to achieve disciplinary acculturation. However, I would argue that the exact conceptualisation and interpretation of writers' voice in any act of writing is not *primarily* affected by the specific literacy type taken up by the writers. After all, successful commercial or professional creative writers are probably accustomed to enacting and performing the kind of identities endorsed by the popular culture prevalent in a particular time and sphere of society. Vice versa, it is not rare to find articles in academic journals on applied linguistics emanating a literary, assertive or even animated voice, often written by well-established scholars (e.g. see Atkinson, 2001; Mason, 2010). Writers are always involved in the negotiation and reconciliation between their own desires and their observation of the outside constraints. The interplay between writers' romantic voice and social voice, as I have perceived, is embodied in the writers' evaluation of the power relations and their possession of 'capital' in the social circumstance surrounding their act of writing, and in how they accordingly assign significance to these external constraints and how they perceive the social or economic consequences of disregarding or flaunting them.

In the next section, the discussion will move on to the second dichotomy, that is, where and how shall we search for writers' voice, through the written texts or through the writing processes?

Voice marked in texts vs. voice displayed in writers' emergent thoughts while writing

Voices exist in written texts as well as in writing processes, as succinctly pointed out in Prior's (2001) statement that writers' voices are represented 'in text, mind, and society' (55). There have been a large number of studies on writers' voices which have managed to analyse various features of *texts*; in contrast, relatively little has been done to interpret writers' voices as shown in their cognitive writing *processes*. This inquiry considers that knowledge of the latter could give us some insight into how the distinctive life stories and personalities writers bring with them vitally impact on their present writing – in particular, to what extent L2 writers' implementation of specific forms, language or content in their creative writing processes are identifiable choices rather than the result of an inexplicable flow of what we might term 'inspiration'. In what follows, I will respectively discuss the orientations and actions taken up by the text-focused approach and the process-focused approach towards unravelling writer voice.

Voice in texts

The text-focused approach could be further split into two strands, i.e. those concentrating on discoursal features in texts, often targeting particular academic genres, and those focusing on ideological and thematic revelations in texts. Of course, there also are those which combine both strands in their scrutiny of texts (e.g. Clark & Ivanič, 1997; Ivanič & Camps, 2001).

For example, regarding the above discoursal strand, recently writer voice has often been investigated through the concept of metadiscourse (e.g. Hyland, 2004; Hyland & Tse, 2004; Hyland, 2005a, 2005b; Abdi, 2002; Gillaerts & Van de Velde, 2010; Li & Wharton, 2012). Metadiscourse, such as hedges, attitude markers and emphatics, refers to 'self-reflective linguistic material' employed by academic writers to 'project themselves into their discourse to signal their attitude towards both the propositional content and the audience of the text' (Hyland & Tse, 2004: 156). A pragmatic and educational overtone could be detected here. Such studies, often quantitative, trace writer voice primarily through counting certain metadiscourse features in written texts, which is sometimes supplemented by insider informant interviews to explore the interesting patterns revealed by statistical analysis. By doing so, the researchers attempt to catch the representative 'voices' expressed by different writer groups coming from diverse language, cultural, disciplinary or temporal backgrounds.

Alternatively, text-focused *qualitative* writer identity studies, given their usually smaller sample sizes compared to the quantitative ones, can often afford to discover how the subtlety of multiple 'voices' are constructed in concrete, personal discursive acts, and gain some insight into the writers' 'skills, attitudes, and values as well as [their] personal psychology' (Maguire & Graves, 2001: 576). In this sense, L2 writers' texts, even those which are seemingly plagiarised (see Ouellette, 2008), shall reflect 'a complex set of linguistic [rhetorical and ideological] strategies through which voices were not just appropriated, but also adapted and contested as writers negotiated the tension between mediational means and their unique use' (Scollon *et al.*, 1998: 229) or alternatively articulated as 'between subjectivity and intersubjectivity' (Maguire & Graves, 2001: 568). The fact that individual L2 writers bring with them idiosyncratic life histories up to the moment of writing determines that voice construction is no formulaic or normative activity, but rather a personal and situated engagement (e.g. Clark & Ivanič, 1997: Chapter 6; Vasudevan *et al.*, 2010; Skinner & Hagood, 2008; Yi, 2007, 2010; Hull & Katz, 2006; Maguire & Graves, 2001; Le Ha, 2009; Hirvela & Belcher, 2001). The textual features selectively focused upon here are similar to those investigated by the quantitative studies on writer voice, e.g. 'syntactic analysis' (e.g. Maguire & Graves, 2001), 'self-referential pronouns' (e.g. Matsuda, 2001), modality, lexis, nominalisation, the use of the first-person pronoun 'I' (e.g. Clark & Ivanič, 1997: 142–152, also see Tang & John, 1999).

Other than textual features, evidence of writers' voices is also looked for in certain ideological revelations of the written texts; a sociopolitical overtone could often be detected in such studies. For example, Pavlenko (2004) investigated the relationship between immigrant authors' construction of identities and their experiences with the English language in American societies at the turn of the 20th century. She found that the 'images of enthusiastic voluntary Americanization' and the trope of 'individual achievement' were dominant (49). The immigrant authors' depiction of their English learning experiences was 'relatively painless' (55) and even joyful. Pavlenko concluded that, under that specific sociohistoric context in America, i.e. the Great Migration, these immigrant writers managed to position themselves as 'legitimate Americans' (55), alongside the Anglo-Saxon race. As a result, the 'racial inequities in American identity politics' (49) were obscured and linguistic discrimination was intriguingly omitted. In the same study Pavlenko points out a contrast with several *contemporary* immigrant writers' autobiographies which often express 'problematic and ambivalent' attitudes concerning their language learning and socialisation experiences as foreign speakers of English in American societies. Their writing 'depicted Americanization as an enforced and coercive process' (49) where the authors vigorously contested their linguistic identities. Apparently, Pavlenko's (2004) insightful undertaking in extracting writers' voices without resorting to discursive features of texts is enabled and facilitated by her comprehensive sociohistoric knowledge of American societies at that particular time. She, embracing a poststructuralist and sociohistoric perspective, powerfully illustrates the various external, macro forces behind the immigrant authors' identity negotiation and self-positioning as revealed in their narrative accounts. However, such an approach, I believe, is rather uncommon among the text-focused writer identity studies investigating ideology, as explained below.

The distinctiveness of the above study is its target L2 texts. Published text is a privileged form of writing; autobiography is a particular emotional and identity-revealing creative writing genre; and immigration is a major social, historical, political, economic and ethnic issue. Justified by the significance and prestige afforded by her target texts, e.g. 'a corpus of narratives that has not been previously discussed in the field' (Pavlenko, 2004: 34), the published L2 autobiographies were the only source of data (with no writer interviews or observations) on which the analysis of writers' voices was predicated. Such an approach was criticised by Stapleton (2002) as 'anecdotal' and less convincing for its suspicious reliance on stereotypical sociocultural, sociohistoric knowledge. For example, in Pavlenko's (2004) study, she made frequent references to the 'ideologies of language and identity' (35) dominant in American societies at the beginning of the 20th century, e.g. the 'trope' of 'the self-made man' (44), 'the rags-to-riches formula' (44), 'the narrative of "luck and pluck"' (45), and 'the "melting-pot" success' (45).

So far, I have discussed how text-focused writer identity studies operate on the theoretical construct that written texts are constitutive of writers' discoursal and ideological choices 'signalling the development of identity negotiation' (Ouellette, 2008: 259). Based on the same theoretical assumption, I would like to demonstrate below how identity construction can also play out in a cognitive writing process.

Voice in writers' emergent thoughts while writing

The conceptualisation fundamental to this approach is that writer voice is seen as 'doing' (Ouellette, 2008), 'performative' (Hull & Katz, 2006) and choice-making. The word 'performative' connotes deliberate expression. For example, actors perform on theatre stages, for large or small audiences, to convey a portrayal of dramatic incidents and vivid characters. In writing, 'performing' suggests writers undertaking actions to construct a certain image or character that they intend to associate with themselves, to the eyes of a scrutinising or appreciative but often judgmental audience, in a wide or restricted community.

Hull and Katz (2006) discuss the 'performative moments' in creative writing which occur 'when an intense awareness of the opportunity to enact one's identity to self and others comes to the fore' (Urciuoli, 1995, cited in Hull & Katz, 2006: 54). Therefore, throughout the actual writing process, writers will sense such opportunities arising for conducting meaningful performative acts of 'self-fashioning' (Hull & Katz, 2006) and will accordingly make decisions to situate the 'self' as part of certain sociocultural groups through performing their ideologies and practices. In this way, individual writers' sense of self as 'isolated' is decreased (47). This, I would argue, propels the progress of their writing, prevents so-called 'writer's block' and brings to them a sense of empowerment, belongingness and pleasure. Along this line of argument, voice construction could thus be seen as exhibited in the writer's endeavour in *generating* and *questioning* opportunities for ideological expressions and discursive representations, in *choosing* the most appropriate option for expressing his/her commitments and affiliations, and in *rehearsing* or *evaluating* the persona the writer intends to construct for him/herself in front of an audience. For this reason, attention in this inquiry will be given to uncovering writers' voices through looking into their cognitive writing processes, which is achieved through think-aloud protocols (a detailed discussion in Chapter 3).

I now intend to develop my argument through illustrating it with some examples from the research previously conducted for my Master's dissertation (Zhao, 2006) which also investigated L2 creative writers' cognitive writing processes (through think-aloud protocols) and which has served as a useful empirical base for my current conceptualisation of writers' instantiations of 'voices' in their immediate writing processes.

In my Master's research, three L2 creative writers were asked to write two short stories in English (i.e. a free-writing task and a story-continuation task) on the spot while thinking aloud. One writer, Kota, displayed a conspicuous pattern of writing processes. In comparison to the other two participants, whichever the task, Kota demonstrated distinctly more metacognitive attention to evaluating plot development, narrative structure, specific wording or the avoidance of repetition; and cognitively she also demonstrated distinctly more attention to choosing the most appropriate ideational, linguistic or rhetorical item, and to verbally rehearsing potential choices. Traditional cognitivist L2 writing researchers might attribute such writing behaviours to Kota's writing expertise or language proficiency and might even correlate her writing behaviours with the quality of her texts in order to prove that she is an advanced writer (for such an approach, see Rijlaarsdam & van den Bergh, 2006). However, I would argue that such writing behaviours actually also signify, in discoursal and ideological ways, powerful negotiations and declarations made by Kota of her linguistic and writer identities, i.e. an agentive and artistic L2 creative writer, a capable English language user and an insightful human being.

As described by Kota in the interview, she had not enjoyed or succeeded in learning English during her formal education. However, she had become very enthusiastic about short story writing in English after she participated in a creative writing module offered by the UK university where she was doing her Master's degree. Before participating in my Master's research, she had already produced a portfolio of short stories exclusively written in English. It is worth speculating here that Kota's story writer identity was constructed or enabled by the emancipative power she had found in L2 story writing for realising and performing a competent, legitimate and agentive L2 self in a way learning English in school had not allowed her. Most of Kota's stories were based on personal experiences. She tapped into her life experiences, along with what she had learnt in the creative writing module, as significant symbolic resources, compensating for her perceived lack of formal L2 linguistic competence, to engage in 'legitimate peripheral participation' (Lave & Wenger, 1991) in the creative writing community. Through such literacy practices, her past sense of self as a somehow ineffective L2 learner and L2 writer was effectively reconstructed and replaced by the self-identity as a blossoming L2 story writer.

For example, as shown in Kota's think-aloud utterances, she meticulously engaged in choosing the most appropriate linguistic item in the process of composition. One example is provided below (',' indicates pausing):

> 'cute beautiful kissable charming charming lovely desirable, too formal, charming charming I wanna have, more, charming it's ok charming'

In the above utterance, a series of synonyms all expressing the meaning of 'attractiveness' were put out for comparison and selection. Kota's attention to the nuances and connotations of lexis as shown above positions her as a creative writer who values and discriminates between aesthetic qualities, at least in the lexical aspect. On the other hand, the desire-statement 'I *wanna* have, more' signals Kota taking control of her own search for the most apt English word to deliver a particular intended effect (though the specific aesthetic intention remains unstated).

Two more examples which respectively signal Kota's negotiation of 'voice' rhetorically and ideationally are given below for further illustration (the exact categorisation of the think-aloud utterance is in brackets):

> 'there is a problem the story is like not a creative writing but unconditional writing'
> (Evaluating what had been written down)
> 'this man this man golden necklace I said tall man yeah a tall man walked toward him coming'
> (Tentative attempt)

The first example shows Kota's awareness of, and seeming willingness to abide by, a well-endorsed discourse convention associated with creative writing, i.e. exercising aesthetic control and imagination in expression or plot design rather than being over-expressive or self-centred in spontaneous 'venting-out' of feelings. Next, as shown in the second example, Kota's verbal rehearsal of the description of a particular scene in her story shows her attempt to stimulate an imaginative and vivid response in her reader, e.g. 'this man *golden necklace*', 'I said *tall man* yeah a tall man'. Notwithstanding subjective issues of literary quality in the product, the two examples above, I would argue, position Kota as a legitimate creative writer who attempts to stimulate some response in her reader through her compositional choices.

In the preceding paragraphs, with a few examples from my Master's research, I have tried to illustrate my conceptualisation of how identity construction can also play out in a cognitive writing process. Some readers might object that my above illustration appears somewhat selective, interpretative and subjective, rather than comprehensive and objective. In response to this, I would say that this inquiry examines the L2 creative writers' identity constructions in a hermeneutic and perhaps inevitably subjective manner (more about this in the next chapter).

Conclusion

This chapter has reviewed the ideological shifts in L2 writing studies and in L2 motivation and identity studies respectively. In particular, I have discussed comparative studies on L1 and L2 writing; then, I have also discussed the CoP theory and poststructuralist perspective which are deemed essential to the conceptualisations and interpretation of data in the present research. I have compared these two theories' slightly different points of departure in explaining the dynamic between agency and structure in identity constructions.

With the background theoretical stage set up, this chapter has then explained and justified the particular theoretical approaches for the two aspects of L2 creative writer identities explored by this inquiry, namely, (1) the discursive construction of autobiographical identities and (2) writers' voices as embodied in their cognitive writing processes. Each of these two approaches has been justified by illustrations of a certain gap in the relevant field of writer identity studies and also by discussions on the possible pedagogical gain.

As has been noted several times throughout this chapter, existent identity or writer identity research has demonstrated different ontological views (i.e. relativism or positivism) and accordingly divergent epistemological stances towards interpreting the particular phenomena (i.e. how can our knowledge of 'L2 writer identity' be acquired? Or what counts as plausible data?). On the one hand, there is the objective, scientific cause-and-effect investigation of writer identities. Such studies meticulously correlate particular criteria of a carefully controlled writer population with certain specificities of this population's identities as portrayed by the statistical data. Such studies, with their strict criteria samplings and scientific procedures in data collection and analysis, are likely to produce clear and definite results; results which are, however, subject to suspicions of charges of determinism and reductionism. In contrast, there is the hermeneutic analysis of identities of individual writers. This model perceives individual writers as unique human beings bringing with them complicated yet essential sociocultural experiences. It is a double-edged sword. Precisely because of this model's sensitivity to personal circumstances, one problem lies in that decisions on writer identities in the particular data analysis sometimes differ from one researcher to another. It was boldly pointed out by Taylor and Bogdan (1998) that '[t]here are no guidelines in qualitative research for determining how many instances are necessary to support a conclusion or interpretation. This is always a judgment call' (56). This 'judgment call' is not only subject to the purpose and goals underpinning the particular research and the specific profiles of the research participants, but more importantly, it is subject to the question of what, after all, is the ultimate drive behind a particular indication of writer identity. Does the writer make a conscious, voluntary decision? Or might it be attributed to the general social conventions and definitions attached to the nested contexts? The next chapter elaborates on this inquiry's methodological frameworks, which are informed by a sociocognitive direction.

3 Methodology

Introduction

In Chapter 1 I listed the procedures of this inquiry and the analytical frameworks (Table 1.1, Table 1.2). The overarching methodological principle asserts that L2 creative writers' literacy practices and identity issues can be systematically investigated by the innovative quantitative and qualitative instruments used in this inquiry. It adopts a sociocognitive perspective on writer identity research, which aims to understand how L2 writers' instantaneous psychological behaviours while performing a story writing activity (i.e. their emergent 'writers' voices') could be related to the writers' self-perceptions of their past sociocultural experiences (i.e. their 'autobiographical identities'). In other words, the inquiry takes up the epistemological stance that L2 creative writing is simultaneously a cognitive construct and a social phenomenon and these two are mutually inclusive. This integration is supported by Vygotskyan theory which acknowledges the significant 'role of semiotic or symbolic mediators in the regulation of psychological behavior' (Englert *et al.*, 2006: 213). Hence, one's appropriation and practice of creative writing are mediated by the one's interpretation of the multiple discourses and social worlds (containing particular semiotic or symbolic resources) available to one.

Predicated upon the above overall theoretical framework, the following research questions are addressed:

(1) How do L2 creative writers construct their autobiographical identities in their retrospective accounts of their literacy, linguistic, educational and professional experiences?
(2) In the two differently conditioned story writing tasks set up by this inquiry, what is the nature of L2 creative writers' on-line writing processes in terms of their attention allocated to different writing behaviours?
(3) What are the connections between the L2 creative writers' constructions of their 'autobiographical identities' revealed in their retrospective life-history accounts and their 'writers' voices' enacted in their on-line writing processes?

More specifically, the methodology of this inquiry embodies specific ontological and epistemological stances. The ontological question considers how L2 creative writer identities shall be perceived and consequently categorised. The epistemological question focuses on how the knowledge pertinent to L2 creative writer identities shall be acquired. To illustrate the above point, the ontological stance of this inquiry is a relational, sociocultural view of 'identities'. Accordingly, the epistemological stance is a sociolinguistic approach as well as a 'Sociocultural Psycholinguistics' (Roebuck, 2000: 80) approach to identity constructions. The sociocultural psycholinguistic approach treats 'psychological and linguistic processes' in a particular context 'as a unified phenomenon' (Roebuck, 2000: 80). The relevance of the above two theoretical approaches to the conceptualisation of the methodology will be discussed in more detail in the following sections.

The ontological stance: A relational, sociocultural view of identities

This research takes on an 'identity-centred' relational method and ontology which perceives L2 creative writers as experiencing an idiosyncratic configuration of macro and micro contexts. L2 creative writer 'voices' (or 'emergent identities') reside in the interaction among the writers' self-consciousness, their literary 'habitus' previously formed in a variety of social sites and the immediate story writing task.

Chapter 2 concluded with the Positivism–Relativism debate (Zuengler & Miller, 2006). Regarding the methodology exploring L2 autobiographical identities, the positivistic stance would believe that there are only a few valid theoretical frameworks to explore L2 identities whose relations with L2 achievement and learning behaviours are regarded as somewhat definite, rule-governed and thus pre-determined. Therefore extraneous variables (such as mother tongue and educational degree) need to be controlled. Although such highly controlled and standardised data collection and analysis methods help to alleviate the research's susceptibility to subjectivity and biases, they compromise the opportunity for investigating the complexity of 'a person's motivational *response* to particular events and experiences in their life' (my italics, Dörnyei & Ushioda, 2009: 355). Regarding L2 'writer voices', Positivist and Relativist researchers reach an agreement that voices are not largely random or innate, waving along unpredictable individual inspirations. On the other hand, the Positivist–Relativist opposition is critical. This opposition resides not necessarily in the process–product, or cognitivist–rhetoric, or cognitivist–cultural, or scientific–romantic contrasts, but primarily in how the research conceptualises writing. Does the research conceptualise writing practices, and hence writer voices, as mainly relating to concrete and transferable techniques, objective and definite textual features which are causally linked to certain criteria of writer groups (such as L1 background, L2 proficiency, L2 study background, writing expertise or educational degree)? Or does the research see writing mainly as literacy practice which is 'intimately tied to social, cultural, economic, historical, and political contexts' (Schultz, 2006: 360)? Given the non-deterministic relational view on writer voices and social factors, research on L2 writers' voices has its 'emphasis on description and investigation, and its focus on explanations rather than cause and effects' (364).

With regard to both L2 identity and L2 writing studies, a convergence of the 'positivist–interpretive' trends might be a little too ambitious to be easily achieved; but a combination of quantitative and qualitative data collection and/or data analysis methods is not rare. For example, in L2 identity research, several studies have combined quantitative and qualitative data collection/analysis methods to balance the broad brushstrokes of learner groups' motivational patterns with the portrait of individuals' particular experiences and perceptions (e.g. Lamb, 2004, 2007). Similarly, in some L2 writing research, concrete features of texts or writing processes are quantitatively marked and counted to capture the general trend; meanwhile, insider informant interviews have been conducted to elicit people's perceptions and establish specific contexts (e.g. Hyland, 2005a, 2005b, 2005c; Wang, 2003) and in-depth, qualitative analysis of the purposes and functions of particular utterances or textual features have been conducted (e.g. Abdi, 2002; Wang, 2003). This inquiry employs a combination of quantitative data analysis methods aiming to portray the general trends shown among the entire 15 participants and qualitative, in-depth examinations of five focal participants' specific perceptions of their life experiences and their think-aloud utterances while writing under the tasks.

The epistemological stance: A sociolinguistics approach and a sociocultural psycholinguistics approach

This inquiry focuses on the sociolinguistic perspective of identity constructions – 'see[ing] language as playing the central role in both interpreting and proclaiming identity' (Omoniyi & White, 2006: 2). In this research, the execution of the in-depth interviews eliciting the L2 creative writers' retrospective life-history accounts is intended to provide an emic view of the writers' sociocultural experiences particular to their own agentive interpretations. Thus, the examination of the discursive constructions of 'autobiographical identities' is the epistemological stance this inquiry has adopted towards interpreting L2 creative writers' self-recounts of their linguistic, literacy, educational and professional experiences. Next, in relation to this sociolinguistic perspective, this inquiry also takes a 'sociocultural psycholinguistic' approach (Roebuck, 2000: 80) in its interpretation of the L2 creative writers' think-aloud writing processes. That is to say, L2 creative writers' psychological activities enacted throughout the process of performing a specific L2 writing activity are interpreted as simultaneous self-positioning movements in a specific social context influenced by the writers' previously formed 'habitus' up to the moment of writing. Thus, the concept of 'emergent identities' is the epistemological approach the inquiry has adopted towards interpreting the L2 creative writers' real-time cognitive writing processes.

As previously mentioned, pre-existing, comprehensive yet essentialistic analytical models are approved by positivists for such models' assured consistency across numerous differently contextualised studies, where the frameworks are employed to produce valid and reliable correlations. However here, as the participants are regarded as bringing with them unique sociocultural experiences, a hermeneutic and explanatory model for analysing identities is needed. Regarding the quantitative data analytical tools of I-statement analysis and think-aloud protocol analysis, the coding systems were developed inductively and recursively, which went on simultaneously with the coding of these two sources of data. In particular, the coding of each I-statement and of each think-aloud utterance ultimately comes down to my own judgement on whether the particular data under examination reveals primarily the participant's agency in fashioning a particular self-image or alternatively some social forces influencing the individual's perceptions and practices.

For example, when one participant, Eliza, a passionate L2 fanfiction writer, stated in the in-depth interview, 'I would not show them [her friends on the internet] my fanfiction', did the I-statement present a deliberate action which contributed to her self-representation as a rather private L2 creative writer, or was it meant to be a resigned suggestion of some surrounding social constraints? Another example, extracted from Eliza's think-aloud protocol under the Autobiographical story-writing task, shows the creative writer considering the climax of her story which describes the first person narrator's fatal discovery of a secret diary. Eliza's think-aloud went as follows (my explanation is provided in square brackets to fill in the ellipses): '[compared to films] for real [life] there is no audience no audience audience audience there is no music to warn the audience [of unpredictable danger in one's life], for you [the person who leads the life] are at once the actor and the watcher'. A decision has to be made regarding whether the above think-aloud utterance, to a higher extent, reveals Eliza agentively *planning* what to write next, driven by a clear protagonist in mind, or alternatively, *evaluating* and justifying her conceptualisation of the plot/characterisation which might be influenced by certain social values (e.g. ideology of fatalism).

Participants

The participants were recruited through the following channels: (1) public appeals for participants through advertising, (2) liaising with a professor from the English and Comparative Literary Studies Department and his Creative Writing course members and (3) through personal contacts. People responding to my call for volunteers were carefully vetted by my enquiring into the details of their creative writing experiences (mainly through email correspondence). Questions asked included: exactly what types of creative writing had they done and in which language; how long had they practiced creative writing and how often had they done it; what did they intend to achieve by engaging in creative writing; and who were their audience. I aimed to screen out those who had, in reality, little or no experience of creative writing, no matter how much they claimed to be interested in such literacy practice.

The 15 finally selected participants were students (except for one participant who was a volunteer carer at the university) from a variety of sociocultural backgrounds and academic fields. The participants' basic profiles are displayed in Table 3.1. Among them are published L2 story writers, creative writing degree students, including an Afghan asylum seeker who had escaped the Taliban, and writers with diverse life trajectories including a philosophy undergraduate from Malaysia who had subsisted as an immigrant worker in Chinese restaurants in Britain for more than a decade. The inquiry welcomed the possibilities of having L2 creative writers from diverse sociocultural and educational backgrounds. Nonetheless, the participant writers needed to meet the level of advanced English proficiency (i.e. IELTS 7.5 or above). Whilst relatively high levels of proficiency are not a pre-requisite for second language creative writing, this project required the participants to engage in think-aloud story writing tasks completely in English (mainly for the reasons of transcribing, coding and comparing the data, which are explained later). It was felt that participants with an advanced English proficiency would be better able to meet the linguistic demands of such tasks.

Data Collection

In-depth interview on the L2 creative writers' sociocultural life histories

The in-depth interview aimed not only to draw out the L2 creative writers' first-person retrospective accounts of their particular experiences but also, more importantly, to elicit the writers' own perceptions and evaluations of such experiences where negotiations of their autobiographical identities happened. I memorised the final list of interview questions (Appendix A) in advance of my interviewing the first participant. Memorising the interview questions helped me bear in mind the interview structure and the target topics when conducting the in-depth interview in real time. However it should be noted that, in the actual interview, questions were not read from the list, nor were they dictated by their original order in the list. Some issues were talked about by the interviewee without my having to ask the question; at other times, certain topics or issues raised by the interviewee but not covered by the question list were also explored.

Table 3.1 Basic background information of the 15 participants (all the names are pseudonyms)

Name	Gender	Age	Nationality	Country of Origin	L1(s) including dialects (the order of the L1s or dialects reflects how closely they were positioned to the participant)	Other languages	Degree course taken at the time of the inquiry
Derek	Male	30	Argentinian	Argentina	Spanish	English	MA in English Language Teaching
Teng	Male	30	British	Malaysia	Chinese (Mandarin, Cantonese, & Hakka) & Malay	English	BA in Philosophy
Fai	Male	20	Malaysian	Malaysia	Chinese (Hakka, Cantonese, & Mandarin) & Malay	English	Bachelor of Law (LLB)
Teri	Female	21	British	Afghanistan	Farsi	English, Russian & Hindi	BA in English Literature and Creative Writing
Maggie	Female	25	German	Germany	German	English	Diploma in English Literature
Angeles	Female	18	Spanish	Spain	Spanish (Catalan)	English & French	BA in English Literature and Creative Writing
Jingjing	Female	19	Hungarian	China	Hungarian & Chinese	English & French	BSc in Economics, Politics and International Studies
Ho	Male	28	Malaysian	Malaysia	Chinese (Mandarin, Hokkien, & Cantonese) & Malay	English	PhD in Educational Studies
Ankita	Female	25	Indian	India	Hindi	English	LLB
Yi	Male	20	Singaporean	Singapore	Chinese (Mandarin)	English	LLB
Dong	Male	30	Taiwanese	Taiwan	Chinese (Mandarin & Hokkien)	English	PhD in English Literature
Marjorie	Female	24	French	France	French	English & Latin	MA in English Literature
Eliza	Female	18	French	France	French	English	BSc in Management
Anna	Female	26	Latvian	Russia	Russian & Latvian	English & German	MA in English Literature
Sebastian	Male	19	German	Germany	German	English & Latin	Volunteer carer of disabled students

Two think-aloud story writing sessions

Different story-writing tasks

The study examined and compared the cognitive writing processes of L2 creative writers when writing under relatively free conditions, i.e. the Autobiographical writing task, and when writing under a certain control and constraint, i.e. the prompted Story-continuation task. The design of these two differently conditioned story-writing tasks intended to tease out, from different angles, the L2 creative writers' instantiations of their writers' voices in the course of the cognitive writing processes. For each participant, the Autobiographical writing task always came before the prompted writing task, as the former is considered less stressful inasmuch as it allows for more freedom and liberty. For both writing tasks, the stories had to be written and finished on the spot.

In the Autobiographical writing task, each participant was explicitly asked to compose from the first-person point of view. Nevertheless, the participants were told their story did not have to be based on a real-life incident. My intention behind this decision was that the participants should not feel their creative or personal space restricted or intruded upon due to the potential face-threatening effects associated with writing about particular topics, especially in my presence. The story could be partially or even totally fictional, but it should be recognisably within the realist autobiographical genre.

The prompted writing was meant to be more constrained than the Autobiographical task. A story opening was extracted from William Boyd's 'Love Hurts' (2008: 157–168), a published short story written by an English writer. The story's language is accessible and vivid. Its content expresses some of the most familiar themes in people's experiences, e.g. friendship, love and marriage. My reason for choosing this as the prompt is that the L2 creative writer participants should not feel encumbered by the story's language, nor should they find that its content poses unfamiliar knowledge or world views. The participants were required to continue and complete the story in English in the most coherent and logical way that they could manage.

L2 think-aloud writing

To catch the movements of the emerging thoughts, each participant was instructed to think aloud in English while writing – that is, to 'say aloud everything they think and everything that occurs to them while performing the task' (Hayes & Flower, 1980: 4). Potential problems of requiring L2 writers to think aloud while composing have been adequately addressed (Smagorinsky, 1994; Brown & Rodgers, 2002: Chapter 3; Ericsson & Simon, 1993). For example: this process, being unnatural, puts constraints on the writers' mental processing, especially L2 writers' limited working memory; the human mind is too capricious to capture; the researchers' interpretation of the think-aloud protocols might be misled by their judgement of the writers' personality or writing ability; and, finally, think-aloud is a potentially face-threatening practice, particularly for an L2 writer. Despite the above criticism, the popularity of think-aloud protocol in process-oriented L2 writing research does not seem to diminish (see Hayes, 2012; Quinlan *et al.*, 2012; de Milliano *et al.*, 2012; Alhaisoni, 2012; Latif, 2009; Sharon, 2013). The prevailing idea is that a proper training session on think-aloud could be conducted to reduce, to a large extent, the influence of possible interfering variables and the 'effects of the protocol conditions themselves on the emergence of process' (Smagorinsky, 1994: 16).

The elicitation of the think-aloud protocol was carefully prepared in this enquiry. Before the first writing session, the L2 writer was given a 30-minute think-aloud training. The training consisted of two parts. In the first part, the writer was asked to think up a topic, within any genre, for me to write on for five minutes while thinking aloud. This was intended to demonstrate what think-aloud writing could be like. In the second part of the training, the participant would practice think-aloud in English for 15 minutes while creating a fictional 150-word reference letter for a friend to work with foreign teenagers. The L2 writer was told not to worry about grammar or sentence completion and to analyse no more than they would do normally. All the participants finished the think-aloud training without any major sign of deviation from the instruction. Then immediately after the training, the L2 writer was instructed to carry out his/her first story writing task. The writers' think-aloud speeches were audiotaped and then later transcribed for examination. Understandably, this think-aloud approach might still strike as unnatural, or even stressful, to some creative writers for whom ideas sometimes came out of the blue when they were concentrating on a completely different topic or activity such as taking a shower or walking. Hence, the participants were given the choice to think about their stories in advance of the think-aloud writing session, yet asked not to go to the length of drafting.

Potential limitation posed by the English-only think-aloud writing sessions

The decision to instruct the 15 participants to think-aloud entirely in English while writing was made for two reasons: (1) the practical exigencies of participant recruitment and (2) my own language limitation of speaking just two languages, i.e. Chinese as my L1 and English as my L2.

Firstly, given that the context of this research was embedded in a UK university and its target participants were English L2 creative writers, it was not feasible to recruit 15 L2 creative writers who exclusively spoke the researcher's L1 (i.e. Chinese) at an advanced level and meanwhile were interested and experienced in certain forms of creative writing. In addition, as previously mentioned, this research, with its exploratory nature, welcomes the possibilities of having L2 creative writers coming from diverse sociocultural backgrounds.

Secondly, although my language ability is limited to Chinese and English, I did not wish to enlist others' help to transcribe the think-aloud protocols which might have been generated in other languages. The reasons are twofold: the research purpose requires verbatim transcriptions of the audio-recordings of the think-aloud verbalisations in the most accurate manner possible; and such highly accurate transcribing processes sometimes require the transcriber to speculate on the intentions behind the participants' particular utterances, pausing or tones. This kind of speculation calls for a certain understanding of the participants' 'habitus' (which, to a certain extent, was achieved by the researcher through the in-depth interviews). Secondly, the processes of transcribing the audio-recordings of the think-aloud verbalisations are simultaneously the processes of increasing the researcher's understanding of the L2 creative writers' cognition, contextualised practices and feelings. Such an increased understanding could facilitate the researcher's later segmentation and coding of the think-aloud protocols. In view of the hermeneutic and explanatory model of analysing identities adopted by this inquiry, the transcribing and coding processes of the think-aloud protocols both demand a high level of sensitivity in the transcriber/coder in interpreting the nuance of meanings decided by the interrelationship between the participants' self-agency and the surrounding contexts.

As countermeasures to the limitation potentially posed by the English-only think-aloud writing processes, the research (1) recruited only L2 creative writers with fairly advanced English proficiency and (2) conducted an English-only think-aloud training session with each participant before the first task. In the training session, I particularly observed if the participant appeared uncomfortable with thinking aloud exclusively in English while writing. In addition, upon the completion of the training, I checked each participant's feelings about thinking aloud entirely in English. By doing so, I intended to verify that the participant's English proficiency could meet the linguistic demands of such tasks and would not discernibly divert their valuable intellectual resources from L2 story creation.

Transcribing the think-aloud audio-recordings with the help of a keystroke logging tool, Inputlog

A keystroke logging tool – Inputlog – was used in the present research. This tool is particularly convenient as it can be easily run under the Windows XP system and in Word. That means the participants could compose in Word and use the internet just as they might normally do on their own computers. Inputlog automatically generates the keystroke logging files, displaying, in a linear order, all the actions of keystrokes, mouse movements and the duration of each pause of above two seconds. The keystroke logging files, along with brief pre- and post-writing interviews, were utilised as data triangulation methods to assist the transcribing of the audio-taped think-aloud verbalisations, for more accurate segmentation and coding of the think-aloud protocols. In the pre-writing interviews, I briefly explored the participants' advance planning activities, such as how the plot was originally conceived and what preparation was made. The post-writing interviews explored participants' feelings and thoughts about the particular writing process they had just been through and the story they had produced. It also allowed me to explore issues arising from my observation of their writing processes. A small extract from one keystroke logging file is given in Figure 3.1 for illustration.

As can be seen in the figure, each numeral within the braces indicates the length of pausing. For example, in the line of 00:00:45, there is one pause which lasts roughly two seconds. 'BS' means backspace, and the numeral following 'BS' indicates the number of times the writer had pressed the Backspace key. The '·' between strings of letters indicates the pressing of the Space key. The keystroke logging files were particularly helpful when I could not decipher from the audio-recordings of the think-aloud speeches what had been uttered by the L2 writers when they were typing. The keystroke logging files were also helpful when I was coding the think-aloud protocols, e.g. when I needed to distinguish the writers' verbalisation of their writing (i.e. ongoing writing) from their oral rehearsals of what was going to be written down (these are two of the 42 coding items for the think-aloud protocols, which will be explained later).

00:00:40	T
00:00:45	ick{2125}·t·
00:00:50	TACK[BS4]tack[BS3]
00:00:55	[BS]ack·[BS3]t
00:01:00	ac[BS]ck[ENTER]·t
00:01:05	ick·tack·[ENTER]{6406}
00:01:10	
00:01:15	[Movement][LeftButton][BS7]·z
00:01:20	[BS]{2844}[CTRL+SPACE]{4641}
00:01:25	[BS9]
00:01:30	[BS]tick·tack·ti
00:01:35	a[BS]ck·tiack[BS3]ck·t
00:01:40	ickack{2547}[BS3]t
00:01:45	ackticka[BS]tacktica[BS]k

Figure 3.1 Example of an extract from an Inputlog keystroke logging file

Data Analysis: The Quantitative Analysis

I-statement analysis of the in-depth interviews

As discussed in relation to the theoretical framework of the discursive construction of identities (Chapter 2), I-statement analysis, developed by Gee (1999), is a discourse analysis tool to quantify the patterns of speakers' or writers' underlying movements of self-fashioning in speech or texts. This section will illustrate how I-statement analysis has been employed as a major data analysis method in several studies with differing research foci in order to explore people's self-identities, self-evaluations and awareness, and how exactly the present inquiry has utilised I-statement analysis for its own investigative purposes.

Gee's study on the social language of American middle-school teenagers from different socioeconomic classes

The first study under discussion here is part of Gee and his team's sociolinguistic research. It aimed to uncover 'how the working-class and upper-middle-class teenagers build different socially-situated identities in language' (Gee, 1999: 124). In Chapter 2, I briefly introduced Gee's research projects on unravelling the socially situated identities constructed by people from different social classes and professions in interviews. Gee (1999) coined the term 'I-statements' in explaining the type of discourse analysis he had conducted on the transcripts of interviews undertaken with American middle-school teenagers from different socioeconomic backgrounds. In the interviews, the teenagers from the two strands of socioeconomic backgrounds were asked about their 'lives', 'communities' and 'interests', as well as their views on some 'societal issues such as racism and sexism' (137). Through recursive scrutiny of the interview transcripts, Gee and his team categorised the teenagers' I-statements mainly 'in terms of the type of predicate that accompanies "I"', such as 'cognitive statements' (e.g. 'I think ...', 'I know ...'), 'affective statements' (e.g. 'I want ...', 'I like ...'), 'state and action statements' (e.g. 'I am mature', 'I hit him back'), 'ability and constraint statements' (e.g. 'I can't say anything to them') and 'achievement statements' (e.g. 'I want to go to MIT or Harvard'). They then counted the number of I-statements under each category and calculated the percentage of each category in the total number of I-statements each interviewee had uttered. Based on the findings, Gee concluded that '[t]he upper middle-class teenagers are focused on knowledge claims, assessment, evaluation, their movement through achievement space' and meanwhile '[t]he working-class teens are focused on social, physical, and dialogic interactions' (Gee, 1999: 146). The implication is: the social language of the upper middle-class teens tends to concern rather abstract goals and self-envisioned achievements relating to the individuals' idea of the adult world; meanwhile the working-class teens' social language seems to be primarily about their concrete and immediate daily activities and relationships within their local, perhaps somewhat narrow, contexts (144). This in turn decides that the teenagers build differently textured identities 'in and through language' (147).

Ushioda's study which traced Chinese university academics' self-awareness in English language learning

In another study, Ushioda (2008) investigated 'how Chinese university academics think about the process of developing their English language skills and how they think about themselves as learners and users of English' (1). Her study was embedded in a large-scale Sino-UK eLearning project between two universities in the UK and some leading universities in China. The project aimed to improve Chinese university teachers' English for Academic Purposes (EAP) skills in teaching, professional interactions and development. The training, developed by the UK side, was carried out through on-line self-studies complemented by face-to-face teaching to a selected group of Chinese academics who came to the UK for the course. It was hoped that this combination could promote the participants' autonomous learning and metacognitive knowledge throughout their EAP learning processes. Throughout some key stages of the training, the Chinese academics were asked to reflect on their English learning experience and motives, in particular, the difficulties encountered, their individual goals and practical plans for improving their English language abilities and finally their evaluation of their own learning throughout the programme. Ushioda's study focused on the above issues through prompted reflective writing and on-line feedback forms. To systematically examine the subtleties and patterns of the Chinese academics' self-perceptions and evaluation, I-statement analysis was used on the entire corpus of the participants' reflective writing and feedback submissions.

The coding processes were inductive; Ushioda (2008) developed the I-statement categories 'through detailed examination of the data as well as consideration of the particular research focus' (9). According to her, as explained by Gee (2005) himself, the coding categories for I-statement analysis are not 'randomly chosen but depend on an overall consideration of the data, context and particular research focus' (Ushioda, 2008: 5). Therefore, she employed recursive coding of the data by focusing on the research concern of looking into 'aspects of [Chinese university academics'] language learning awareness, autonomy and change' (9). Eventually, seven I-statement categories, encompassing 'beliefs and feelings', 'personal gains', 'needs', 'future goals', 'constraints', 'actions' and 'suggestions about the programme' were finalised after multiple scrutinies of the texts and ongoing discussions of the coding schemes with her colleagues. Ushioda then coded the entire corpus of I-statements, counted the number of I-statements falling under each category and calculated the percentage each category took out of the total number of I-statements. Accordingly, the I-statement analysis results enabled the researchers and course designers to understand the effects of the training on the Chinese university academics' language learning awareness and self-regulatory skills.

Fang and Warschauer's exploratory project on Chinese university undergraduates' learner autonomy in the English for Tourism class

In this study, which was also conducted with Chinese participants, 'to quantify learner autonomy in the "English for Tourism" class', Fang and Warschauer (2004) 'conducted an I-statement analysis on student self-evaluations written at the end of the semester' (311). Their goal was to find out how the Chinese university students 'use language to fashion themselves' as learners participating in and responding to the group-work research projects (e.g. in hotels, tourist bureaux) assigned by the 'English for Tourism' class as an innovative instruction method. Their I-statement coding categories comprise 'action', 'state', 'ability' 'constraint', 'cognition' and 'success'. Given their focus on students' learning to take control and responsibility for their work as active project-participants in this newly adopted teaching method, the 'action' I-statements were of particular importance to the researchers' concerns in that they reveal students' perception of 'themselves as taking initiative in learning the subject matter' (312). The patterns that emerged in Fang and Warschauer's analyses of the students' I-statements provided valuable insights into the students' self-evaluation and self-positioning tendencies in this learner-centred, reformist course experience. The researchers found that, broadly, the students generated rather positive self-images – for example as resourceful and pragmatic EFL speakers, as skilled modern technology users or as members of collective yet autonomous learners.

The above three studies have shown that I-statement analysis could be adapted to suit a diversity of research concerns in various social and institutional contexts, with differently constituted groups of individuals, in exploring aspects of their identity issues based on their verbal utterances or written texts.

I-statement in this inquiry

In this study, I-statement analysis was used on the transcripts of the in-depth interviews conducted with all 15 L2 creative writers. The objective was to investigate how the L2 creative writers had constructed their autobiographical identities through recounting their unique sociocultural life histories and to draw an overall picture of the patterns that emerged. The I-statement examination of the writers' sociocultural life histories was selective, as it focused on five content areas: (1) the individuals' writing experiences, (2) language-related experiences, (3) educational experiences, (4) professional experiences and (5) reading experiences. Before presenting the I-statement coding categories, it is necessary to briefly explain the procedures that were adopted to carry out I-statement analysis in the inquiry.

The first issue concerns I-statement segmentation in spoken texts. As spoken language often contains sentence fragments, I-statements were segmented and counted at basic clause level, rather than sentence level. That is to say, in a hypotactic clause relation, the main clause and the subordinate clause are counted and coded separately; and in a paratactic clause relation, the two paralleling clauses are also counted and coded separately. In addition, when 'I don't know' and 'I mean' serve as fillers, they are not counted as I-statements.

The second issue concerns the hermeneutic and inductive approach fundamental to the present I-statement analysis. By focusing on how the L2 creative writers positioned themselves in specific contexts retrospectively when negotiating the five identities (suggested by the five content areas mentioned above), the process of generating the I-statement coding scheme occurred simultaneously with the process of examining and coding the data. It should be noted here that my initial coding of each I-statement did not rely on the specific verb in the predicate, but rather depended on the overall connotation embedded in the predicate. For example, the seemingly action-oriented verb 'speak' in 'hopefully I don't speak that way' (uttered by one participant, Teng, in the in-depth interview) does not put the above I-statement in the 'action' category. Instead, the adverbial 'hopefully' plays a dominant role in deciding the implication suggested by this I-statement, in indicating that the speaker was expressing a 'desire or intention' about the image or impression he would avoid constructing for himself as a particular type of ESL speaker.

This inquiry's I-statement coding scheme is presented in the following list. To illustrate each category, examples are provided. In the brackets following each example, the particular content area (among the five areas) and the participant (all the names are pseudonyms) who uttered the I-statement are also indicated.

(1) Actions and experiences
'I have been <u>writing</u> a play, in English' (Writing experience, Derek)
'I <u>use</u> Mandarin <u>to interact</u> with my father' (Language experience, Teng)
'I <u>read</u> mostly fiction' (Reading experience, Maggie)

(2) Passives
'well he didn't <u>make me</u> write it' (Writing experience, Angeles)
'and I <u>got accepted</u>' (Educational experience, Jingjing)
'then I <u>was offered</u> a job in America' (Professional experience, Teng)

(3) States

'so I <u>am</u> quite a literature person' (Reading experience, Dong)

'when I <u>was</u> in primary school' (Writing experience, Ho)

'so emm I <u>was</u> born in Afghanistan' (Language experience, Teri)

(4) Affordances and relations

'I did <u>have a teacher</u> in high school who was actually very <u>good to me</u>' (Writing experience, Teri)

'first I <u>have English literature</u> from the fourteenth fifteenth, no fifteenth sixteenth or seventeenth centuries' (Reading experience, Derek)

'I mean I <u>have a lot of friends</u> who actually <u>speak English</u>' (Language experience, Sebastian)

(5) Ability, success and achievement

'I <u>got a very good result</u> in my chemistry and quite good in physics as well' (Educational experience, Ho)

'I was I was <u>quite good</u> in Hungarian writing' (Writing experience, Jingjing)

'I am <u>more critical more professional</u>' (Reading experience, Anna)

(6) Constraints, limitations and problems

'and I actually go for <u>too long sentences</u>' (Writing experience, Sebastian)

'because I <u>don't really have this really clear idea</u> about English history' (Educational experience, Dong)

'because it's like I am <u>not used to those kinds of speech acts</u>, speech events so to speak' (Language experience, Derek)

(7) Obligations, self-regulations and requisite

'because some part I <u>have to</u> pick up a dictionary again' (Writing experience, Teng)

'so I <u>have to</u> speak all the time in English' (Language experience, Anna)

'I <u>have to</u> keep myself very busy ... so I'm right now I'm not actually reading as in reading literature for pleasure' (Reading experience, Marjorie)

(8) Desires and intentions

'I <u>got this urge</u> I, at least this urge to write more fictional more open' (Writing experience, Sebastian) 'so I <u>want to</u> go back to do some like really traditional literature here in PhD' (Educational experience, Dong)

'and I <u>need</u> my little book thing and I feel a lot more comfortable reading than going out' (Reading experience, Eliza)

(9) Cognition

'and I <u>think</u> that my writing improves every year every day' (Writing experience, Derek)

'when I <u>get an idea</u> it bursts it's like a burst' (Writing experience, Eliza)

'but surprisingly I actually <u>remember</u> all the stories' (Reading experience, Teri)

(10) Feelings and affect

'I <u>hate</u> writing in French, it's so difficult, so many accents' (Writing experience, Angeles)

'and I really feel like quite <u>happy</u> with that story' (Writing experience, Derek)

'I just drew a boundary in a way, like <u>hatred</u>' (Language experience, Anna)

Creative writers' sense of belonging: We- and You-statements

We- and You-statement analyses were developed in this inquiry for the purpose of gaining insight into the L2 creative writers' sense of membership to particular communities as revealed in their interview comments. My conceptualisation of the We- and You-statement analyses in the present inquiry was inspired by Fairclough (2003). Fairclough (2003) discussed how the representations and classifications of social actors are achieved by speakers through their naturally shifting among pronouns like 'I', 'You' and 'We' when talking about their sociocultural experiences. Fairclough illustrated how 'we-community' and 'you-community' are depicted in texts to signify social relations and to 'represent and construct groups and communities' (149) – for example, exactly which social group is represented by a particular 'We' and how this 'we-community' is positioned to other social groups (148–150); in short, the social significance of inclusion and exclusion.

It is not difficult to see that when people speak in the first person plural 'We', they instantly identity themselves as belonging to a certain community and signal this sense of belonging to the listener(s). On the other hand, the type of You-statements focused on in the present study is when people speak in the generic 'You'. For example, in the in-depth interview conducted with one participant, Maggie, she commented on the discomfort she felt in reading out her work in front of other people and tried to explain such feelings by saying that:

> if *you* chose to write a short story of course it's not always very good or very nice, and *you* always feel if *you* are presenting like a story to someone, *you* always feel like *you* have this strange claim of a strange idea it needs to be very nice.

As demonstrated in Maggie's above comment and as stated by Fairclough (2003), the generic 'You' is employed to reference ordinary experience (150), which, I would argue, further conveys the speaker's belief in the well-accepted nature of the practice concerned or the pervasiveness of the particular phenomenon under discussion. In Maggie's case, she employed the generic 'You' to talk about a particular creative writing experience of her own. That is to say, she perceived her personal experience of feeling ill at ease when reading out her work in public as ordinary and shared by most of the other creative writers. Also, by aligning the other creative writers' problems with hers, Maggie immediately identified herself as one of them. Therefore, when people speak in the generic 'You', they are simultaneously expressing a strong identification with particular values, beliefs, practices and experiences by claiming that such values, beliefs, practices or experiences are of common sense. This subsequently shows the speakers' self-perception of belonging to the community of practice (CoP) which defines such values or experiences.

Similarly to the I-statement segmentation, the We-statements and You-statements were also segmented and counted at basic clause level. Each We- or You-statement was first coded based on its indication of the specific type of community, e.g. student writer group in a particular (disciplinary or sociocultural) context, member of a language learning community or member of a particular nationality or ethnicity. The coding categories of the community types are meant to be descriptive and explanatory. Again, similar to the approach I had adopted in examining and coding the I-statements, I employed inductive analysis of the We- and You-statements. The process of establishing the community types went simultaneously with the process of data examination and coding. Eventually, a total of 19 communities were identified, as displayed in Figure 3.2 (for illustrations of the 19 communities established through coding the participants' We- and You-statements, see Appendix B). Each participant expressed his/her belongingness to some, not all (ranging from 6 to 12 communities), of the 19 communities. The We- and You-statement coding results (displayed in Chapter 6) facilitated my selection of the focal participants, all of whom have demonstrated some conspicuous tendency of social situatedness.

1	Professional identity	10	Member of a particular ethnicity
2	Educational community	11	Member of a socialising community
3	Community of L2 speakers	12	Community of readers
4	Student writer group in a particular context	13	Individuals with a particular skill
5	Community of L1 student writers	14	Individuals with insight
6	Community of L2 (or L3) student writers	15	Member of immigrants
7	Community of bilingual (or multilingual) student writers	16	Member of computer game players
8	Community of creative writers	17	Member of experienced Internet users
9	Member of a particular nationality	18	Member of British society
		19	Gender identity

Figure 3.2 The 19 communities identified in the entire We- and You-statement coding

So far, I have explained the quantitative treatments of the interview transcripts. The next section discusses the quantitative coding of the think-aloud protocols.

Coding of the think-aloud utterances

In each story-writing process, the individual participants were required to speak out their immediate and natural thoughts all the way through. The 15 L2 creative writers' audio-taped think-aloud verbalisations were then transcribed verbatim in standard English, and consequently 30 think-aloud transcripts (two writing processes and hence two transcripts per writer) were produced. Generally, each think-aloud transcript was coded into indications of four major types of writing behaviours: Planning, Composing, Monitoring and Revising. Obviously, a notable portion of any writing process would be taken by the Composing activities, which consist primarily of the writer rehearsing what is to be written down, verbalising instantaneously what is being written down and him/her re-reading what has been previously composed. Meanwhile, the writing behaviours of Planning, Monitoring and Revising accentuate the L2 creative writers' problem-solving and decision-making moments. In particular, the writing activities of Monitoring address any evaluative comments uttered by the L2 writer in his/her story-creation process.

In this inquiry, the recursive nature of writing is demonstrated in almost every think-aloud protocol. That is to say, there is no linear order among Planning, Composing, Monitoring or Revising. Under each of these four major writing behaviours, the think-aloud utterances were further divided according to their focus on different aspects of writing. The aspects of writing are generally put as 'language', 'content or ideas', 'literary technique' or 'writing procedures'. In Table 3.2, I illustrate the coding scheme of the think-aloud protocols with examples. Some symbols are used here. The underlined parts are writers' instant verbalising of their writing; the double underlined parts are the revisions actually made to the written text; the parts within [ ] are writers' readings of what has been written down; a comma indicates pausing. When necessary, in order to illustrate the context where the particular think-aloud example is embedded, the adjoining think-aloud unit is provided within '( )'. In the '{ }' following each think-aloud example, I have specified, in this order: the L2 writer who made the think-aloud utterance, the specific writing task and the sequence of the specific think-aloud unit in the think-aloud protocol.

Ultimately, connections between the I-statement coding results and the think-aloud protocol coding results among the 15 participants were analysed.

Data Analysis: The Qualitative Analysis

The in-depth interviews

The five focal participants' identity constructions were inspected through an integration of *content* and *discursive* analyses, both facilitated, to some extent, by a *critical* perspective so as to unravel why the individuals prefer to conduct creative writing in their L1 or L2 in certain ways in a given situation and how such choices might relate to their sense of empowerment, self-liberation, self-esteem and status. Certain critical discourse analysis tools are employed to qualitatively tease out the focal participants' discursive identity constructions at the *textual* level and the level of *discursive strategies*.

At the *textual* level, I mainly focus on the use of pronouns and modality. The use of first-, second- or third-person pronouns in the focal participants' talk about themselves and other people, through active or passive voice sentences, could reveal their self-positioning in the power relations of particular social sites. Next, modality choices also play an important role in the construction of identities. Fairclough (2003) states that 'what you commit yourself to is a significant part of what you are' (2003: 166). There are two types of modality: (1) epistemic modality, which shows the speaker's 'commitment to truth'; and (2) deontic modality, which shows the speaker's 'commitment to obligation/necessity' (166–167). Epistemic modality, indicating one's commitment to truth or claims, is most often realised through tense, hedges or amplifiers. Next, deontic modality, showing obligation and necessity, is usually activated through modal auxiliary verbs such as 'should', 'must', 'may', 'can', 'have to', or modal adverbs such as 'certainly', 'always', 'perhaps', 'maybe', or modal adjectives such as 'possible'

Table 3.2 Coding categories of the think-aloud protocols

	1. Idea-generating	e.g. *'emm, why why why would she why would she say that how can I how can I give introduction, emm how can I give an introduction to to Noah to the story'* {Jingjing, Autobiographical writing, 133}
		e.g. *'no wait, emm does he meet someone on the way as he walks down the road, where is she where can he meet'* {Yi, Autobiographical writing, 177}
	2. Goal-setting on ideas	e.g. *'and yeah we can have a little description of the wedding'* {Jingjing, Story-continuation writing, 21}
		e.g. *'first point OK, body text is about emm what is game-based learning and what a game-based learning specialist do.'* {Ho, Autobiographical writing, 13}
Planning	3. Looking for language	e.g. *'oh what do you say, relaxing no that's not relaxing what do you say when you, it's healthy no it's huh well I would say, therapeutical thera there we go, I hope it exists, no it doesn't so let's see the options therapeutic oh, therapeutical therapeutic, oh there we go yes therapeutic just a matter of spelling'* {Derek, Autobiographical writing, 100}
		e.g. *'the two groups, what I want to write emm one making fun of the other being weird beatniks weird beatniks or, sh, emm, couldn't be listened no,'* {Maggie, Autobiographical writing, 330}
		e.g. *'not how precise but, it's a word, but how but how ah it's not preciseness, but they are gentle they are having strength they are strong'* {Sebastian, Autobiographical writing, 339}
	4. Goal-setting on literary technique or text format	e.g. *'OK there should be some emm, problem faced, problem faced and then climax of the story, then final confrontation and then the ending'* {Ho, Autobiographical writing, 17}
		e.g. *'OK and then I can I normally plan the number of words OK, require for example normally the body text will take emm 80% and this is 10% 10% that means it's 40 words 40 words and then this is 80% 320 words'* {Ho, Autobiographical writing, 5}

Composing	5. Tentative formulations: verbal rehearsals of what is to be written down	e.g. 'she had nothing she could not she wouldn't she wasn't able to do anything else she' {Jingjing, Story-continuation writing, 184}
		e.g. '(she what,) I just wanted to hit her, (I can't say I wanted to hit her) {Majorie, Autobiographical writing, 140}
	6. Verbalising one's writing: concurrently verbalising what is being written down	
	7. Reading what's been written down previously	
	8. Reviewing the story's beginning provided in the prompted writing task	
	9. Evaluating writing procedures	e.g. 'emm first of all I, my usual my usual way of planning emm that is I create a table, table' {Ho, Autobiographical writing, 3}
		e.g. 'OK number of words so far 299, OK' {Ho, Autobiographical writing, 32}
	10. Evaluating content or ideas	e.g. 'oh god I hope it makes sense too many riddles err' {Angeles, Story-continuation writing, 154}
		e.g. '(she what, I just wanted to hit her,) I can't say I wanted to hit her {Majorie, Autobiographical writing, 141}
Monitoring	11. Evaluating language	e.g. '"what really got on my nerves" is better "grated on my nerves" is weird' {Angeles, Autobiographical writing, 505}
		e.g. 'emm oh no you can't switch tense, the story is written in the present tense and past' {Angeles, Story-continuation writing, 113}
		e.g. 'emm maternity I don't really like that word' {Angeles, Autobiographical writing, 337}
	12. Evacuating literary technique	e.g. 'the style was really jerky' {Teri, Story-continuation writing, 11}
		e.g. 'can I capitalise "true love", yes I can and I will' {Eliza, Story-continuation writing, 149}

13. Trying alternative language	e.g. '([and comma naturally she had had the ma the maternity card going for her]) the the woman trump card the mom emm the maternity card' {Angeles, Autobiographical writing, 341}
	e.g. '(heat heat emm you could see the heat glowing glowing off the tarmac roads) glowing radiating' {Angeles, Autobiographical writing, 310}
	e.g. '(I looked her in her eyes and emm through tear filled eyes I knew what she was afraid of emm but did not did not want to emm) I looked her her in the eyes in her eyes I looked into her in the eyes' {Ankita, Story-continuation writing, 101}
14. Trying alternative content	e.g. '([to me they had been arguing for years although now that I think back, although now that I think back it can't have been going on for more than, for more than a a half a year]) no for more than a couple of months' {Angeles, Autobiographical writing, 21}
	e.g. (of course I made excuses of course I made, emm I'm not good at excuses not relevant) [of course, I made of course I made] emm, an effort' {Teri, Story-continuation writing, 305}
15. Revising language	e.g. '([though I see her only for see her for only a few fleeting seconds]) for a few lingering seconds' {Yi, Autobiographical writing, 236}
	e.g. '([a teenager dressed in a grey sweater and baggy pants, comes to a halt almost comically] with an almost comical expression on his face' {Yi, Autobiographical writing, 246}
16. Revising content	e.g. '([his expression is sagging] his hair is in a mess after running his hands through it again and again' {Yi, Story-continuation writing, 124}
17. Revising text format	

Revising

or 'probable' (170). Taking one of Derek's statements as an example, he said: 'I just feel like I should direct in Spanish'. 'Should' expresses a relatively high level of his commitment to the necessity of doing creative writing in his L1, and this in turn is part of Derek's identity construction.

At the level of *discursive strategies*, the focus is on the L2 individuals' use of (1) legitimation and (2) the logic of difference/equivalence (Fairclough, 2003: 98–103) in the process of identity construction.

Strategies of legitimation are employed by the speaker to justify his or her claims, propositions or opinions. For example, in the in-depth interview, another participant, Maggie, gave the following comment concerning why she did not like to show her work to others:

> I mean I could still write it but I don't need to read it out and I have that coz' I did one which involves like it didn't involve real people I know it didn't really involve them it's sort of you could recognise it's like ok it's like too much men who says in his foreword like any resemblance to characters and feeling and you know that, that's how they something about actual people but I did the story nevertheless and just never showed it to anyone.

Maggie referred to authority to justify her claim. That is, to justify her own claim that her audience could recognise the real-life prototype of her story even if the story 'did not involve real people'; and also to justify her reluctance to show her work to others, she referred to a common practice of professional creative writers who are also wary of an observant audience when they adapt real life incidents into their stories.

The logic of difference, which 'creates differences and divisions', and the logic of equivalence, which 'subverts existing differences and divisions', are strategies employed by the speaker to reflect his or her positioning in social classification (Fairclough, 2003: 100). By aligning with or opposing a certain ideology, the speaker's identification with some social values and self-positioning *vis-à-vis* the different social groups are revealed. The logic of equivalence is achieved by putting together text items expressing similar ideologies to strengthen certain ideological importance; here is an example from Derek's interview:

> we would be given a text and we have to write a story based on that title or we would be given a situation and then we would develop that situation and we would be given I don't know a dialogue and we had to expand and create a story based on that dialogue.

The above comment has an interesting three-part list structure of 'we would be given something by the teacher and we have to do something as students'. By putting these three sentences of paratactic relations together,

Derek was suggesting (consciously or unconsciously) the power of the teacher over students' classroom creative writing practices. Consequently, two kinds of identities are constructed here, i.e. the teacher in control and the students who had to fulfil their obligations. On the other hand, the logic of difference is realised by putting together text items expressing contrasting ideologies to highlight one's affiliation to certain ideological positions.

Think-aloud utterances: Knowledge construction and demonstration

Discussions of the five focal writers' think-aloud utterances focus on several major issues that have been addressed in existent L2 creative writing literature. They are: (1) how L2 creative writers' life histories and personalities vitally impact on their writing, (2) how L2 creative writers' implementation of specific forms, language or content in the writing processes are identifiable choices based on certain rules, (3) in what sense L2 creative writing, compared to academic writing, puts a premium on L2 writers' sociocultural heritage and personal knowledge and (4) how L2 creative writing empowers L2 writers to take creative and meaningful ownership of the language.

To examine the above issues, particular attention is paid to how the L2 creative writers' tangible think-aloud utterances can provide evidence of intertextuality and interdiscursivity; that is, how writers are able to reaccentuate and reword the language, discourse and ideology of others from previous discourses and thus to perform unique ways of self-articulation in the current cognitive writing processes. Subsequently, with an eye to the L2 creative writers' autobiographical selves, certain concrete features in the writers' think-aloud utterances may be seen as embedding specific sociocultural, sociopolitical significance resonant of the writers' previous experiences in particular milieux.

Conclusion

This chapter has carefully explained this inquiry's methodology, presenting the rationale for the methods employed. It reveals a tentative and critical stance towards the data methods adopted by this exploratory research. To check and also to improve the validity and reliability of the quantitative coding, I managed to involve a colleague who works in the field of applied linguistics and asked him to code randomly selected samples of the I-statements and the think-aloud data. Before that, I explained to him my definitions of the coding schemes and showed him some examples of my coding of the other participants' data (not those in the samples). When his coding of the samples was completed, our disagreements were settled through discussion. I then re-coded the entire datasets of the 15 participants twice. In this process, revisions were made to the coding of some data but not to the coding categories themselves.

The next chapter will commence the 'Results and Discussion' section of the book. In particular, through demonstrating the quantitative analyses, Chapter 4 discusses how the 15 L2 creative writers' *voices* enacted in their cognitive writing processes are related to their *autobiographical identities* constructed in their personal narratives. This is achieved by locating the connections between the I-statement analysis results and the think-aloud protocol analysis results.

4 Quantitative Analyses of the Connection between L2 Creative Writers' Autobiographical Identities and Their Creative Writing Processes

This chapter will illustrate how the *autobiographical identities* textured by the L2 creative writers through I-statements in their self-recounts of life histories are related to the writers' *emergent identities* (also referred to as 'writer voices') which are enacted through conspicuous tendencies of the participants' cognitive writing processes throughout the two writing tasks. To do so, this chapter will firstly demonstrate the self-positioning trends shown in the 15 participants' autobiographical identities. These were quantitatively teased out through the I-statement analysis. The chapter then undertakes another quantitative analysis: it presents the coding results of the 15 participants' think-aloud protocols generated in the two different L2 story-writing sessions and subsequently discusses some global trends emerging in such analysis results. I will illustrate how four general strands of 'writer voices' are identified through examination of conspicuous proportions taken by different cognitive writing behaviours in the writing processes. The four strands of the writer voices identified are: the Proactive Voices, the Retroactive Voices, the Spontaneous Voices and the Uncharacteristic Voices. Building on the above categorisation, relationships between the writer voices and the autobiographical identities depicted by the I-statement results will be illustrated. Ultimately, the suggestion is that there might be a pedagogical value for L2 teachers to try to understand their students' identity issues which underlie the learners' creative writing practices.

Self-Positioning Tendencies in Autobiographical Identities: I-Statement Analysis

As Gee (1999) comments on his I-statement inquiry, 'the numbers … are not meant to be "significant" in themselves … we use such numbers simply to guide us in terms of hypotheses that we can investigate through close scrutiny of the actual details' (125). The central issue is how to achieve a representative picture of the overall trends among a reasonable sample pool (i.e. 15 writers) while also avoiding the obscuration of the individual circumstances when determining identities. As explicated in the previous chapter, I-statements occur when speakers 'refer to themselves by speaking in the first person as "I"' (Gee, 1999: 124). When constructing I-statements (e.g. 'I' who acts or thinks or feels or evaluates etc.), people inevitably reveal their (often subconscious) discursive movements of self-positioning. In this section, the quantitative findings are illustrated with I-statement examples of particular L2 creative writers, displaying the investigative strength of this instrument in comprehensively yet also sensitively examining how the speakers make agentive interpretation of their roots.

The I-statement coding results are displayed in Table 4.1. With regard to all 15 participants, the categories of 'Actions and Experiences' and 'Cognition' take evidently larger percentages than any of the other I-statement categories. The suggestion is that the participants' discursive constructions of their autobiographical identities are primarily achieved through their recounting of (1) specific and tangible actions they had engaged in or particular activity-oriented experiences they had negotiated their way into and through (2) their knowledge, memory, thinking or perceptions regarding their participation or social existence in certain communities. In particular, other than participant Fai, all the other 14 participants' I-statements falling under the Actions and Experiences category unanimously represent the biggest proportion in their total number of I-statements, occupying as much as nearly half of the total (i.e. 48.4% in Yi's case) and only as low as more than a third of the total (i.e. 36.5% in Marjorie's case). In what follows, some participants' Actions and Experiences I-statements (also referred to as the action I-statements) are discussed; after that, the Cognition I-statements are exemplified.

Self-representations achieved through descriptions of one's actions

I-statements of actions and experiences can help to construct a certain image of the speakers as proactive or experienced individuals engaging in tangible activities. Abstract numbers only make sense when they could lead us to examining some conspicuous details. Here, three participants, Angeles, Teri and Yi, are chosen to illustrate the above point. Table 4.2 shows the respective distribution of these three writers' action I-statements among the five content areas focused on in the in-depth interview.

It could be seen that these three writers' action I-statements embody some individual features. As regards Angeles, a rather high proportion of her action I-statements concerns her 'Writing' practices, texturing a dynamic writer identity. Meanwhile, Teri's action I-statements pay noticeable

Table 4.1 The coding results of the 15 participants' I-statements uttered in the in-depth interviews

	Actions and Experiences	Passive	States	Affordances and Relations	Abilities, Successes and Achievements	Constraints, Limitations and Problems	Obligations, Self-Regulations and Requisite	Desire and Intentions	Cognition	Feelings and Affect
Jingjing	40.4%	0.7%	9.6%	4.5%	1.1%	1.0%	2.0%	1.8%	27.2%	11.7%
Marjorie	36.5%	1.1%	9.9%	2.2%	5.1%	3.0%	4.3%	6.4%	22.5%	9.0%
Derek	45.3%	1.3%	8.0%	4.5%	2.4%	2.0%	3.5%	5.3%	22.0%	5.8%
Dong	44.4%	0%	6.2%	1.1%	3.4%	1.6%	3.4%	8.2%	26.2%	5.4%
Eliza	41.7%	0.3%	11.5%	1.1%	2.6%	2.6%	2.3%	3.8%	23.0%	11.2%
Anna	37.8%	0.9%	6.0%	2.4%	2.9%	4.8%	6.3%	7.0%	24.5%	7.4%
Sebastian	38.8%	1.1%	8.9%	2.2%	2.9%	5.1%	3.2%	10.8%	23.1%	3.9%
Yi	48.4%	0.3%	9.4%	2.3%	2.3%	1.0%	2.8%	3.5%	25.5%	4.7%
Teri	42.2%	3.9%	9.4%	3.3%	3.9%	2.1%	5.2%	5.7%	18.7%	5.5%
Fai	31.9%	1.0%	9.4%	2.0%	4.0%	5.9%	2.7%	3.7%	38.4%	1.0%
Teng	43.0%	0.7%	8.8%	3.3%	1.9%	1.1%	2.9%	6.9%	26.3%	5.2%
Angeles	44.9%	0.5%	5.7%	1.4%	1.7%	1.9%	2.1%	4.8%	18.9%	18.1%
Ankita	41.0%	0.4%	4.8%	1.2%	1.0%	3.4%	6.2%	5.0%	27.5%	9.4%
Ho	38.7%	0.9%	13.3%	2.6%	4.8%	3.1%	6.8%	7.6%	19.2%	3.1%
Maggie	38.3%	0.8%	5.1%	2.5%	3.8%	5.8%	3.0%	2.8%	28.4%	9.4%

Table 4.2 The ideational distribution of Angeles, Teri and Yi's action I-statements

		Action and Experience I-statements				
	Total	Writing	Language	Education	Profession	Reading
Angeles	**44.9%**	35.3%	3.1%	0.5%	0.7%	5.3%
Teri	**42.2%**	29.8%	3.1%	1.5%	0.3%	7.5%
Yi	**48.4%**	35.2%	3.1%	1.6%	4.5%	4.0%

attention to her 'Reading' engagements. Finally, the intensity with which Yi described his 'Professional' actions and experiences is conspicuously higher than the other two, suggesting a certain relevance of his professional identity to his (creative) writer identity.

Angeles

Angeles, for example, expressed the following I-statements. The underlined words were the clues upon which I coded the I-statements. For convenience, the following I-statements are numbered 1 to 10; however, in the actual interview they were not uttered consecutively in this order.

(1) I would <u>write</u> about how we go into a haunted house or stuff like that
(2) so I <u>would write</u> little stories
(3) I <u>started going</u> to the internet
(4) and <u>put</u> in my blogs and little websites and stuff like that with writing
(5) I <u>write</u> like competitions now and then
(6) you know the story of Pandora's Box, well I <u>was writing</u> a story about that, like involving Pandora's Box
(7) and then I <u>was writing</u> about how she tried to steal it and the box was not what it seemed
(8) and I <u>was</u> just <u>developing</u> that how she was stealing it finding it and then getting it open
(9) well I <u>wrote</u> a little story about trees the other day about this magic forest that if you walked into it and went into the shadow of the tree
(10) I <u>started writing</u> that foresty shadow tree story

The above action-oriented I-statements portray a variety of Angeles's self-initiated creative writing moments. They show her performing a particular type of creative writing – fantasy and 'little stories' – for her own pleasure; and they depict her voluntarily sharing her stories with an audience in social space and publicly pronouncing her creative writer membership through participating in creative writing competitions 'now and then' (I-statements 3–5). Furthermore, they describe her innovatively appropriating, re-accentuating and thus engaging in a 'dialogue' (Bakhtin, 1986) with the ideology from a previous discourse – i.e. Pandora's Box or 'magic forest' (I-statements 6–10) – and performing unique ways of self-representation through her own stories. Angeles, through indicating her engagement in intertextuality in her creative writing practices, not only fortifies her fantastical story writer identity but also her self-agency.

Teri

Teri's self-sovereignty as a creative writer is manifestly projected through her description of the executive or dynamic actions she had taken. When Teri was attending secondary school in the UK, she wrote stories of her childhood memories as an Afghan asylum seeker who had escaped the Taliban and emigrated to Russia and then the UK. Her stories attracted attention from her secondary school teacher back then, as well as a UK publisher. This writing experience was described by Teri in the following action I-statements. Below, within ( ), the adjacent I-statement is provided to illustrate the contexts; in addition, my explanations are given within < > to fill in the ellipses in the I-statements.

(11) and I <u>didn't allow</u> for the whole piece to be published
(12) I only <u>allowed</u> the first section of it which was just my childhood to be published as a short story
(13) and that was the only part I <u>allowed</u> for her <Teri's secondary teacher> to read after the class or for it to be published
(14) but it was ten thousand words that I eventually <u>ended up writing</u>
(15) and I <u>allowed</u> (I think) the two thousand words or three thousand words to be published
(16) but I <u>wrote</u> it in a few weeks
(17) because once I <u>started writing</u>
(18) it goes like I <u>could write</u> three thousand words in one night or two thousand words in one night (if I find an idea)

First of all, as revealed in I-statements 11, 12, 13 and 15, Teri's self-positioning of her creative writer status is situated in two different power relationships: the power relationship between her and her teacher and that between her and the publisher. The 'effectivity of agency' and 'the capacities of the agent' (Fairclough, 2003: 161) are highlighted through Teri's juxtaposition of the actions she had respectively taken in the above two contexts with the social relations normally legitimised by such contexts. In the educational context of a UK secondary school, Teri's identities as a secondary school student and an immigrant child (indicated in the in-depth interview though not in the above I-statements) conventionally put her in a less powerful subject position in the teacher–student relationship. However, when Teri activated her creative writer identity through producing substantial work, which caught the attention of a UK publisher, in a naturally flowing and vibrant manner as depicted in the action I-statements 14, 16, 17 and 18, the power relation between her and her teacher was somehow reversed. The student–teacher relationship was transformed into the relationship between a creative writer and an appreciative reader. Teri's creative writer identity was bolstered by the significant symbolic capital she already possessed: i.e. her early childhood in Afghanistan and her living experiences all over the world as an asylum seeker (indicated in the in-depth interview). Teri's sense of empowerment as a creative writer was pronounced when she described her actions of authoritatively allowing only specific parts of her work to be published by the publisher or read out by the teacher in class.

Next, as indicated by Table 4.2, more than one-sixth of Teri's action I-statements (i.e. 7.5% out of 42.2%) refer to her reading activities, which is visibly higher than the respective equivalents of Angeles's and Yi's. Teri's academic identity as a student in the final year of her BA programme in English Literature and Creative Writing might have nurtured her self-image as a cultivated reader:

(19) I read the *Economist*
(20) and I read the *Times*
(21) I read a lot of writing from abroad from native writers
(22) so at the moment I'm reading stories from the partition of India
(23) but in terms of literature I've read a lot of Shakespeare
(24) I read the European novels of George Eliot emm *Crime and Punishment* obviously
(25) I read Fyodor Dostoevsky
(26) I've sort of read medieval writing
(27) so I read Greek mythology
(28) I read romanticism
(29) and I'm also reading biographism autobiographism
(30) I read Joseph Conrad
(31) because stream of consciousness when I read that
(32) the reason I picked World War Two Literature (was because I thought I need to read literature that isn't so engrossed in Afghanistan and Asia)
(33) but I reread all the classics

Teri perceives her future self as a political writer who tells a global audience the lived stories of Afghan people (more details on Teri are given in Chapter 7 where she is one of the focal cases). With this audience and purpose in mind, Teri was conscious of herself as an assiduous reader assimilating and engaging with various established literary discourses. Her self-agency is embodied in her actions of building a solid foundation for her stylistic sensitivity and capital of literary criticism. This in turn empowers her self-esteem as an L2 creative writer who has been 'classically' prepared and fortified.

Yi

Yi's I-statements of actions and experiences take a larger proportion than the equivalent of any of the other 14 participants, occupying nearly half of the total amount of his I-statements. Yi was an undergraduate Law student; his creative writing activities had never been related to his academic studies. In fact, Yi's self-portrait of his actions as a writer fashions the identity of a highly self-reliant and versatile writer who values conceptual power and ingenuity over rules. Yi often conducted creative writing in English to enjoy wider audiences on social networking websites where his work would be published. His creative writing practices ranged from poems, stories, to comic strips and even scripts for documentaries. He wrote for pleasure and self-expression, but sometimes also for money as a self-advertised freelance writer. Some examples of Yi's action I-statements are listed below.

(34)   \<the writing teacher> gave me a structure \<for stories>, in junior college, so 16 to 18, for A level but I never <u>followed</u> the structure

(35)   I don't <u>use</u> like very big words

(36)   I <u>try to make</u> my sentences very short

(37)   when people read \<journal articles> they just read and they try to get the information out, but for me when I <u>read</u> (I will see what's the techniques being used, what's the author trying to say, and why is the structure of his writing)

(38)   but for my creative writing I <u>try not to follow</u> too many rules or it would be very boring

(39)   because for me it\<creative writing>'s a personal hobby so I don't <u>go for</u> like the degree or whatever

(40)   but now I <u>am doing</u> comics, is comics a kind of creative writing?

(41)   as now I'<u>m trying to pick up</u> like drawing, because drawing is a different way of showing ideas as well

(42)   I <u>put on</u> \<social networking websites> \<advertisement of> writing illustrating services, so writing is freelance writing and drawing

(43)   they \<people responding to his advertisement> gave me the \<freelance writing> job so I just <u>wrote</u> it

(44)   (they \<his clients> said I need you to do this I pay you 200 dollars) I <u>said</u> OK

(45)   I just <u>gave</u> them \<his clients> the very rough idea

(46)   because I <u>was doing</u> it for the \<film> director

(47)   so I would <u>draw</u> these angles where he \<the film director> wanted and the people inside

Yi contrasted his own actions with some ratified writing practices (I-statements 34–36, 38) or peer practices (I-statements 37, 39), which in turn reflect his confidence to be recognised as a legitimate writer endowed with insight though not always following the rules.

Yi was one of the few participants who had had some full-time working experience before coming to study in the UK. He worked as a journalist for a major newspaper in Singapore:

(48) because I <u>worked</u> there as a reporter plus an artist
(49) so in the morning I <u>would go out</u>
(50) and I <u>would interview</u> people
(51) and in the afternoon when I <u>finished</u> all my interview
(52) afternoon I <u>went back</u> to my office
(53) and I <u>wrote</u> my story
(54) then after I <u>finished</u> my story
(55) I <u>sent</u> it to editor
(56) so I <u>stayed</u> late after writing
(57) and I <u>drew</u>
(58) and then I <u>went</u> home very late, emm so that's one day

When asked about his working experience, interestingly, Yi uttered a series of concise I-statements (shown above) which might suggest a certain self-fashioning as an independent or self-contained writer.

Self-representations achieved through descriptions of one's cognition

I-statements of cognition indicate the individuals' views, memory, knowledge or thoughts regarding certain dialectics between themselves and particular semiotic/symbolic mediators (e.g. what the writers have read, written, heard or witnessed) in the contexts concerned. Concerning the 'Cognition' I-statements and taking participant Derek as an example, he expressed the following I-statements to portray his writer identity:

(59) I really I always <u>remember</u> the words that the teachers of mine said to me (when I was in secondary school, and this is a teacher I am still in contact with, she said if you want to be a good writer first of all you have to be a very good reader)
(60) and I <u>think</u> that my writing improves every year every day (because of all the amount of reading that I do)
(61) (I was in the States that was in Portland, well and I have some friends and I wanted to go to the Pacific Ocean so they took me to Cannon Beach, a lovely village and so I saw this man teaching his boy how to fly a kite) and I <u>began</u> like <u>day-dreaming</u>

(62) and I <u>began</u> you know <u>thinking about</u> an old man who is watching that scene

(63) some stories <in Derek's published books> they have this open ending style, like I was <u>imaging</u> the life of the character this way as if it were you know part of a film

(64) sometimes I <u>know</u> something begins to grow in my head

(65) yes, it is the play <written by Derek for his students> so you see the language is different it's easier, and because I <u>know</u> children would be performing it

(66) (most of the time I write my emails now I write them in Spanish) if I <u>know</u> the other person knows English (I might code-switch)

The above I-statements represent different facets of Derek's cognition, i.e. memory (I-statement 59), knowledge (I-statements 65, 66), thinking (I-statements 61–64) and perception (I-statement 60), and consequently they construct Derek's autobiographical identity as a writer from slightly different angles. First of all, in I-statements 59, 65 and 66, *social relations* are evidently projected in Derek's portrait of the memories and knowledge he recalls in association with his role as a writer, e.g. his memory of his secondary school teacher's advice to him, his understanding of his young-learner actors' language ability for his English play and his knowledge of his friend's capacity for handling L1–L2 code switching communication. By representing his cognition in the context of various social relations, Derek not only articulates the symbolic mediators available to him (e.g. the advice he received and the teacher who offered him the advice), but also accentuates the depiction that the knowledge and memory he possesses as a writer are in close connection with his social existence and social agent status. In I-statements 61–64 above, Derek, through his detailed descriptions of his thinking processes, aligns himself (though probably subconsciously) with the value of imagination, a quality which is considered to be axiomatically inherent in the creative writer community. Finally, in I-statement 60, Derek articulated his alignment with another major belief and knowledge practice endorsed in the creative writer community, i.e. writers are simultaneously readers and their reading and writing activities are reciprocally beneficial.

So far we have quantitatively analysed how the 15 L2 creative writers enact particular autobiographical identities in the I-statements they uttered when recounting their previous literacy, linguistic or educational experiences. Next, we will quantitatively examine the participants' writer voices revealed in their think-aloud story writing processes.

Writer Voices in Cognitive Writing Behaviours: Coding Results of the Think-Aloud Writing

In Table 4.3, the coding results of the 15 L2 creative writers' think-aloud protocols are presented. Some figures are shaded in grey and some are boxed. Such differentiations are made as a result of the horizontal comparisons that were conducted on the proportions taken by each major writing activity (i.e. Planning, Composing, Monitoring and Revising) across the entire 15 participants. Regarding the percentages taken by each major writing activity performed by the 15 L2 creative writers in each writing task, those among the top four highest are boxed and those among the bottom four lowest are shaded in grey. The above measure helps me identify the most conspicuous writing behaviours of each writer, i.e. the major writing activities to which the individual writer allocated markedly more/less attention than most of the other participants. In what follows, I will explain how I have identified the four general strands of writer voices through examination of the L2 creative writers' characteristic writing behaviours under the two story-writing tasks.

L2 creative writers' voices enacted in their cognitive writing processes

To accentuate the characteristic writing behaviours of the 15 writers, I focused on how significant or noticeable a participant's certain *major writing activity* becomes when compared with its counterparts exhibited in the other participants' cognitive writing processes. Consequently, I managed to locate each writer's conspicuous writing behaviours across the two story-writing tasks that quantitatively and consistently 'stand out from the crowd'. The most conspicuous writing activity is seen as the individual's 'pillar writing activity' (termed by me as such and used in this way from now on). The pillar writing activity 'props up' the writer's whole cognitive writing process and plays a significant role in how the other major writing activities function. To identify the *writer voices*, it is essential to establish each participant's pillar writing activity which remains relatively stable across the two different story-writing task conditions. This data enables me to attempt a categorisation of this cohort of 15 participants into four strands of writer voices, with each embodying similar characteristic writing processes. They are: the 'Proactive Voices', the 'Retroactive Voices', the 'Spontaneous Voices' and finally the 'Uncharacteristic Voices'.

My focus in identifying the participants' pillar writing activity is on their 'Planning', 'Composing' and 'Revising' activities. That is to say, the impetus which engineers the L2 writers' story-writing processes could be the directing and goal-oriented Planning activity, or the spontaneous and

Table 4.3 The coding results of the 15 participants' think-aloud protocols generated in the Autobiographical writing task and the Story-continuation task

Participants 1–5	Jingjing		Marjorie		Derek		Dong		Eliza	
Task approach	Autobiographical	Story-continuation	Autobiographical	Story-continuation	Autobiographical	Story-continuation	Autobiographical	Story-continuation	Autobiographical	Story-continuation
Total Think-Aloud Units	**428**	**276**	**231**	**193**	**333**	**151**	**104**	**64**	**261**	**242**
Planning	9.8%	12.0%	7.4%	21.2%	17.1%	13.9%	5.8%	12.5%	6.1%	5.4%
Idea-generating	3.7%	5.7%	3.4%	8.8%	6.6%	5.2%	2.9%	3.1%	1.9%	0.8%
Goal-setting on ideas	5.6%	6.3%	1.7%	10.4%	8.4%	6.0%	2.9%	7.9%	1.5%	2.1%
Looking for language	0%	0%	2.3%	2.0%	1.8%	2.0%	0%	1.5%	2.3%	2.1%
Goal-setting on literary technique or text format	0.5%	0%	0%	0%	0.3%	0.7%	0%	0%	0.4%	0.4%
Composing	63.1%	61.2%	53.2%	56.0%	57.7%	60.3%	66.3%	75.0%	51.0%	54.1%
Tentative formulations	5.1%	5.4%	2.6%	1.6%	8.7%	7.3%	0%	0%	6.9%	10.7%
Verbalising one's writing	28.7%	29.0%	26.4%	31.6%	31.8%	27.8%	38.5%	40.6%	21.8%	21.9%
Reading what's been written down	29.2%	24.6%	24.2%	20.7%	17.1%	23.8%	27.9%	31.3%	22.2%	20.7%
Reviewing the prompt	0%	2.2%	0%	2.1%	0%	1.3%	0%	3.1%	0%	0.8%
Monitoring	15.9%	14.5%	29.4%	19.2%	18.6%	18.5%	14.4%	7.8%	19.2%	18.2%
Evaluating writing procedures	2.3%	2.9%	7.8%	1.5%	3.9%	4.6%	4.8%	4.7%	4.3%	5.4%
Evaluating content or ideas	8.7%	6.5%	10.0%	8.9%	5.4%	2.0%	2.9%	3.1%	3.1%	2.9%
Evaluating language	3.7%	3.3%	11.6%	8.8%	7.5%	11.9%	4.7%	0%	11.1%	7.0%
Evaluating literary technique	1.2%	1.8%	0%	0%	1.8%	0%	2.0%	0%	0.7%	2.9%
Revising	11.2%	12.3%	10.0%	3.6%	6.6%	7.3%	13.5%	4.7%	23.8%	22.3%
Trying alternative language	3.8%	5.0%	3.0%	1.0%	2.7%	2.0%	2.9%	1.6%	12.5%	11.1%
Trying alternative content	0.2%	0.4%	0%	0%	0.6%	0.7%	0%	0%	1.1%	2.9%
Revising language	4.7%	4.0%	6.5%	2.0%	1.5%	4.6%	8.7%	3.1%	8.0%	5.4%
Revising content	2.3%	2.5%	0%	0%	1.5%	0%	1.9%	0%	1.1%	2.9%
Revising text format	0.2%	0.4%	0.5%	0.6%	0.3%	0%	0%	0%	1.1%	0%

Participants 6–10	Anna		Sebastian		Yi		Teri		Fai	
Task approach	Autobiographical	Story-continuation	Autobiographical	Story-continuation	Autobiographical	Story-continuation	Autobiographical	Story-continuation	Autobiographical	Story-continuation
Total Think-Aloud Units	**209**	**163**	**561**	**451**	**250**	**354**	**486**	**445**	**470**	**366**
Planning	**9.1%**	**8.6%**	**13.5%**	**10.4%**	**20.0%**	**9.6%**	**11.9%**	**15.7%**	**11.9%**	**9.8%**
Idea-generating	4.8%	4.4%	1.1%	2.2%	10.8%	5.3%	5.3%	8.1%	2.1%	3.7%
Goal-setting on ideas	2.9%	2.4%	7.2%	4.9%	9.2%	3.1%	5.6%	5.8%	7.4%	5.5%
Looking for language	1.4%	1.2%	4.1%	2.9%	0%	1.2%	0.4%	0.4%	2.2%	0.6%
Goal-setting on literary technique or text format	0%	0.6%	1.1%	0.4%	0%	0%	0.6%	1.4%	0.2%	0%
Composing	**54.5%**	**58.3%**	**52.6%**	**60.8%**	**45.2%**	**61.9%**	**60.9%**	**57.3%**	**54.7%**	**53.0%**
Tentative formulations	0.5%	1.2%	2.7%	8.2%	3.6%	4.2%	3.9%	2.7%	4.7%	4.1%
Verbalising one's writing	27.8%	27.6%	28.7%	27.5%	22.8%	30.2%	25.3%	24.0%	19.8%	19.9%
Reading what's been written down	26.3%	28.2%	21.2%	23.7%	18.8%	25.4%	31.7%	30.3%	30.2%	29.0%
Reviewing the prompt	0%	1.2%	0%	1.3%	0%	2.0%	0%	0.2%	0%	0%
Monitoring	**18.7%**	**19.6%**	**22.2%**	**16.6%**	**14.8%**	**6.5%**	**17.7%**	**18.7%**	**8.1%**	**4.6%**
Evaluating writing procedures	6.3%	4.9%	3.3%	3.1%	1.6%	0.6%	3.6%	4.2%	4.4%	1.6%
Evaluating content or ideas	4.3%	4.3%	5.7%	6.2%	11.2%	3.3%	6.6%	6.9%	1.0%	2.8%
Evaluating language	8.1%	10.4%	12.8%	6.2%	1.6%	2.3%	5.9%	5.5%	2.7%	0%
Evaluating literary technique	0%	0%	0.4%	1.1%	0.4%	0.3%	1.6%	2.1%	0%	0.2%
Revising	**17.7%**	**13.5%**	**11.1%**	**12.2%**	**20.0%**	**22.0%**	**9.5%**	**8.3%**	**25.3%**	**32.5%**
Trying alternative language	2.4%	1.8%	5.5%	5.3%	3.2%	3.7%	3.9%	2.2%	5.1%	6.8%
Trying alternative content	0.5%	0%	0.4%	1.8%	1.6%	1.1%	0.8%	0.4%	1.1%	1.4%
Revising language	9.1%	5.5%	4.1%	3.6%	8.4%	12.7%	3.4%	2.3%	14.5%	15.6%
Revising content	3.8%	3.1%	0.9%	1.1%	6.8%	4.2%	0.8%	2.5%	4.6%	8.7%
Revising text format	1.9%	3.1%	0.2%	0.4%	0%	0.3%	0.6%	0.9%	0%	0%

Participants 11–15	Teng		Angeles		Ankita		Ho		Maggie	
Task approach	Autobiographical	Story-continuation	Autobiographical	Story-continuation	Autobiographical	Story-continuation	Autobiographical	Story-continuation	Autobiographical	Story-continuation
Total Think-Aloud Units	200	162	611	425	512	420	122	86	356	243
Planning	1.5%	1.9%	5.2%	9.6%	2.7%	4.5%	18.0%	29.1%	3.9%	1.6%
Idea-generating	1.5%	0%	2.8%	4.0%	1.0%	3.7%	6.5%	12.9%	3.0%	0.8%
Goal-setting on ideas	0%	1.3%	1.5%	4.5%	0.2%	0.4%	6.5%	13.9%	0%	0.8%
Looking for language	0%	0.6%	0.7%	1.1%	1.3%	0.2%	0%	0%	0.6%	0%
Goal-setting on literary technique or text format	0%	0%	0.3%	0%	0.2%	0.2%	5.0%	2.3%	0.3%	0%
Composing	67.5%	75.3%	52.0%	59.1%	46.5%	61.0%	40.2%	40.7%	57.6%	63.8%
Tentative formulations	5.5%	8.0%	7.2%	7.8%	1.6%	2.6%	0.8%	0%	3.1%	3.3%
Verbalising one's writing	29.5%	36.4%	15.5%	25.4%	13.3%	24.3%	13.1%	24.4%	21.1%	24.7%
Reading what's been written down	32.5%	29.6%	29.3%	24.9%	31.6%	33.3%	26.2%	11.6%	33.4%	35.8%
Reviewing the prompt	0%	1.2%	0%	0.9%	0%	0.7%	0%	4.7%	0%	0%
Monitoring	12.5%	9.3%	14.2%	13.6%	15.8%	10.0%	20.5%	29.1%	15.4%	3.3%
Evaluating writing procedures	5.0%	4.8%	0.9%	2.1%	1.9%	1.3%	12.4%	12.7%	10.1%	2.9%
Evaluating content or ideas	2.5%	0%	2.7%	5.1%	3.3%	3.9%	0.8%	14.0%	2.2%	0%
Evaluating language	5.0%	4.5%	9.0%	6.2%	9.6%	4.8%	3.2%	2.4%	3.1%	0%
Evaluating literary technique	0%	0%	1.6%	0.2%	1.0%	0%	4.1%	0%	0%	0.4%
Revising	18.5%	13.6%	28.5%	17.6%	35.0%	24.5%	21.3%	1.2%	23.0%	31.3%
Trying alternative language	3.0%	3.1%	10.6%	4.6%	14.8%	9.6%	1.7%	0%	5.6%	7.1%
Trying alternative content	0.5%	0.6%	3.1%	1.9%	0.8%	0%	0%	0%	0.6%	0.4%
Revising language	10.0%	6.2%	10.1%	6.9%	15.1%	11.8%	13.9%	0%	10.9%	15.2%
Revising content	3.5%	3.1%	2.9%	3.3%	3.3%	2.1%	4.1%	1.2%	5.9%	8.6%
Revising text format	1.5%	0.6%	1.8%	0.9%	1.0%	1.0%	1.6%	0%	0%	0%

improvisational Composing activity, or the meticulous and compensatory Revising activity. On the other hand, the Monitoring activity, i.e. evaluative comments or any kind of metacomments, is considered as attaching to any of the above three major writing activities for the effect of strengthening that particular writing activity's pillar function.

To locate each participant's pillar writing activity, I looked for that particular major writing activity, among Planning, Composing and Revising, the percentage taken by which generally and consistently ranks higher among the 15 writers than the other two major writing activities have done. To achieve this, for each participant, I noted the respective rankings taken by his/her Planning, Composing and Revising writing activities after comparing each of them with their respective counterparts exhibited in the other participants' cognitive writing processes. I established a rank order of each participant's writing activities in terms of bands; that is, does the percentage taken by this individual writer's Planning or Composing or Revising activity rank among the top four highest, or among the middle seven, or among the bottom four lowest. Consequently, Table 4.4 was produced. In Table 4.4, with each of the above-mentioned three major writing activities as the unit of examination, the rankings of the percentages respectively taken by the 15 writers are displayed. The letter

Table 4.4 The respective rankings of the 15 participants' Planning, Composing and Revising writing activities

The writing activity of Planning

Top 4	Marjorie S; Derek A, Derek S; Sebastian A; Yi A; Teri S; Ho A, Ho S
Middle 7	Jingjing A, Jingjing S; Marjorie A; Dong A, Dong S; Eliza A; Anna A, Anna S; Sebastian S; Yi S; Teri A; Fai A, Fai S; Angeles S
Bottom 4	Eliza S; Teng A, Teng S; Angeles A; Ankita A, Ankita S; Maggie A, Maggie S

The writing activity of Composing

Top 4	Jingjing A; Dong A, Dong S; Yi S; Teri A; Teng A, Teng S; Maggie S
Middle 7	Jingjing S; Marjorie A; Derek A, Derek S; Anna A, Anna S; Maggie A Sebastian A, Sebastian S; Teri S, Fai A, Angeles A, Angeles S; Ankita S;
Bottom 4	Marjorie S; Eliza A, Eliza S; Yi A; Fai S; Ankita A; Ho A, Ho S

The writing activity of Revising

Top 4	Eliza A, Eliza S; Fai A, Fai S; Angeles A; Ankita A, Ankita S; Maggie S
Middle 7	Jingjing A, Jingjing S; Dong A; Anna A, Anna S; Sebastian S; Yi A, Yi S; Teri S; Teng A, Teng S; Angeles S; Ho A; Maggie A
Bottom 4	Marjorie A, Marjorie S; Derek A, Derek S; Dong S; Sebastian A; Teri A; Ho S

Table 4.5 The four strands of writer voices

The Proactive Voices	Derek, Ho, Marjorie, Teri, Sebastian
The Spontaneous Voices	Dong, Teng
The Retroactive Voices	Fai, Ankita, Eliza, Maggie, Angeles
The Uncharacteristic Voices	Yi, Anna, Jingjing

'A' following the participants' names refers to the Autobiographical writing process; the letter 'S' refers to the Story-continuation writing process. For some writers, a major writing activity ranks in the same league across the two story-writing tasks; and in such cases, the two ranking results are framed together in shaded boxes.

A participant's pillar writing activity should rank in the top four range, at least in one of the two story-writing processes (the Autobiographical and the Story-continuation tasks). On the other hand, a participant's non-pillar writing activities performed in the two story-writing processes, by and large, locate in the middle seven and bottom four ranges. Using the analysis method illustrated above, four strands of writer voices are established among the 15 participants and the results are shown in Table 4.5.

With the global trends emerging in the think-aloud coding results established, in the next section, I will explore if any connection could be found between the distribution of these four strands of writer voices among the 15 participants and the writers' I-statement tendencies for constructing their autobiographical identities (shown earlier). The intention is to show that the L2 creative writers' story-creation processes are not coincidental or formulaic, but mediated by the writers' socioculturally formed evaluative lens through which they interpret and perform the current literacy activities.

Relationships between L2 Creative Writers' Voices and Their Autobiographical Identities
Category-by-category comparisons of the four strands of writers' I-statement tendencies

Previously, I have established the four strands of writer voices. Now, I will compare these four strands of writers' I-statement coding results category by category. The comparisons are displayed in Figure 4.1: the 10 line charts respectively focus on the ten I-statement categories; each line of a specific colour represents a particular strand of writer voice; and each dot in each line represents a particular participant embodying that voice. It should be noted that regarding each of the four lines which represents a particular strand of writer voice, there is no particular arrangement regarding which participant's result comes first, or second, or third, yet the specific dot in each line, throughout the ten line charts, consistently corresponds to the same participant. In addition, the sequence for writers in each line is the same as the sequence in which writers are displayed under each strand of writer voice in Table 4.5 shown earlier. Finally, the reason I have threaded the dots into lines, rather than leaving them in the form of dots of different colours, is that I consider lines a more effective form of demonstrating the differences among these four strands of writers' I-statement approaches and thus highlighting any pattern revealed in such comparisons. The ultimate aim is to see the connection between the participants' particularly characterised writing behaviours and the particularly characterised configuration of their various I-statement types.

In Figure 4.1, if we consider the four strands of writer voices together, we could hardly see any pattern throughout the ten charts. However, if we focus only on the solid black line (the Proactive-Voice Writers) and the white line (the Retroactive-Voice Writers), a discernible pattern can be observed in most of the categories except for Actions and Experiences (Figure 4.1a). Consequently, Figure 4.1 reveals that the Proactive-Voice Writers and the Retroactive-Voice Writers show distinct I-statement tendencies for constructing their autobiographical identities. Overall, the emerging picture is that (1) the L2 creative writers who expressed *proactive voices* in their story-writing processes employed a more assertive, more socially textured and also more self-assured I-statement approach in constructing their autobiographical identities than the Retroactive-Voice Writers, and (2) the L2 creative writers who revealed *retroactive voices* employed a more implicit, more expressive and also more self-critical I-statement approach in their self-representations. This observation will be elaborated upon in the following sections firstly through a chart-by-chart comparison of the Proactive-Voice Writers and the Retroactive-Voice Writers' I-statement approaches. Subsequently, concerning each of these two strands of writers who have enacted the proactive and the retroactive voices, a summative yet refined picture will be drawn synthesising the writers' I-statement tendencies in constructing their autobiographical identities.

The Proactive-Voice Writers' and the Retroactive-Voice Writers' respective employment of the varied types of I-statements

Figure 4.1a on the Actions & Experiences I-statements shows no perceptible difference between the percentages respectively taken by the Proactive-Voice Writers and the Retroactive-Voice Writers. The suggestion is that these two types of writers, despite their different writing 'habitus' revealed in the cognitive writing processes, equally recount their actions so as to fashion their autobiographical identities from a dynamic and agentive angle.

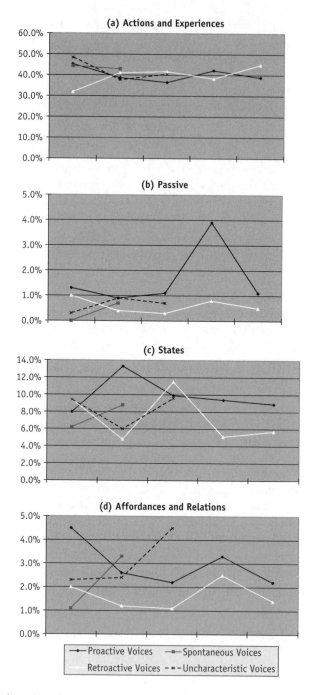

Figure 4.1 (Continued)

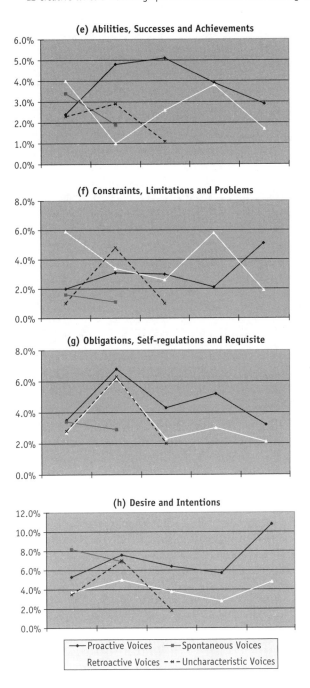

Figure 4.1 (Continued)

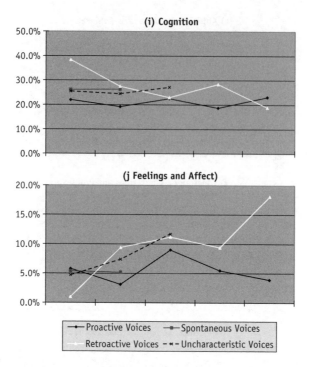

Figure 4.1 Category-by-category comparisons of the four strands of writers' I-statement coding results

In Figure 4.1b on the Passive I-statements, it can be seen that the Proactive-Voice Writers' solid black line constantly rises above the Retroactive-Voice Writers' white line. As the passive voice often accentuates particular social relations (examples given later), especially power relations, the implication is that the Proactive-Voice Writers more visibly reveal their awareness of the dialectic between their self-agencies and the surrounding social structures.

In Figure 4.1c on the States I-statements, the Proactive-Voice Writers' solid black line generally rises above the Retroactive-Voice Writers' white line. Although there are two peaks in the white line which rise above the black line, their particular margins are noticeably narrower than the margins by which the three remaining solid black dots rise above the white line. The indication is that the Proactive-Voice Writers generally display a higher tendency for articulating the I-statements on their own physical or social circumstances or on their personal characteristics (examples given later). Consequently, the Proactive-Voice Writers somehow, to a higher extent, reveal their awareness of their own social positioning.

In Figure 4.1d on the Affordances and Relations I-statements, again, the Proactive-Voice Writers' solid black line constantly rises above the Retroactive-Voice Writers' white line with an evident margin all the way through. The suggestion is that the Proactive-Voice Writers conspicuously demonstrate a higher tendency for pointing out their possession of varieties of 'capital' in the communities concerned, e.g. their materialistic or symbolic 'capital' such as private language courses, attentive teachers or dictionaries and books, and their social 'capital' such as friendships, professional relationships or social contacts.

In Figure 4.1e on the Abilities, Successes and Achievements I-statements, the Proactive-Voice Writers' solid black line largely rises above the Retroactive-Voice Writers' white line. The implication is that the Proactive-Voice Writers seem more amenable to revelations concerning their positive self-esteem and status and consequently, to a high degree, represent themselves as self-assured individuals.

Figure 4.1f on the Constraints, Limitations and Problems I-statements shows that the Retroactive-Voice Writers display a higher tendency than the Proactive-Voice Writers for employing a self-critical approach in constructing their autobiographical identities, i.e. explicitly voicing their deficiency in respect of the sanctioned knowledge practices or values of the communities they perceive themselves belonging to. This corresponds with what is exhibited in the previous chart where the Proactive-Voice Writers display a higher tendency for stating their strengths and achievements.

In Figure 4.1g on the Obligations, Self-regulations and Requisite I-statements and Figure 4.1h on the Desire and Intentions I-statements, the Proactive-Voice Writers' solid black line constantly rises above the Retroactive-Voice Writers' white line by perceptible margins. Hence, the Proactive-Voice Writers reveal a higher tendency than the Retroactive-Voice Writers for not only articulating their 'ought selves' but also for expressing their 'ideal selves' (Higgins, 1987, cited in Dörnyei, 2009: 13). However, it should be noted that the present research's take on the notions of the 'ought self' and the 'ideal self' is somewhat different from Higgins's conceptualisation of these two issues. Cited in Dörnyei (2009: 14), Higgins defined the 'ought self' as *someone else's* vision for the individual' (my italics). However here, when an 'ought self' is suggested in an I-statement, it refers to the individual's *own* sense (without any emphasis put on some else's vision) 'of duties, obligations or moral responsibilities' (Dörnyei, 2009: 13) – in other words, what 'one believes one *ought to* possess to meet expectations and to *avoid* possible negative outcomes' (original italics, 29). Regarding the 'ideal self', Higgins (1987, cited in Dörnyei, 2009) and Dörnyei (2009) both conceptualised such a concept as a somewhat imaginary or ambitious picture of what one would like to become or do in the future. However, in this inquiry when the participants depicted their 'ideal selves' in their I-statements, they could either refer to their rather tangible or specific desires which are readily achievable or refer to their fairly substantial or abstract aspirations and wishes which are left for future realisation (examples will be provided later).

In Figure 4.1i on the Cognition I-statements and Figure 4.1j on the Feelings and Affect I-statements, the trend is reversed. We can see that the Retroactive-Voice Writers' white line generally rises above the Proactive-Voice Writers' solid black line in both charts. The indication is that in their I-statement approaches for identity constructions, the Retroactive-Voice Writers not only display a higher tendency than the Proactive-Voice Writers for demonstrating the various aspects of their *cognition* (i.e. knowledge, memory, thinking and perception), but they also seem more willing to express their *feelings* and *emotions* when negotiating their particular identities. The specifics of the participants' *cognition* (e.g. perception or knowledge of certain issues, thinking about or imagining certain things) or *emotion* (e.g. happiness, awkwardness, hatred or enjoyment) subtly reflect the individuals' alignment or disagreement with particular interest or knowledge practices associated with specific social groups.

Next, I will discuss respectively the overall characteristics of the Proactive-Voice and the Retroactive-Voice Writers' autobiographical identities. Examples of I-statements will be provided as illustrative support. Examples of think-aloud utterances illustrating the four strands of writer voices will be used in the next chapter's discussions on task influences.

The Proactive-Voice Writers' constructions of their autobiographical identities: Assertive, self-assured and socially textured

A more socially textured I-statement approach by the Proactive-Voice Writers

Compared with the Retroactive-Voice Writers, the Proactive-Voice Writers more intensely suggested the social relations and social circumstances they were immersed in, particularly through showing higher tendencies for making the following three types of I-statement: I-statements in the *passive* voice, I-statements on one's *affordances and relations* and I-statements on one's *states*. The *passive* voice often accentuates authority or power issues in particular social relations (see Fairclough, 2003: 145) and accordingly the privileges afforded by certain social parties, i.e. either the privileges afforded by the social parties who made the speaker 'I' do particular things or the privileges regarded by the speaker 'I' as afforded by him/herself who was asked or offered to do certain things. To illustrate this point, some I-statement examples uttered by the Proactive-Voice Writers are provided below. The content area and the participant who uttered the specific I-statement are indicated within '{ }'; sometimes the adjacent I-statement is provided within ( ) to illustrate the context; in addition, my explanations are given within < > to fill in the ellipses in the I-statements.

Passive voice

(1) so I <u>was invited</u> to read some stories to the public {Writing, Derek}

(2) (doing a PhD is part of my work) because I'<u>m sponsored</u> by Malaysian government to to do to get a PhD in 3 years {Profession, Ho}

(3) (I think my problem is because in academic writing) I <u>have been constrained</u> to plan things so much (that now I just hate planning) {Writing, Marjorie}

(4) but I <u>wasn't allowed</u> to continue with it <stream of consciousness> {Writing, Teri}

(5) and since I <u>got invited</u> to his family already (I had like an insight into English culture) {Language, Sebastian}

(6) and I <u>was allowed</u> to have like examples of of culture English experienced in a family and stuff {Language, Sebastian}

In I-statements 1 and 2 above, the dialogue between the specific social relation and the speaker's sense of self respectively results in the positive representations of Derek's creative writer identity and Ho's professional identity, both of which are imbued with a sense of pride and self-esteem. To be more specific, Derek and Ho perceived themselves to be in a mutually beneficial joint-partnership with a superior social party which possesses significantly greater authoritative power and social influence than themselves, i.e. the book publisher who made money out of publishing Derek's stories and the Malaysian government who funded Ho to do a PhD in the UK and in turn required his future service in Malaysia. In contrast, as shown in I-statements 3 and 4, the society–agency dialogue respectively leads to the negative representations of Marjorie and Teri's student writer identities. Marjorie and Teri positioned themselves as the subjugated social members whose agency was deprived in their engagements with the more authoritative social members (e.g. teachers, examiners). The discontentment or even rebellious sentiment of Marjorie and Teri towards their social positioning is noticeable. Finally, in I-statements 5 and 6, Sebastian positioned himself as a non-native speaker living in Britain entering a friendship with a British family. The gratification he felt in negotiating his access into the English culture and the English language in a personal and also meaningful context is evident. On the other hand, Sebastian's agency is implied in his awareness of how this social relation could shape his identity formation, as connoted precisely by the passive voice 'I was allowed to'. That is, Sebastian perceived that his interaction with these more experienced social members in this context allowed him to accumulate 'capital' as an ESL speaker who was in the process of a 'centripetal participation in the ambient community' (Lave & Wenger, 1991: 100) of bilingual speakers.

In what follows, I will discuss how the I-statements on States and on Affordances and Relations similarly demonstrate the speakers' awareness of the surrounding social relations playing a role in their identity formations.

First of all, some examples of the States I-statements made by the Proactive-Voice Writers are provided below.

States

   (7)   though of course when I <u>was at university</u> (I had to write in English for everything) {Writing, Derek}

   (8)   (I think) I'<u>m very very fortunate</u> to be born as a Malaysian Chinese {Language, Ho}

   (9)   well I <u>could</u> speak a bit of German like A-level German a little bit of Spanish {Language, Marjorie}

  (10) (what they usually say is that emm they couldn't say) I'<u>m French</u> {Language, Marjorie}

  (11) (and it <her creative writing work> concentrated on the recent <u>experiences) that I had</u> in Kabul {Writing, Teri}

  (12) (so I really tried to get into that English literature) when I <u>was here</u> <in this particular UK university> {Reading, Sebastian}

The States I-statements include two sub-branches, i.e. announcement of one's personal characteristics, as exemplified in I-statements 8, 9 and 10, and indication of one's sociocultural circumstances, as exemplified in I-statements 7, 11 and 12. We can see that in I-statements 8, 9 and 10, the participants straightforwardly spoke out the characteristics they considered associated with themselves, i.e. Ho's self-perceived fortunate status as a Chinese–Malaysian bilingual; Marjorie's ability to speak some German and Spanish; and Marjorie's national and L1 identity as a French person. As shown in this inquiry, such categorical declarations are the most straightforward and forceful I-statement approach employed by the participants to convey their social identities. Furthermore, such declarations sometimes also signal the individuals' awareness of the qualities and practices associated with the particular social groups from where their social identities derive, e.g. the qualities that make Ho feel 'fortunate' to be a member of a Malaysian Chinese community (e.g. bilingual instinct and cultural diversity) or the qualities that Marjorie considered revealed by French people (such as accent) when they speak in English with British people. On the other hand, the States I-statements depicting one's circumstances, such as I-statements 7, 11 and 12, display the speaker's awareness of the shaping effect of the specific social contexts on his/her own knowledge practices. For example, in I-statement 7, Derek indicated his awareness that his university degree course shaped his L2 writing activities. In order to be a legitimate member of this context, Derek had to comply with the rules of engaging intensively in English writing.

Now, we will turn to some examples of the I-statement on Affordances and Relations which are declarations made by the speakers of their social capital.

Affordances and Relations

(13) (I always remember the words that the teachers of mine said to me when I was in secondary school and this is <u>a teacher</u>) I <u>am still in contact with</u> {Writing, Derek}

(14) and, I <u>have some lecturers</u> from Jordan from India India {Education, Ho}

(15) later on I <u>had a teacher</u> who kept reading my essays or my creative writing in front of the class {Writing, Marjorie}

(16) and I <u>know people</u> who work for the Persian BBC {Writing, Teri}

(17) so I'<u>m in contact with them</u> <the people who work for the Persian BBC> (when if they come to my house) {Writing, Teri}

(18) I mean I <u>have a lot of friends</u> who actually speak English {Writing, Sebastian}

In I-statements 13–18 on Affordances and Relations, the Proactive-Voice Writers notably suggest the facilitating effect of some social relations. For example, I-statements 14 and 15 respectively show Ho's and Marjorie's somewhat proud self-identity due to their engagements with certain more powerful and recognised others.

A more direct and self-assured I-statement approach by the Proactive-Voice Writers

The Proactive-Voice Writers evince a higher tendency for making Affordances and Relations and Abilities, Successes and Achievements I-statements. It is self-explanatory how the above two types of I-statements texture confident self-identities. Hence, in what follows, I will concentrate on how the Proactive-Voice Writers, through generally displaying a higher tendency than the Retroactive-Voice Writers for voicing the Obligations, Self-regulations and Requisite I-statements and the Desire and Intentions I-statements, have established a more direct and assertive I-statement approach in their identity constructions. Let us first look at some examples of the Proactive-Voice Writers' I-statements on Obligations, self-regulations and requisite.

Obligations, Self-regulations and Requisite

(19) I <u>should</u> review it my own writing (but I don't know when I might have it published) {Writing, Derek}

(20) (for emm my modules are Shakespeare) which I'<u>m supposed to</u> read a lot of good plays {Reading, Teri}

Desire and Intentions

(21) if I <u>want to</u> write something in which humour is involved (I'll prefer English) {Writing, Marjorie}

(22) I'll <u>prefer</u> English {Writing, Marjorie}
(23) but if I <u>want to</u> work on specific puns, (I'll probably choose French) {Writing, Marjorie}
(24) (but if I want to work on specific puns), I'll probably <u>choose</u> French {Writing, Marjorie}

Fairclough (2003) stated that 'what you commit yourself to is a significant part of what you are – so modality choices in texts can be seen as part of the process of texturing self-identity' (166). Thus, declaring one's commitment to certain practices or attributes in the I-statements is an assertive identity-construction strategy. For example, in I-statement 19 above, by speaking out his responsibility of conducting revision of his own writing before attempting any publication, Derek represents himself as a practiced creative writer who understands that spontaneity and writing for instant pleasure cannot get one's work published, and consequently positions himself as a legitimate member of the publishing creative writer community.

Regarding the I-statements on Desire and Intentions, how the speakers represent their aspirations, intentions or passions reveals the possibilities they perceive in their own initiatives or abilities for achieving particular results. In I-statements 21–24, the Proactive-Voice Writer Marjorie, by indicating her desire to work on humour in the English language and puns in the French language, pronounces her ability to wittily switch between her L1 and L2 at her own will in order to achieve particular literary effects.

The Retroactive-Voice Writers' constructions of their autobiographical identities: Implicit, expressive and self-critical
A more self-critical I-statement approach by the Retroactive-Voice Writers

Firstly, compared to the Proactive-Voice Writers, the Retroactive-Voice Writers adopt a more self-critical I-statement approach in their identity constructions in that they display a higher tendency for pointing out their deviations or discrepancies from certain valued attributes or knowledge practices (i.e. their self-perceived 'constraints, limitations and problems') associated with the communities that they committed themselves to. A few examples of the Retroactive-Voice Writers' I-statements on Constraints, Limitations and Problems are given below to illustrate this point.

Constraints, Limitations and Problems
(25) I'm <u>not good at</u> that <recalling stories> {Reading, Fai}
(26) because I can't <u>practice</u> <law>, (you still need the LLB to practice) {Education, Ankita}
(27) (and do draft then rewrite and stuff) which I <u>have great difficulty</u> to do {Writing, Eliza}

(28) maybe I <u>wasn't as good as</u>, wasn't like so good <u>in oral communication</u>
{Language, Maggie}
(29) (and then I could see the story in my mind) but I <u>couldn't write it</u>
{Writing, Angeles}

For example, in I-statement 25, Fai states the discrepancy between his 'actual reader self', who had constraint in recalling the stories he had previously read, and the 'ideal literature reader', as perceived by Fai, who possesses a remarkable memory and knowledge. In I-statement 27, Eliza indicates the discrepancy between her self-perceived actual self – an academic writer who had problems with revision and multiple drafting – and the ideal writer perceived by her.

However, if we compare the above I-statements on Constraints, Limitations and Problems with the I-statements on Obligations, Self-regulations and Requisite previously illustrated, we can see that, although the above I-statements construct rather self-critical images of the Retroactive-Voice Writers who identified their less-than-ideal practices or abilities, such I-statements do not necessarily show the speakers' motives to reduce the discrepancy between their 'actual selves' and their self-perceived 'ideal selves' sanctioned by the social sites they are situated in. As shown in the above I-statements, the Retroactive-Voice Writers do not demonstrate what the Proactive-Voice Writers manifest in the I-statements on Obligations, Self-regulations and Requisite and on Desire and Intentions – that is, the desire to maintain or improve one's legitimate peripheral participation in a particular community through articulating one's motivation (extrinsic or intrinsic) to commit to certain beliefs or practices valued by the communities they are, or aspire to be, members of. Therefore, I would argue that the Retroactive-Voice Writers, through displaying a higher tendency for making the Constraints, Limitations and Problems I-statements, display a self-critical but also implicit approach in negotiating their autobiographical identities.

A more implicit and personal I-statement approach by the Retroactive-Voice Writers

The Retroactive-Voice Writers take an implicit yet expressive I-statement approach in constructing their autobiographical identities. This subtlety and expressiveness resides in that the Retroactive-Voice Writers display a higher tendency for exploring various aspects of their *cognition* (i.e. knowledge, memory, thinking and perceptions) and *emotion* in response to particular practices or values. As the Cognition I-statements have been discussed earlier (section 4.1.2), the following part illustrates the Emotion I-statements.

Emotions are generally treated as private, natural and spontaneous, and thus often understood as self-justified and cannot always be rationalised.

When suggesting their social positioning, people's expressions of their emotions are less likely to be challenged or contested by their listener(s) in the way their articulations of their *perceptions* might have been. Fairclough (2003) distinguished 'between personal and social aspects of identity – **social identity and personality**' (originally in bold, 160). He claimed that people's 'personality' enables the individuals to personify their 'social identity' with their 'primary and ultimate concerns' and enact their social identity 'in a distinctive way' (161). With people coming from a variety of sociocultural contexts, their diverse life histories undoubtedly lead to dissimilar *cognitions* and *emotions* held by the individuals regarding particular social phenomena or issues. On the one hand, it is generally acceptable to challenge other people's *cognition*, perceptions and knowledge in particular, as evidenced by the value placed on public debate. On the other hand, the Feelings and Affect I-statements, I would argue, allow the speakers subjective space to inject personality and idiosyncrasy without feeling considerable social strain. By expressing their positive or negative emotional responses to certain social practices, the participants signalled their alignments or disagreements with particular social groups.

To illustrate the above point, I provide below a few examples of the Retroactive-Voice Writers' I-statements on Feelings and Affect.

Feelings and Affect

(30) but I <u>like</u> adjectives yeah {Writing, Fai}
(31) I <u>feel more comfortable</u> speaking in English still {Language, Eliza}
(32) I <u>feel embarrassed</u> <reading out her own stories> because when there are close friends which know each other {Writing, Maggie}
(33) but usually I <u>like</u> writing for myself because it makes me happy (because I can forget about everything and then I'll be like forgetting everything) {Writing, Angeles}
(34) because I <u>can forget about everything</u> {Writing, Angeles}

In the above examples, one negative emotional response can be seen in I-statement 32 by Maggie, concerning a practice sanctioned by the creative-writer group she was a member of. In this I-statement, Maggie expressed her uneasiness concerning the practice of reading out her work in a local community of creative writers, whose members are 'close friends [who] know each other'. Maggie's personality, i.e. a shy and sensitive person, and her social identity, i.e. a member of this creative writer community, are constructed in dialectic. More importantly, such agency–context dialectic is represented more from the angle of Maggie, through accentuating her feeling, justifying her ambivalence towards this community practice of work-sharing. Through such an *emotion* I-statement, Maggie injects her idiosyncrasy into this particular social identity she has adopted, with her personality individualising her social identity rather than the other way around. Regarding such affect I-statement approach, in a way, the social circumstances and social practices associated with the speakers' identities are not as much to the fore in shaping the individuals' self-positioning as we have seen earlier in some other types of I-statements, for example, the I-statements uttered in the *passive* voice, the I-statements on Affordances and Relations.

Conclusions on the Connection between Autobiographical Identities and Writer Voices

This chapter quantitatively locates the connection between the L2 creative writers' constructions of their autobiographical identities and their persistent writer voices. Based on the think-aloud coding results, I have demonstrated how four general strands of writer voices are identified through examination of the L2 creative writers' cognitive writing processes under these two story-writing tasks. A discernible pattern can be seen when the Proactive-Voice Writers and the Retroactive-Voice Writers' I-statement coding results are compared category by category. I have discussed how the Proactive-Voice Writers, compared with the Retroactive-Voice Writers, employ a more direct, socially textured and self-assured I-statement approach in discursively constructing their autobiographical identities. I have also discussed how the Retroactive-Voice Writers, in comparison with the Proactive-Voice Writers, employ a more implicit, expressive, idiosyncratic and self-critical I-statement approach in their identity constructions. I have illustrated my above two observations with concrete I-statement examples respectively uttered by the Planners and the Revisers. L2 creative writers' story creation processes are sometimes considered to be capricious rhapsodies of inspiration, especially when compared with the ratiocination of argumentative or persuasive writing composition; however, the quantitative examination performed in this chapter suggests that the writers' self-representations and hence their past life histories systematically inform the characteristics of their cognitive writing processes. The next chapter will explore the connection between the 15 participants' constructions of their autobiographical identities and the *changing* of their writer voices influenced by the switching of the story-writing task types (from the Autobiographical writing task to the Story-continuation task). Chapter Five, through exhibiting the particularities of the think-aloud utterances, will provide illustrations of these four strands of writer voices in vivid details. It shows how exactly the L2 participants' cognitive story writing processes are enactments of distinct writer voices.

5 Quantitative Analyses of Task Influences on L2 Creative Writing Processes and Their Relationship to the Writers' Autobiographical Identities

This chapter, also building on quantitative analyses, will display how the switch of story-writing task type from the Autobiographical writing task to the Story-continuation task influences the L2 creative writers' cognitive writing processes. The writers' changing cognitive writing behaviours are related to their varying self-positioning acts embodied in the stories under creation (e.g. what they consider as acceptable ideas or language) and the writers' perceptions of their reader's reception of the work. Given their different autobiographical identities, L2 creative writers' considerations of the above issues vary. It can be expected here that the participants in this inquiry would exhibit different adaptions of their cognitive writing processes in reaction to the change of the story-writing task type. In this chapter, through highlighting some quantitative trends, I will discuss how these two different story-writing tasks exert some universal influences on the L2 creative writers' cognitive writing processes, i.e. an increase in improvisational 'Composing' activities and a decrease in supervisory 'Monitoring' activities when switching to the fictional Story-continuation task. Consequently, I will comment on how the autobiographical genre brings with it an underlying appeal for authenticity and reality and thus certain closeness between the story and the writer and a sense of accountability, while the Story-continuation writing task signals fictitiousness and thus suggests a rather flexible distance between the story and the writer and a sense of anonymity and playfulness. Subsequently, I will examine how the L2 creative writers, who have shown different I-statement tendencies, characteristically tune their cognitive writing processes across the two story-writing tasks. The discussion concentrates on how those writers who accentuate their proactive and spontaneous writing behaviours when engaging with the fictional Story-continuation task, also consistently construct more straightforward, socially textured and self-assured autobiographical identities in the interviews on their past experiences. Hence, a quality of certainty, directness or even boldness could be seen threading through these writers' autobiographical identities and their adaption of writers' voices.

Universal Task Influences on the L2 Creative Writers' Cognitive Writing Processes

An overall picture

The 15 L2 creative writer participants come from a diversity of sociocultural and educational backgrounds. Hence it is interesting to find some universal task influences which occur generally across the board when changing from the Autobiographical writing task to the Story-continuation task. Overall, under the Story-continuation task, there are increases in the proportions taken by the spontaneous Composing activities and meanwhile decreases in the evaluative Monitoring activities.

The Autobiographical writing task seems to allow the participants considerable sovereignty regarding the plot, the protagonist and literary style. This leaves the writers opportunities for performing a range of self-fashioning acts; in other words, the participants could meaningfully and satisfactorily enact certain values and identities to themselves as well as to their readers. This consequently brings the L2 writers a sense of control and responsibility. On the other hand, the Story-continuation task, despite its laying down the main characters, the setting and an ideological foundation for the story, might have led to a sense of uncertainty and unpredictability for the participants. This is possibly because the L2 creative writers need to somehow align their own sense of selves with the kind of writer voices they see as appropriate, empowering or convenient to negotiate in this particular fictional story-writing context. Embedded in this fictional writing, there are ideologies such as calamitous love, intricate relationship and ominous prospect of marriage, Americanism and materialism, as suggested by the opening of William Boyd's 'Love Hurts' (2008: 157–168). These ideologies might have caused indecision for the participants when they were comparing their own experiences and values with the writer images which, as they considered, were expected of them by the task. The participants possibly sensed that they were more closely situated towards their Autobiographical writing than their Story-continuation writing. This distance between the participants' sense of selves and the self-images to be fashioned in their story creation process might not easily propel the progress of their writing. However, this distance could also lead to casualness and even playfulness in the creation process.

Now I will briefly explain the procedures I have gone through to establish the task influences on the participants' cognitive writing processes across the two story-writing tasks. In Chapter 4, I categorised the 15 L2 creative writers into four strands of writer voices based on the individual writers' distinctive writing behaviours which consistently stand out in the crowd across the two story-writing tasks. These four strands of writers' voices are: the Proactive Voices, the Spontaneous Voices, the Retroactive Voices and the Uncharacteristic Voices. To locate the magnitude of the task influences on the participants, I treat these four strands of writer voices as the foci of comparisons. I investigated the changes occurring, between the two story-writing tasks, in the percentages respectively taken by the major writing activities of Planning, Composing, Monitoring and Revising. To be more specific, the change is measured through deducting the percentage taken by the participant's particular writing activity in the Autobiographical writing task from its counterpart percentage in the Story-continuation task and then dividing the resultant figure by the percentage taken by this major writing activity in the Autobiographical writing task. For example, let us turn to Table 4.3 in Chapter 4 and find Participant 1 Jingjing. It shows that Jingjing's Planning activity takes 9.8% of her total think-aloud units in the Autobiographical writing task and 12.0% in the Story-continuation writing task. The task influence is then measured through deducting 9.8% from 12.0% and then dividing the resultant 2.2% by 9.8%, which finally comes to 22.4%. That is to say, Jingjing's Planning activity has a 22.4% increase when switching from the Autobiographical writing task to the Story-continuation task. After the task influences are measured in this way for all the participants, embracing the four strands of writer voices, the results are presented in Figure 5.1. Here the writing activities of Planning, Composing, Monitoring and Revising are separately represented in the four column charts from Figure 5.1a to Figure 5.1d. The four strands of writer voices are respectively represented by the four different patterns: *dotted* – the Proactive-Voice Writers, *stripes* – the Spontaneous-Voice Writers, *gray* – the Retroactive-Voice Writers and *black* – the Uncharacteristic-Voice Writers. Each column of a specific pattern represents a particular writer included in the strand of writer voices concerned. The sequence in which the writers from each strand are represented in the columns of a particular pattern is shown in Table 5.1.

In Figure 5.1 we could see that, when switching from the Autobiographical writing task to the Story-continuation task, a majority of the participants – whichever the strand of writer voices they embrace – display a stronger tendency towards the Composing activity (shown in Figure 5.1b) and a weaker tendency towards the Monitoring activity (Figure 5.1c).

Previously I commented that such manifestations of the task influences suggest that the participants possibly feel, on the one hand, more personally authentic and thus more responsible for the constructions of their Autobiographical stories than in their Continued stories, and on the other hand, more distanced from their Continued stories than their Autobiographical ones and thus more casual or improvisational

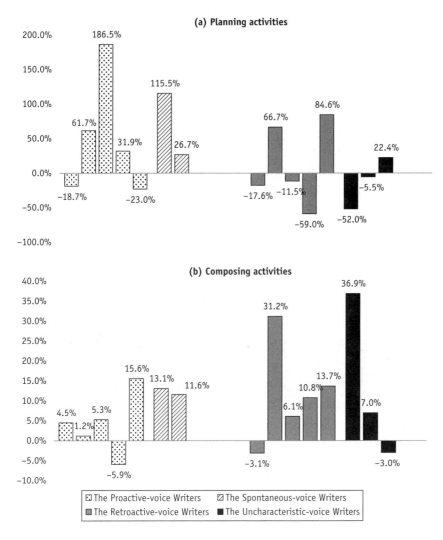

Figure 5.1 Task influences on the four strands' of writers' Planning, Composing activities

(Continued)

in the Story-continuation writing processes. Obviously, what underlies the characteristic changes in the individual L2 writers' Composing and Monitoring activities is individual. For example, some of the L2 writers might have felt free and motivated in the Autobiographical writing task as they valued taking full charge of the story. Some others might have felt liberated in the Story-continuation task as they were able to maintain a flexible distance between them and their stories which allowed them a certain degree of anonymity and randomness. That is to say, although

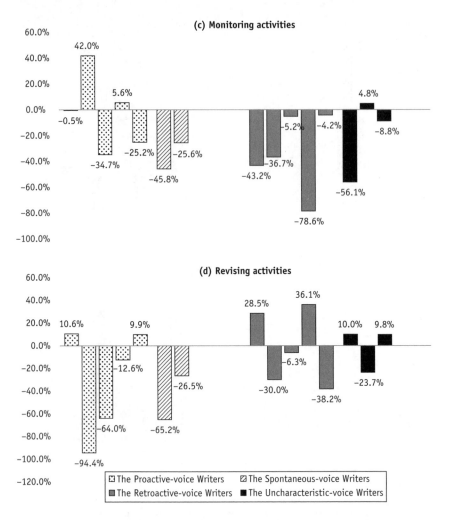

Figure 5.1 (Continued) Task influences on the four strands' of writers' Monitoring and Revising activities

both of the above two types of writers demonstrate a higher tendency for performing the spontaneous Composing activity and a lower tendency for the vigilant Monitoring activity in the Story-continuation task than in the Autobiographical one, the writers' self-consciousness behind such cognitive writing behaviours and such performances of their writer voices might be idiosyncratic. They are idiosyncratic because the participants bring to their present writing various literary and language practices which the individual writers have been immersed in and imbued with in their past experiences.

Table 5.1 The sequence of the representations of writers in each strand of Writer Voices in Figure 5.1

Pattern of column	Writer Voices	Writers
The DOTTED Columns	The Proactive-Voice Writers	Derek, Ho, Marjorie, Teri, Sebastian
The STRIPES Columns	The Spontaneous-Voice Writers	Dong, Teng
The GRAY Columns	The Retroactive-Voice Writers	Fai, Ankita, Eliza, Maggie, Angeles
The BLACK Columns	The Uncharacteristic-Voice Writers	Yi, Anna, Jingjing

Such literary and language practices consequently constitute the writers' senses of their roots (this is better dissected by the qualitative discussions on the selected focal participants in Chapter 7 than here).

To give a quick example to illustrate the above argument, let us look at the following comments which were respectively given by participants Sebastian and Yi in the individual in-depth interviews. Sebastian, from Germany, was a 19-year-old volunteer carer of disabled students at this UK university. Yi, aged 20 and from Singapore, was an undergraduate Law student. They were explaining their individual motives behind their self-initiated creative writing practices:

> **Sebastian**: I think creative writing is an important part emm I plan to do it really like like till the very end [of his time in England] and and further on and more English and I mean even these letters in German I sent home I want to probably do it in English, because I want to do this exam [Certificate in Advanced English] at the end of this year in the UK, I'm feeling that when I write, everything that I don't get from reading it's being it's coming to me …
>
> **Yi**: I like to write about stories, because I had read a lot of books then I wanted to try my try writing as well, so I read a horror book and then I would try to write a horror story, if I read some other book I would write other story as well, so more of trying all different things …

Sebastian's utterance suggests that he was encouraged by the opportunities to practice and improve his English through writing in a personal and meaningful way, i.e. reflecting on his immediate life experiences in the UK. It is worth speculating here that Sebastian's L2 creative writer identity was associated with the realisation of a competent

L2 self in a way learning English in school back in Germany had not allowed him. In comparison, Yi's comments portray his avid exploration of different creative writing genres, which might imply that creative writing, whichever the language, helps him to construct a certain self-image of an adventurous and resourceful writer unhindered by language issues, as well as the identity of a keen reader.

Interestingly, Sebastian and Yi, despite being L2 creative writers of very different agenda, both increased their attention to the Composing activities and reduced their Monitoring effort in the Story-continuation writing processes (see Participants 7 and 8 in Table 4.3: Chapter 4). In Table 4.3, if we look into the subcategories of Monitoring, we can see that Sebastian has halved his Monitoring effort (from 12.8% to 6.2%) on his *language* when writing under the Story-continuation task; meanwhile Yi has eased up on Monitoring the *content or ideas* of his story (a drop from 11.2% to 3.3%). Such different foci respectively shown in the changes of Sebastian and Yi's Monitoring exertion correspond with the two writers' previous comments which portray their certain self-perceptions as L2 creative writers. In the Autobiographical writing task, as the writer is situated rather close to the story, for Sebastian his treatment of the language and for Yi his handling of the story's ideas become crucial to each of these two L2 creative writers' construction of their writer images. That is to say, Sebastian cared if the writing strengthened his identity as a L2 writer who can use refined language to deliver genuine, subtle emotion. Similarly, Yi cared if he could be perceived by the reader as an innovative L2 creative writer with insightful, unexpected ideas.

When the distance between the story and the writer gets elastic in the Story-continuation task, both writers seem to have become less cautious in controlling the linguistic or ideational texture of the story and more playful and spontaneous with what can be summoned to their minds. If we look into the subcategories of Composing in Table 4.3, we can see that Sebastian's increased spontaneity resides in his adventurously trying out phrasing or ideas before writing anything down (i.e. a dramatic increase in 'Tentative formulations', from 2.7% to 8.2%). Meanwhile, Yi's Planning effort has considerably dropped and his reliance on the spur-of-the-moment to create his story has increased (a visible increase in 'Verbalising one's writing', from 22.8% to 30.2%); so has his tendency for retracing his previous writing – as a 'springboard' strategy (Roca de Larios *et al.*, 1999: 20) – to stimulate the creational flow (the increase in 'Reading what's been written down', from 18.8% to 25.4%).

In the next two sections, I will look into some details of the task influences on the participants' Composing and Monitoring activities by focusing on the four strands of writer voices compared in Figure 5.1.

Increases in the attention directed to the improvisational Composing activities

As shown in Figure 5.1b on the Composing activities, the Proactive-Voice Writers, compared to the other three strands of writer voices, demonstrate rather minor increases in their attention directed to the Composing activities when switching from the Autobiographical writing task to the Story-continuation task. Close scrutiny of the Composing subcategories of these four strands of writers in Table 4.3 of Chapter 4 (the categorisation of the writer voices is displayed in Table 4.5) suggests that the Proactive-Voice Writers, compared to the other three strands of writers, show little tendency for collective increases in 'Tentative formulations', or 'Verbalising one's writing', or 'Reading what's been written down'. It is particularly worth noticing that, regarding 'Tentative formulations', decreases, rather than increases, happen to four out of the five Proactive-Voice Writers, i.e. Derek, Marjorie, Ho and Teri, when changing to the Story-continuation task. The implication is that the Proactive-Voice Writers, when required to continue the fictional storyline initiated by the Story-continuation task, have not increased their inclination towards improvisation or spontaneity to bring their stories into being as much as the other strands of writers have done.

Previously, I mentioned the task influences on Yi's writing behaviours. Yi is one of the three Uncharacteristic-Voice Writers. Figure 5.1b shows that Yi's Composing activities have a staggering 36.9% increase when changing to the Story-continuation task, revealing the largest magnitude of growth among the participants. Two excerpts of Yi's think-aloud utterances extracted respectively from his Autobiographical and Story-continuation writing processes are displayed in Excerpts 1 and 2. The intensification of Yi's Composing activities when continuing the provided fictional story, as revealed in Excerpt 2, is rather representative of what happened in many of the other participants' Story-continuation writing processes.

Yi's 'Composing' activities are all highlighted in grey. The two think-aloud excerpts are taken from the very beginning of his two story-writing processes. When writing for his Autobiographical story (in Yi's case, a fictional first-person narrative), Yi was creating a monologue – rather cynically toned – going through the mind of a fictional protagonist who is a policeman foot-patrolling the high street. In Excerpt 1 we can see that Yi articulated the goals and the questions which were intended to orient and spur his later creational flow. He planned the ideologies underlying his seemingly every-day policeman character – in particular, the themes of 'justice' and 'are the truly good people good people' (quoted from Excerpt 1, second think-aloud utterance). The underlined parts are Yi's instant verbalising of his writing; the double underlined parts are the revisions actually made to the written text; the parts within [ ] are the writer's reading of what has been written down; a comma indicates pausing. The number in the left column shows

Excerpt 1 Yi's s think-aloud utterances from the Autobiographical writing task

Think-aloud utterances	Categorisation of writing activities
1. OK, what's this story about	Planning: Idea-generating
2. this story was about, justice this was, the good and bad are the truly good people good people, what's the difference between a policeman and, yeah so the protagonist is a policeman	Planning: Goal-setting on ideas
3. how does it start, how that shows his evilness emm	Planning: Idea-generating
4. his feel for an evil policeman but in the sense that you can't tell it, you can't really tell tell this he has this, but policeman is human so they have got urges as well	Planning: Goal-setting on ideas
5. so how he was walking down the street, he on patrol, how it starts emm, there is something over on the street when he's walking down and he sees people, how it starts	Planning: Idea-generating
6. it's a quiet sunny day	Composing: Tentative formulations
7. no that's too cliché umm, emm, shall I be cliché shall I start with a quiet sunny day, OK then	Monitoring: Evaluating content or ideas
8. I'm walking down, Warwick Avenue, yeah I just write Warwick Avenue, I'm walking down the street the same street	Composing: Verbalising one's writing
9. emm [I'm walking down the street, I'm walking down the street the same street]	Composing: Reading what's been written down
10. that I have, for the, the God knows how many times, many how God knows how many	Composing: Verbalising one's writing
11. [I'm walking down the street]	Composing: Reading what's been written down
12. the same street	Revising: Revising language
13. yeah [walking down the street]	Composing: Reading what's been written down
14. for how many times for God knows how many times	Revising: Trying alternative language
15. I patrol the street	Revising: Trying alternative language
16. this I walk down this street many many times because he is a policeman on patrol	Monitoring: Evaluating content or ideas
17. [walking down the street]	Composing: Reading what's been written down
18. this is	Composing: Verbalising one's writing
19. I know every building	Revising: Trying alternative content
20. OK I just show I know this street	Planning: Goal-setting on ideas
21. I know every building on this street, I know the people the shops, I can, I can tell from memory the order of the shops in my mind	Composing: Verbalising one's writing
22. [I can tell the order of the shops]	Composing: Reading what's been written down
23. the exact order of the shops lining its cobbled, [lining its] cobbled path	Composing: Verbalising one's writing

Excerpt 2 Yi's s think-aloud utterances from the Story-continuation task

Think-aloud utterances	Categorisation of writing activities
1. OK so I'll start at the very end, emm, the protagonist is consoling Lamar	Planning: Goal-setting on ideas
2. Lamar how to say	Planning: Idea-generating
3. just start Lamar emm, emm	Composing: Verbalising one's writing
4. it's the day so I'll start the evening when everything is already done, everything is done every-thing is, Lamar is	Planning: Goal-setting on ideas
5. it it is the first time	Composing: Verbalising one's writing
6. I've never seen Lamar like this emm, [first time], emm, I'm not used to this un unused to this	Composing: Tentative formulations
7. [self-confidence surrounds him like a force field]	Composing: Reviewing the prompt
8. it's the first time I see Lamar like this, err, there have been many firsts today, there have been many firsts today	Composing: Verbalising one's writing
9. I'll talk about, emm, in terms of Lamar	Composing: Tentative formulations
10. [there have been many firsts], emm, [there have been many firsts]	Composing: Reading what's been written down
11. for me [today] in terms of Lamar, in terms of my	Composing: Verbalising one's writing
12. acquaintance with Lamar, of us	Composing: Tentative formulations
13. [there have been many, firsts for me today]	Composing: Reading what's been written down
14. related to Lamar, emm	Composing: Verbalising one's writing
15. [there have been many firsts] for Lamar	Revising: Trying alternative language
16. [there have been many firsts for me today]	Composing: Reading what's been written down
17. in terms of my relationship with Lamar in terms of my relationship with Lamar, in the morning, in the morning	Composing: Verbalising one's writing
18. emm, after in the morning OK it's been quite later in the morning the wedding, after my bed at night	Monitoring: Evaluating content or ideas
19. [in the morning]	Composing: Reading what's been written down
20. Lamar would be travelling to church	Planning: Goal-setting on ideas
21. on the way to the church in the car, emm I saw	Composing: Verbalising one's writing
22. the shell of confidence	Composing: Tentative formulations
23. the force field of confidence around him	Composing: Verbalising one's writing

the sequence of the specific think-aloud utterance in the whole think-aloud speech. In the right column, the major and the sub-categorisations of the particular think-aloud utterances are presented.

In Excerpt 2, Yi's compositional process in the Story-continuation task shows him working with elements of uncertainties, especially shown in his rehearsals of the seemingly trivial details of the descriptive phrasing. In the story opening provided by this task, the fictional narrator 'I' kicks off his retrospective testimony of Lamar and Cherylle's (the two main characters') ominous relationship. Here, Yi's writing process concerns the fictional narrator 'I's account of his friend Lamar's disastrous wedding. The bridegroom, Lamar, is a methodical and driven-to-succeed American businessman who suffers a severe blow to his ego when his bride stands him up.

Yi did not conspicuously map out the general ideology or goal underpinning his story as he did in the beginning of his Autobiographical story writing process. After attempting to generate some ideas for his story in Utterance 2 of Except 2, Yi dived rather straight into Composing, later making several spontaneous attempts at formulating the phrasal and ideational possibilities for what was to be written down. He frequently used rereading to stir the creational flow.

Decrease in the attention directed to the metacognitive Monitoring activities

The Monitoring activity constitutes metacomments and any evaluative comments made on particular aspects of writing (e.g. content or ideas, language or writing procedures). The general decrease in the writers' metacognitive exertion when writing under the Story-continuation task suggests that most of the participants adopted a less supervisory or controlling approach in their cognitive writing processes than they did in the Autobiographical writing task. This movement corresponds with the participants' generally increased tendency for taking on a spontaneous and improvisational approach (i.e. the Composing activity) when writing under the Story-continuation task as illustrated previously.

However, such decreases in the L2 writers' attention directed to the Monitoring activities, when switching to the Story-continuation task, are shown to occur selectively across the Monitoring subcategories. For example, Figure 5.1c shows that the Spontaneous-Voice Writers and the Retroactive-Voice Writers manifest unanimous drops in Monitoring. Yet, closer examination of the Monitoring subcategories (Table 4.3) of the two Spontaneous-Voice Writers, Dong and Teng, indicates that the decrease in Dong's metacognitive exertion is fairly language oriented (a drop from 4.7% to 0% in 'Evaluating language') while the reduced intensity of Teng's metacomments is primarily content related (a drop from 2.5%

to 0% in 'Evaluating content or ideas'). Inspection of their think-aloud protocols reveals that, when engaging with the Autobiographical story writing task, Dong was driven to strike the linguistic appearance of a meticulous L2 user and Teng the ideological aura of a seasoned individual who has endured much hardship in life (Teng's experience and writing will be further discussed in Chapters 6 and 7 as he is one of the five focal participants). In a similar vein, through examining the five Retroactive-Voice Writers' Monitoring activities, I discovered that, when changing to the Story-continuation task, the respective decreases in Ankita's and Angeles's attention directed to Monitoring are mainly due to 'language' issues (Table 4.3). In Fai's case, there are perceptible drops in his monitoring the 'writing procedures' as well as the 'language'. Finally, comprehensive decreases could be seen in Maggie's metacognitive control which involve the 'writing procedures', 'content or ideas' and 'language', when switching to the Story-continuation task.

To illustrate the concept that the participants' specific adjustments of their Monitoring effort actually indicate particular self-positioning acts, I will look at two excerpts of think-aloud utterances respectively generated by Ankita (a Retroactive-Voice Writer) and Jingjing (an Uncharacteristic-Voice Writer) while writing under the Autobiographical writing task.

Jingjing

Jingjing's Autobiographical writing narrates a fictional teenage romance which seemed to evoke traces of *The Twilight Saga*. The fictional narrator 'I', a strong female protagonist, is a high-achiever in school. Coming from a single-parent family, this first-person narrator is nonchalant and cynical about love. The male protagonist, Noah, athletic and talented in everything, is a new student in the school who falls in love with the narrator 'I' at first sight. Jingjing was articulate and meticulous about the story's fundamental themes in her visualisation of it, e.g. 'love–hate relationship', 'the importance of family', 'selfishness', 'threat of death', 'illness', 'music' and 'sports' (see Utterances 45–50 in Excerpt 3). As shown in Excerpt 3, in Jingjing's writing process, she regularly monitored (highlighted in grey) the ideologies which underlie her development of the story and distinctive characterisation.

The excerpt suggests that Jingjing's Autobiographical story-writing process instantiated values of westernised, intellectual and vibrant young adults and consequently situated her 'self' as part of this social group. It can be inferred that her story-writing process possibly brought her a sense of belongingness and self-identification. In Jingjing's Story-continuation writing process, her Monitoring activities had a modest 8.8% drop (Figure 5.1c). The implication is that the provided story opening might have confined the room within which Jingjing could personify particular ideologies in her writing to pronounce her individuality.

Excerpt 3 Jingjing's think-aloud utterances from the Autobiographical writing task

Think-aloud utterances	Categorisation of writing activities
45. emm OK so it's all her remembering right now she is alone she is writing down the story and she wants people to understand why she did what she did so I probably have 'love' of course then a bit of love hate relationship and also emm have emm have family very important, family and selfishness	Planning: Goal-setting on ideas
46. yeah selfishness that's very personal I'm kind of selfish	Monitoring: Evaluating content or ideas
47. so she is gonna be very selfish but then something changes there is gonna be death	Planning: Goal-setting on ideas
48. because death makes it interesting or at least threat of death yeah threat	Monitoring: Evaluating content or ideas
49. emm also I want, is it a happy ending well we'll see	Planning: Idea-generating
50. emm family selfishness death also music I don't know how but there's gonna be music or sports could be sports seems could be sports because Noah is very talented I don't know why emm not yet OK let's have him emm with also one from death we have sickness illness or sickness OK	Planning: Goal-setting on ideas
51. [mulling over our past mistakes is the worst torture] yeah [so I won't do that I'll simply give you my account of the past year]	Composing: Reading what's been written down
52. emm, I come from a broken family, no wrong word wrong worng word not broken not broken only only not not whole my mom left us when	Composing: Verbalising one's writing
53. yeah give her character good character	Monitoring: Evaluating content or ideas
54. [my mom left us when]	Composing: Reading what's been written down
55. I was three, so I have been kind of I have been, so	Composing: Verbalising one's writing
56. [my mom left us when I was three]	Composing: Reading what's been written down
57. and, so I have always been, always been very close to my dad	Composing: Verbalising one's writing
58. oh very American emm	Monitoring: Evaluating content or ideas
59. [my mom left us when I was three so I have always been very]	Composing: Reading what's been written down
60. close very close [to my dad]	Composing: Verbalising one's writing
61. emm, emm, broken family, I just forget words	Revising: Revising language
62. [broken family no wrong word not broken only, only not whole]	Composing: Reading what's been written down
63. only only different	Revising: Revising language
64. [mom left us when I was three so I have always been very close to my dad]	Composing: Reading what's been written down
65. ah we don't really need a name yeah I don't really need a name for the parents	Monitoring: Evaluating content or ideas

Ankita

Ankita was sensitive to the texture of her L2 phrasing. Her Autobiographical writing process particularly embodied her concern for making sure the language maximally creates an authentic yet also dramatic impression for the story. For example, Excerpt 4 displays the painstaking process Ankita went through to produce a title for her Autobiographical story, which recounts her thrilling adventure of observing some wild elephants in India. Her Monitoring activities are highlighted in grey. It can be seen that Ankita was persistent in reaching a catchy title. Her attempts initially led to some critical evaluation from her – for example, too revealing, 'stupid' or 'not making sense'. Eventually, her relentless try-outs generated

Excerpt 4 Ankita's think-aloud utterances from the Autobiographical writing task

Think-aloud utterances	Categorisation of writing activities
221. OK emm and I can call this the title emm it the the elephant chase no chased by emm	Composing: Tentative formulations
222. the angry elephants	Composing: Verbalising one's writing
223. no, that that gives away everything in the title	Monitoring: Evaluating language
224. the the the the the the the the the night at the	Composing: Verbalising one's writing
225. a night at the park	Composing: Tentative formulations
226. no that sounds stupid not that	Monitoring: Evaluating language
227. the night the elephant ran the night we ran the night the car ran the night the car was chased by an elephant	Revising: Trying alternative language
228. no that's not making sense	Monitoring: Evaluating language
229. the night the day the car the elephant the, park trees birds I'm gonna call this the elephant chase no emm the day emm the the the night the no the night the elephant chased the elephant chase	Revising: Trying alternative language
230. no but that kind of makes sense	Monitoring: Evaluating language
231. the elephant chased us an elephant chased us an elephant chased us an elephant the chase	Revising: Trying alternative language
232. what about the chase	Composing: Verbalising one's writing
233. it's kind of short and sweet	Monitoring: Evaluating language

some satisfactory results, with her issuing evaluations such as 'kind of makes sense' and 'kind of short and sweet'.

Not only did Ankita diligently brainstorm strings of words in quick succession, she also kept careful control of the nuances of words. Ankita's engagements in monitoring the language of the story halved when changing to the Story-continuation task (a drop from 9.6% to 4.8%), which is responsible for the drop in the overall intensity of her Monitoring activities. However, Ankita's reduced linguistic monitoring did not bring her a sense of ease in her Story-continuation writing process. After her continued story, Ankita and I had the following exchange:

Me: OK so now you have finished, what's your feeling about this experience?

Ankita: It's tiring, as it's like because like I was trying to put myself in that position so that sounds like mentally exhausting.

Me: You mean put yourself in the position as if you were the narrator.

Ankita: Yeah, and also like I was trying to imagine like you know what can be going on in his head.

It seems that the fictional writing task did not exactly motivate Ankita to enthusiastically take up an imaginative or playful L2 creative writer identity. The lack of opportunities for articulating genuine feelings affected Ankita's drive to monitor the undertone of her language or to texture the linguistic details.

There have been advocates of fictional, controlled and playful types of creative writing activities in ESL/EFL classrooms, such as role-play improvisation of drama scenes, story-relay activities and various rule-governed 'quirky' poetry writings (e.g. Elgar, 2002; Maley, 2009, 2012; Tin, 2011, 2012; Cook, 2000). Such creative writing activities certainly have their place in L2 classrooms. The activities embrace some evident constraints so as to push the students out of their comfort zone. They particularly elicit the learners' nonconformist use of language and form, compared to their staple writing practices. However, while some L2 students feel liberated by such opportunities for creative language use, some others might feel exhausted or even embarrassed doing it in front of their peers. When incorporating certain rules/constraints into the design of L2 creative writing tasks, we need to look into the students' adjustments of their creative writing processes in reaction to different types of writing activities. This could be achieved by asking students to perform think-aloud writing in their own space and to record their individual think-aloud speeches. Through listening to the students' think-aloud creation processes, L2 teachers could subsequently design the creative writing task rubrics specifically tailored to the students' learning and creative needs. Such highly targeted L2 creative writing activities could offer surprising insights for teachers regarding the students' language competencies and self-identities, which helps to promote both language learning and teacher–student communication.

So far, I have discussed the two universal task influences on the four strands of writers' cognitive writing processes – namely, general increases in the intensity of the Composing activities and decreases in the Monitoring activities. We shall not forget the L2 creative writers' autobiographical identities. In the next section I will focus exclusively on the connection between the characteristic task influences revealed respectively in the Proactive and the Retroactive Writers' cognitive writing processes and these two strands' distinct I-statement tendencies (previously analysed in Chapter 4).

Characteristic Task Influences on Writers' Voices and the Connections to the Writers' Autobiographical Identities

Characteristic task influences on the Proactive-Voice and the Retroactive-Voice Writers

To reveal the connections between the characteristic task influences and the writers' autobiographical identities, the relevant trends emerging in Figure 5.1 will be related to those in Figure 4.1 (Chapter 4), which shows these two strands of writers' specific I-statement tendencies in identity constructions. The central idea is that the L2 creative writers' particular adjustments of their cognitive writing processes between the two tasks are not entirely random or whimsical but somehow identity-indicative. This notion will be further illustrated in the qualitative discussions in Chapter 7.

In Figure 5.1, I noted that when writing under the Story-continuation task, the Proactive-Voice Writers engaged even more vigorously in Planning and meanwhile reduced the intensity of their Revising activities further. On the other hand, the Retroactive-Voice Writers increased their cognitive exertion on the Composing activity and curtailed their involvement in the Monitoring activity. This adjustment corresponds with the task influences universally exhibited across all the participants discussed previously, but especially so among the Retroactive-Voice Writers. Subsequently, a division can be observed: with the Retroactive-Voice Writers on one side and the Proactive-Voice Writers on the other side.

When switching from the Autobiographical writing task to the Story-continuation task, the Retroactive-Voice Writers have not readjusted their writing behaviours to strengthen their writing 'habitus'. Let me explain this. First of all, when changing to the Story-continuation task, the Retroactive-Voice Writers have not universally increased the intensity with which they engaged in the Revising activities. That is to say, the Retroactive-Voice Writers have not reinforced their habitual writer voices as retroactive, duteous or meticulous writers (see Figure 5.1d). In contrast, the Proactive-Voice Writers have conclusively strengthened their writing 'habitus' when changing to the Story-continuation task. Figure 5.1 shows that the Proactive-Voice Writers have generally reinforced their Planning activities and generally reduced their attention to Revising. The implication is that when writing for the partially pre-set, fictional story, the Proactive-Voice Writers keenly and determinedly reinforced their self-representation as writers who primarily focus on getting the stories written down through structured directions or spontaneity. Differently, the Retroactive-Voice Writers behaved a bit uncertainly regarding whether to maintain their self-representation as writers who rely on retracing and revising their earlier writing so as to shape and stimulate their composition.

To clarify writing 'habitus', in the following I will illustrate the Proactive-Voice Writers and the Retroactive-Voice Writers' respective 'habitus'.

The Proactive Voices

Participant Ho's cognitive writing processes represent the archetype of the Proactive-Voice Writers. Excerpt 5 records the very beginning of Ho's Story-continuation writing process. Ho was seen here making intensive and pragmatic exertion on planning the scenarios continuing from the provided beginning of the fictional story 'Love Hurts'. Again, the Planning activities are highlighted in grey.

Ho's think-aloud speech enacts the image of a fairly controlled and perhaps also logical L2 story writer.

The Retroactive Voices

The Retroactive-Voice Writers are typically represented by participants Eliza and Ankita. Eliza generated Excerpt 6 not long after she started the Story-continuation writing process. It can be seen that some Retroactive Voice was already emerging (highlighted in grey). Eliza was creating the first-person narrator's description of Lamar and Cherylle's wedding scene, where the bridegroom was increasingly agitated by the no-show of his bride.

Three times Eliza went back to read her previous sentence. Although such effort of retracing her previous writing seemed to be made by Eliza in an exertion to generate new text, it notably led to the writer's trying alternative content or language to what she had composed earlier, which could further lead to revising.

Another participant embodying the Retroactive Voice is Ankita who, compared to Eliza, possibly engineered her story more visibly through natural surges of inspiration. Ankita created her initial text in a

Excerpt 5 Ho's think-aloud utterances from the Story-continuation task

Think-aloud utterances	Categorisation of writing activities
1. emm first of all I would like to choose the option I mentioned several options just now now it's time to write I can only pick one emm to develop within one hour	Monitoring: Evaluating writing procedures
2. so my option I think, OK I have three options emm to make, usually I think I will, I will choose a conventional way which is emm, emm, Lamar was hurt in the relationship and OK	Planning: Goal-setting on ideas
3. I'd better write it down, making it bullet points	Monitoring: Evaluating writing procedures
4. Lamar was hurt in the relationship, and the narrator was emm emm felt emm sad because of his failure OK emm because of Lamar's failure, and emm, stubborn, OK? for not accepting emm I think it's she OK her advice	Planning: Goal-setting on ideas
5. OK emm and then what happened to Cherylle, OK this is the the key that I have to develop OK emm that means what are the things Cherylle, emm did which make Lamar emm, Lamar's love hurt OK hurt OK, so I have to list some some things OK it depends on how many points, emm, what are the things emm, OK? escape from marriage or wedding ceremony, emm, escape from wedding ceremony or, making emm extraordinary, actions during the ceremony or disappear or cheat cheating Lamar after marriage, emm, how does she cheat on him maybe, emm decided	Planning: Idea-generating
6. OK I think that's enough emm	Monitoring: Evaluating content or ideas
7. OK you see you can make some points on the on the out-of-work actress so out-of-work actress OK we have to make some points out of it emm out-of-work actress she is being out of work maybe because OK she is beautiful but she is out-of-work there must be something wrong with her characteristic so	Planning: Idea-generating
8. OK wayward is the is the key word wayward OK, that means she did what she, she did what she liked liked to, liked to do without considering others' feeling	Planning: Goal-setting on ideas
9. if that's the case then escape from a wedding ceremony is not very possible and making one OK maybe making extraordinary actions during the ceremony, is that OK? I think cheating Lamar cheating Lamar would be after the marriage would be more interesting	Monitoring: Evaluating content or ideas

Excerpt 6 Eliza's think-aloud utterances from the Story-continuation task

Think-aloud utterances	Categorisation of writing activities
18. [Cherylle is late the priest] <u>has graciously graciously</u> emm [graciously] <u>allowed us</u> allowed <u>Lamar and his best</u> Lamar <u>and I to</u>	Composing: Verbalising one's writing
19. no I don't know what to write	Monitoring: Evaluating writing procedures
20. [Cherylle is late]	Composing: Reading what's been written down
21. I don't know what now emm	Monitoring: Evaluating writing procedures
22. [Cherylle is late]	Composing: Reading what's been written down
23. emm Lamar is in the next room	Revising: Trying alternative content
24. <u>Lamar is in the next room anxiously trying to get a hold of her on the phone, as a best as the best man I should</u>	Revising: Revising content
25. emm as the best man I should do something about something yeah probably I should be helping him	Planning: Goal-setting on ideas
26. emm, I have tried to reassure him	Composing: Tentative formulations
27. <u>I have tried to reassure him that she would show up</u>	Composing: Verbalising one's writing
28. [to reassure him that she would show up]	Composing: Reading what's been written down
29. [to reassure him] that everything would be fine	Revising: Trying alternative language
30. <u>that everything would be fine that she would show up</u>	Composing: Verbalising one's writing

somewhat crude yet truthful manner. However, she habitually reviewed her previous writing which enabled her to get a feel for what to write next; this process might also let her refine the grammar and phrasing of what she had written down earlier, as shown in Excerpt 7. Here Ankita has just begun her Autobiographical story, which recounts her thrilling adventure to catching a rare glimpse of wild elephants living in a forest reserve in India. Two episodes of her emerging retroactive voice are highlighted in grey.

So far, I have illustrated the writing 'habitus' typically shown by the Proactive-Voice Writers and the Retroactive-Voice Writers respectively. Next, I will relate the previous observation regarding the *changing* aspect of

Excerpt 7 Ankita's think-aloud utterances from the Autobiographical writing task

Think-aloud utterances	Categorisation of writing activities
6. we were driving driving around the forest around no [we were driving] deep within within the forest emm in the heart of Kerala a small state, on southern tip of Indian emm	Composing: Verbalising one's writing
7. [we were driving deep within the forest in the heart of Kerala a small state on southern tip of India emm ok so [it's dark we were driving deep within the forest in the heart of Kerala a small state on southern tip of India]	Composing: Reading what's been written down
8. emm OK we now what we do, emm how do I, how do I encounter the emm emm	Planning: Idea-generating
9. Kerala is known, Kerala has a famous emm sanctuary called Periyar which is emm which is known best for its Asian elephant	Composing: Verbalising one's writing
10. emm of one of the largest, emm OK end here	Composing: Tentative formulations
11. [Kerala has a famous sanctuary called Periyar which is known best for its Asian elephant]	Composing: Reading what's been written down
12. this is where emm emm where we were that day that day emm er as a birthday present from my parents to me emm I loved all things wild and emm and my father being a an being an environmental activist emm emm could get access emm to emm parts of	Composing: Verbalising one's writing
13. to access no OK I don't have him to travel with	Monitoring: Evaluating content or ideas
14. emm blah blah blah [from my parents to me] full stop	Composing: Verbalising one's writing
15. [we were driving deeply within the forest in the heart of Kerala a small state on southern]	Composing: Reading what's been written down
16. on the southern	Revising: Revising language
17. [tip of India Kerala has a famous sanctuary called Periyar which is known best for its Asian elephant this is where]	Composing: Reading what's been written down
18. Capitalise Asian	Revising: Revising language
19. [elephant this is where we were that day] emm [that day]	Composing: Reading what's been written down
20. that night	Revising: Trying alternative content
21. that evening	Revising: Revising content
22. next paragraph as we drove deeper	Composing: Verbalising one's writing
23. emm perhaps I should first say it was getting dark	Revising: Trying alternative language
24. coz it's evening it's dark already when we drove further	Monitoring: Evaluating content or ideas
25. it was getting dark OK	Revising: Revising language

these two strands of writers' cognitive writing behaviours to the writers' characteristic I-statement approaches in constructing their autobiographical identities.

The connections to the writers' autobiographical identities

In Chapter 4, through the category-by-category comparisons of the I-statement coding results (in Figure 4.1), I have made two observations. Firstly, the Proactive-Voice Writers, compared with the Retroactive-Voice Writers, employ more direct, socially textured and self-assured I-statement approaches in constructing their autobiographical identities. Secondly, the Retroactive-Voice Writers, in comparison with the Proactive-Voice Writers, employ more implicit, emotional and self-critical I-statement approaches in fashioning their autobiographical identities.

A connection consisting of the L2 creative writers' instantiations of identities can be detected *between* the writers' I-statement tendencies and the writers' adjustments to their writing behaviours when changing to the story-continuation task. For example, a feeling of self-assuredness and directness could be sensed in the Proactive-Voice Writers' constructions of their autobiographical identities and their adjustments to their writer voices. When the task type is changed to the Story-continuation task, the Proactive-Voice Writers conclusively demonstrate an inclination towards the structured, focused yet also spontaneous writing behaviours and a disinclination towards the retroactive, iterative writing approaches. In contrast, a sense of implicitness is detected in the Retroactive-Voice Writers' identity instantiations. The Retroactive-Voice Writers, who adopt more implicit I-statement approaches to construct their autobiographical identities in comparison to the Proactive-Voice Writers, exhibit a less definite or black-and-white image of the task influence exercised on their cognitive writing processes than the Proactive-Voice writers do when switching to the Story-continuation task. The implication is that the L2 creative writers' voices shown in their changing cognitive writing processes – characteristically tuned across different story-writing tasks – actually express and inform the creative writers' constant reformulations of their autobiographical identities.

Conclusion

The insights gained from unravelling L2 creative writers' cognitive writing processes could promote teachers' understanding of how the students' texts, despite using similar language items or discourse devices, might be reached through a diversity of paths. That is to say, language choices or ideas are not simply independent products marked in texts for teachers to scrutinise or assess. The insights gained from looking into the students' creative writing processes could enable the L2 teachers to see how their learners characteristically adjust their self-identities – e.g. primarily as a language learner, or an imaginative maverick, or a high-achiever student writer – through performing the current creative writing activity in particular ways. In other words, looking into the cognitive writing processes enable the teachers to appreciate what intentions the L2 individuals' characteristic allocation of attention or movements of thoughts in their creation processes serve in the writers' constant reformulations of their positioning in particular contexts.

It is important to recognise that L2 creative writing is employed, not only as a fun activity in ESL/EFL classroom, but also as a valuable self-empowering tool for learners. To decide on the constitution of creative writing task types or orientations in the classroom, i.e. how to strike the balance between the relatively free and the relatively constrained creative writing tasks, ESL/EFL teachers need to have some understanding of how the students' engagements with various L2 creative writing activities offer the L2 individuals' particular mediums for negotiating certain self-images. In other words, L2 teachers might adjust their design of the creative writing activities to target the students' most relevant sense of selves in the classroom, be it L2 learners yearning for formal English proficiency, or L2 writers with imagination or critical thinking skills, or L2 writers who like to entertain their reader, or even budding L2 poets. By understanding and hence strengthening these particular self-images which are activated by individual L2 student writers in their creative writing processes, L2 teachers could help develop their students' positive self-esteem, which nurtures confidence and motivation in L2 learning, L2 writing or simply engagements with the L2.

Admittedly, the descriptions so far of the trends and connections between the autobiographical identities and writer voices appear inevitably abstract and general; hence it is necessary to employ qualitative discussions to elucidate the L2 creative writers' concrete and idiosyncratic constructions of their autobiographical identities and their writer voices in specific social circumstances. The next two chapters move on to five selected focal participants. Chapters 6 and 7 conduct descriptive and selective examinations of tangible utterances made by these five L2 creative writers in the in-depth interviews and their think-aloud writing processes for evidence of identity work.

6 L2 Creative Writers' Sense of Social Localities

This and the next chapter will demonstrate how identities are manifested through varied, idiosyncratic forms. This will be achieved through concentrating on the sociohistorical particularities of the L2 creative writers' autobiographical identities and their actually value-laden psychological activities in the story-writing processes. These two chapters will particularly illustrate how the theoretical complexities of writer identities could be studied in a qualitative, empirical and micro manner through looking at concrete utterances. In this chapter I will firstly explain how I have selected five L2 creative writers through applying We- and You-statement analysis. Subsequently, I will portray these five writers' general creative writing and English language learning histories. The descriptions are entirely based on the information gained from the in-depth interviews. I will briefly narrate the stories of how these five L2 creative writers have reproduced their *L2 (or L3) identities* and *creative writer identities* through 'personifying' them and 'investing' them with their primary concerns and needs in specific social circumstances (Fairclough, 2003: 160–161). Throughout such unique socialisation trajectories, each L2 creative writer has gradually developed a certain propensity or capacity to practice particular forms of creative writing. Later, against such portrayals, I will discuss the focal participants' conspicuous tendency for indicating their memberships in particular communities, through conducting some discourse analysis on the individuals' tangible interview comments.

We- and You-statement analysis

I concentrated on the participants' sense of social-political localities, such as student writer status, professional role or national identity, by applying We- and You-statement analysis (previously explained in Chapter 3) to the L2 creative writers' self-recounts of their life stories. The focal participants are drawn from the Proactive-Voice Writers, the Spontaneous-Voice Writers and the Retroactive-Voice Writers (previously established in Chapter 4), as these participants demonstrate *habitual* writer voices across the two story-writing tasks. The coding results of the We- and You-statements in respect of these three strands of writer voices mentioned above are presented in

Table 6.1 where, for each participant, the percentages respectively taken by specific communities are shown.

The five focal L2 creative writers were chosen based on their demonstrating conspicuous alignment with a particular social standing in their personal narratives. Hence, based on the We- and You-statement analysis results, from the strand of Proactive-Voice Writers, Derek and Teri were picked out as the focal participants, as Derek, among the entire three strands of writers, demonstrates the highest percentage of the We- and You-statements taken within the category 'Professional' community (the percentage is boxed) and Teri the highest percentage occupied within the 'Social' community category. From the Spontaneous-Voice Writers, Teng was selected as he demonstrates the highest percentage within the 'L2 Speakers' community. Finally, Maggie and Fai were picked out from the Retroactive-Voice Writers, as Maggie demonstrates the highest percentage in the 'Creative Writer' community classification and Fai the highest percentage occupied in the 'L2 (or L3) Student Writer' community grouping.

Creative Writers' Personalisation of Their Social Identities: L2 (or L3) Speaker Identities and Creative Writer Identities

L2 speaker identities

Derek and Maggie

Derek and Maggie attained advanced English language proficiency in their home countries before coming to the UK for their postgraduate studies: Derek achieved an overall IELTS score of 8.5 and Maggie has an 8.0.

Derek, at the age of 11, started going to a private language institute to learn English 'two days a week three hours a week' (Derek, in-depth interview), as English was not heavily taught in his public school. Neither of Derek's parents spoke English.

Maggie started to learn English when she entered secondary school, where English was a compulsory subject. In addition, Maggie's social circumstances – national, geographical and familial – have provided her different opportunities to access practices and ideologies of English usage outside the classroom boundary. For example, Germany (Maggie's home country) is geographically closer to Britain than Argentina (Derek's home country). Furthermore, and significantly, Maggie's father was a bilingual teacher of German and English at a local grammar school. In his youth he had spent a year living in London, which possibly contributed to his Anglophile status, evidence for which is provided by the fact that he took the family

Table 6.1 The Proactive-Voice Writers', Spontaneous-Voice Writers' and Retroactive-Voice Writers' We- and You-statement coding results

The Proactive-Voice Writers

DEREK

Professional	L2 Speaker	L1 Student Writer (L1 SW)	L2 Student Writer (L2 SW)	Creative Writer	Particular Nationality (National)	Socialising Community (Social)	Reader	'Individuals with Insight' (Insight)
23.8%	9.9%	3.0%	24.8%	19.8%	2.0%	6.9%	8.9%	1.0%

TERI

Professional	Educational	Student Writer in Particular Context (SW Particular)	Creative Writer	Particular Ethnicity (Ethnic)	Social	Reader	Immigrant
3.5%	4.9%	26.4%	35.4%	1.4%	14.6%	4.2%	9.7%

HO

Professional	Educational	L2 Speaker	L1 SW	L2 SW	Bilingual Student Writer (Bilingual SW)	Creative Writer	Ethnic	National	Reader	Insight
7.7%	14.9%	7.2%	3.1%	4.6%	5.1%	43.1%	2.6%	8.7%	2.1%	1.0%

SEBASTIAN

Professional	Educational	L2 Speaker	SW Particular	L1 SW	L2 SW	Creative Writer	National	Social	Reader
3.7%	7.9%	16.6%	2.3%	15.5%	19.8%	15.5%	3.3%	6.0%	9.3%

MARJORIE

Professional	Educational	L2 Speaker	SW Particular	L1 SW	L2 SW	Creative Writer	National	Social	Reader	Individuals with a Particular Skill
2.3%	5.3%	4.6%	4.6%	19.1%	3.1%	38.2%	0.8%	6.1%	13.7%	2.3%

The Spontaneous-Voice Writers

DONG

Professional	Educational	L2 Speaker	SW Particular	L1 SW	L2 SW	Creative Writer	Ethnic	National	Reader	Insight
7.7%	5.0%	11.3%	9.7%	5.3%	9.0%	27.7%	2.3%	3.7%	15.0%	3.3%

TENG

Professional	Educational	L2 Speaker	SW Particular	L1 SW	L2 SW	Bilingual SW	Creative Writer	Ethnic	National	Reader	British
17.4%	10.2%	27.3%	7.2%	2.6%	9.5%	9.2%	11.5%	1.3%	2.0%	1.3%	0.3%

The Retroactive-Voice Writers

FAI

Professional	Educational	L2 Speaker	SW Particular	L1 SW	L2 SW	Bilingual SW	Creative Writer	Ethnic	National	Social	Reader
0.3%	7.8%	11.9%	11.2%	16.0%	25.9%	3.4%	10.9%	1.0%	1.4%	1.0%	9.2%

ANKITA

Professional	Educational	L2 Speaker	SW Particular	L1 SW	L2 SW	Bilingual SW	Creative Writer	National	Reader	Gender identity
6.2%	11.0%	5.5%	15.2%	7.6%	1.4%	2.8%	33.1%	2.8%	13.1%	1.4%

(Continued)

Table 6.1 (Continued)

ELIZA

Educational	L2 Speaker	L1 SW	L2 SW	Bilingual SW	Creative Writer	National	Social	Reader
19.3%	7.9%	14.3%	7.1%	3.6%	27.9%	0.7%	2.9%	16.4%

MAGGIE

Professional	Educational	L2 Speaker	SW Particular	L1 SW	L2 SW	Creative Writer	Social	Reader
2.0%	7.1%	4.0%	2.0%	6.1%	11.1%	58.6%	3.0%	6.1%

ANGELES

L2 Speaker	SW Particular	L2 SW	Creative Writer	Social	Reader
3.9%	17.6%	9.8%	25.5%	7.8%	35.3%

to London and Kent on social visits several times every year. These visits provided Maggie with valuable social opportunities to encounter a wider community of English language speakers outside the language classroom. Maggie's father is evidently a vital 'knowledgeable other', shaping the formation of Maggie's L2 speaker identity.

Both Derek and Maggie's first degree subjects are closely related to English education and literature. Derek received his bachelor's degree in English Education, as well as an honour's degree in Linguistics at home in Argentina. As for Maggie, in Germany she started her five-year teacher diploma programme which prepares future bilingual grammar school teachers of German and English. Furthermore, Derek and Maggie's respective disciplinary subjects at the Midlands University (this is a pseudonym) are also closely linked to English (see Table 3.1 in Chapter 3). Before being awarded a full scholarship to study for a master's degree in English Language Teaching at the Midlands University, Derek had been teaching English in secondary schools in Argentina for eight years. As for Maggie, she was selected to do the final year of her teaching diploma programme at the Midlands University as an exchange student, studying English literature. Apparently, Derek and Maggie's outstanding ability in their respective English-mediated and English-related academic and professional careers was acknowledged through the more or less privileged circumstances under which they had come to the UK. Both Derek and Maggie portray their past and present L2 selves as among those to whom English has come rather naturally through their ongoing participation in the English-mediated or -related CoPs.

Teng and Fai

Both Teng and Fai are Malaysian Chinese; and given this particular multicultural, multiethnic society they grew up in, they are multilingual (i.e. Malay, Chinese and English) as well as multi-dialectalists (Mandarin, Cantonese and Hakka). However, Teng and Fai were born in different sociohistorical times in Malaysia (with Teng 10 years' older than Fai, see Table 3.1 in Chapter 3); in addition, they had also been positioned in distinctive local contexts – mainly, familial and educational. Teng's family and Fai's family hold different attitudes towards children's education and the two families possibly also embody different economic statuses. These differences in their macro and micro circumstances contribute to the divergent paths they had taken in their transformations of their L2 learner/speaker identities and achievements in L2 advanced speaker status. Teng's English language learning practices are performed more purposefully outside than inside the classroom context while Fai's have strong academic purposes. In what follows I will illustrate the above point in summarising aspects of Teng's and Fai's life histories.

Teng

Teng was born in the late 1970s in a Chinese community in Malaysia. When he was a child he perceived little use for English in his future. However, from the mid-1980s, after the first post-colonial flush of rejection of English by the Malay-dominated government had passed, Teng began to sense the increasing resurgence of English in Malaysian society. To keep up with this macro sociohistorical shift in Malaysia, Teng began to learn English more purposefully than before, for example, through devoting more attention to classroom English writing tasks (Teng was a rebellious student; this will be discussed later), listening to English music, watching English films and studying English dictionaries. Regarding the micro contexts surrounding Teng, his English learning activities were also shaped by his positioning at home and in school. At home Teng was not particularly close to his father and thus craved financial independence and self-sovereignty; in school Teng was a rebellious student who disdained homework and had negative relations with teachers. Regarding Teng's family context, there is the implication that his parents did not (or could not) execute strong control over their children's educational realisations. Teng's elder brother left school at the age of 14 and entered full-time work. Teng himself also started working at 14, though on a part-time basis, selling T-shirts in a shopping mall. Hence, possibly in accordance with his rebellious student status in school, Teng devoted minimum time to only the compulsory modules, including English. The indication is that Teng's English language learning experience and opportunities in school were constrained by his less legitimate positioning arising from non-conformity to the social practices or social structures ratified in this context.

After Teng finished secondary school, he distanced himself from his family as well as school. Rather adventurously, he left home on his own and went to Japan and then later to Britain, in 1998. Since then, he had been working full-time, but precariously, in restaurants, hotels and bakeries in Britain till he started his full-time undergraduate course in Philosophy at the Midlands University in 2008. Throughout his decade-long working experience in the food and hospitality industry in the UK, Teng was exposed to a variety of spoken English (i.e. accents and dialects) locally practised in meaningful social situations (if not always by native speakers). Mainly out of socioeconomic motives (i.e. to negotiate recognised social existence and economic return), Teng agentively aligned his practices of English particularly with the discourse norms of spoken English prevalent where he worked, lived and socialised. In this process, he gradually accumulated considerable cultural 'capital'. Thus, Teng's advanced English speaker identity is formed in this process of negotiating 'centripetal participation' in this 'ambient community' (Lave & Wenger, 1991: 100) where he made a living and socialised, against the macro backdrop of British society.

Fai

Fai was born in Malaysia in the late 1980s, by which time, unlike in Teng's youth, English had been re-established as a valued second language which no longer threatened the primary status of Bahasa Malaysia. As for the micro contexts Fai was situated in, his parents played a strong role in maximising their children's educational possibilities and achievements. Despite growing up in a small village in a Chinese community, Fai and his sister, after primary school, were sent away to a private school in Kuala Lumpur. When Fai entered secondary school education, his private school adopted the Singaporean 'English across the curriculum' system, in which science subjects were taught in English. This initially presented difficulties to Fai who felt that his English was not good enough to handle such a practice. Fai also sensed a split between his rather Chinese-oriented 'points of view' and 'ways of doing things' (Fai, in-depth interview) and his private school classmates' enactments of Western ideologies and performances of fluent English. Fai felt peripherally positioned in his classroom community. This experience upset him but also motivated him to learn English more diligently than ever before so as to align with the endorsed knowledge practice of treating English not only as a subject but also as an ideological medium. In secondary school, Fai studied English literature and also extensively practised story writing in English (discussed in detail later), though both for exam-oriented purposes.

Fai scored high in the final English exam of his secondary school education, which exempted him from taking any English proficiency test before being offered a place on the undergraduate programme in Law at the Midlands University in 2007. In this specialised L2 disciplinary context, Fai did not perceive himself as marginally positioned despite the subject-related challenges he sometimes faced. From the above it can be seen that Fai's advanced English speaker identity is mainly negotiated in educational contexts, particularly facilitated by the advantageous educational opportunities he had received since primary school. Consequently, in drastic contrast to Teng, Fai is imbued with the voices and practices of the academic establishment – firstly, with the discourse of English acknowledged in the academic context and, secondly, with that of written or literary English.

Teri

Like Teng, Teri is an immigrant who has settled in Britain. Teri is also multi-lingual, having Farsi as her L1 and speaking fluent Hindi, Russian and English; hence she called herself 'a child of the world'. Teri has a socioculturally and geographically diversified life history. She was born in Kabul. Her father was a political journalist and among the intelligentsia in Afghanistan. Against the political and historical context of the Soviet invasion of Afghanistan since 1979, Teri's family migrated to Russia when Teri was four years old. In Russia, Teri attended primary school; and towards the end of her primary school education, her family moved to Britain for the purpose of securing better education for their children. In Britain, Teri finished secondary school, did her A-levels and, when the in-depth interview was conducted, she was in the final year of her BA in English Literature and Creative Writing.

For Teri, throughout the family migrations from Afghanistan to Russia and then to Britain – three countries with diverse socioeconomic structures, political status and language systems – she has developed a capability to negotiate her positioning from peripheral membership in the communities she walked into for the first time ever to gaining legitimate peripheral participation and even to the extent of achieving recognition from some powerful social agents (e.g. teachers and book publishers, as previously mentioned in the I-statement discussions in Chapter 4). Particularly regarding the educational contexts in which Teri found herself, she determinedly and strategically mastered the target language proficiently so as to improve her legitimate student status and widen her educational opportunities and achievements, especially in competition with the native speakers of the target country. Thus, Teri's transformations of her advanced English speaker identity were sociopolitically necessitated in the macro sense and highly educationally driven in the micro sense.

Summary

The above stories demonstrate the distinctive trajectories of the five focal participants' previous transformations of their English language learner/speaker identities across a variety of social circumstances. These five individuals are imbued with the voices of different L2 discourse types and conventions and accordingly embrace the interests, beliefs and practices of diverse social groups. That is to say, the five individuals' respective L2 advanced speaker identities are manifested in association with a diversity of other social identities formerly or presently held by them. To name a few, there are: Derek's professional identity as an experienced English language teacher in Argentina; Maggie's familial identity as the daughter of an English–German bilingual grammar school teacher and her educational identity as a diploma student majoring in English language and English literature; Teng as an immigrant working in Britain in the hospitality and catering industry for a decade; Fai's identity as a private school student receiving an English-mediated secondary school education; and Teri as an immigrant child from Afghanistan and the daughter of an intellectual political journalist. In what follows, in a similar manner, I will tell the stories of the five focal participants' idiosyncratic transformations of their creative writer identities.

L2 creative writer identities
Derek

First of all, for Derek, narrative writing in his L1 and English had constituted a major part of the classroom writing practices throughout secondary school and the first two years of university. In Derek's description of his L1 narrative writing experience in the classroom, the writing activities were diversified, including, in his own words, '[picture] description and narrative composition' and 'creative writing but following different courses, different approaches and different types' and imitative writing of particular creative writers' styles. Derek employed unconventional, modernist literary techniques in his L1 stories. Such self-initiated deviation from the prevalent story writing practices in the writing classroom was not always appreciated by his teachers. Derek commented that he sometimes purposefully incorporated 'spelling mistakes' into his L1 story writing and he sometimes also created a less-contextualised style of stories which have minimal beginning or no ending. Derek recounted that his teachers often adopted critical stances towards the above practices yet he legitimated his 'avant-garde' attempts to the teachers by explicating his creative intentions or pointing out the existence of such practices in published stories. In the interview, through such recounts of his L1 creative writing practices in a classroom context, Derek fashioned the effectivity of his self-agency in shaping his texts and his own creative writing values. In contrast, in Derek's description of his English story writing experience in the classroom, students obligatorily fulfilled the story writing tasks assigned by authoritative teachers. Derek indicated that the work he had completed had not left much impression on him due to the invariably rule-governed and constraining nature of such imposed narrative writing practices.

From the above, the implication is that Derek's preference for L1 story writing can be connected with his sense of individuality and agency. This assumption is further reinforced by Derek's self-perception of his L2 writer identity. As previously mentioned, Derek is an experienced EFL teacher with eight years of teaching work when the interview was conducted. He incorporated literature reading and creative writing in English into his language class. However, interestingly, his motivation in English creative writing for non-professional or non-academic purposes was relatively low. Derek remarked in the interview that: 'I try to say what's possible I mean that collocation because perhaps it sounds natural to me but for a British person whose first language is English might find just a little bit odd or awkward you know'. Clearly, Derek sensed that English, his L2, could not allow him to express the nuances of meaning in a sensitive and controlled manner to the extent that a native-speaker creative writer could. This self-perceived lack of L2 linguistic and cultural capital, in Derek's view, constrained his power to impose reception on an audience which is crucial to his sense as a self-governed creative writer. Derek felt less comfortable with the possibly peripheral position he might end up negotiating if he attempted to publish in English.

Finally, Derek is a published L1 short story writer. Since finishing his bachelor's degree, Derek had published several short stories in the local newspaper, and had one prize-winning story which was published as 'part of a collection of stories in Argentina', and had also published two collections of his short stories (mainly in his L1). As a relatively experienced published L1 story writer, Derek cannot avoid interactions with his publishers, editors or readers. However, Derek particularly distanced himself (socially and metaphorically) from the social group of professional creative writers when he was back in Argentina. He fashioned his creative writer identity as someone who saw writing as a 'hobby', rather than as a way to make a living.

Maggie

Different from Derek's case, according to Maggie, short story writing or any other form of creative writing practice in either her L1 or English was seldom among the assigned writing activities in the classroom, where literary analysis and expository essay writing dominated. Outside the classroom, Maggie's creative writing activities mainly consisted of diary writing and participation in a creative writing interest group. Her creative writing was realised in both her L1 and L2, though it was indicated that her diary was mainly written in her L1.

Maggie has been keeping a diary since she was 13. She performed diary writing particularly during some emotionally volatile periods of her life, e.g. her teenage-hood, her first overseas study experience in Russia and her second in the UK, at which time the interview was conducted. When Maggie studied in St Petersburg for half a year as an exchange high school student, she suffered from 'cultural shock' and loneliness (Maggie, in-depth interview). To neutralise the negative emotion caused by her marginalised and less powerful social position in that Russian school (compared with how she was positioned in Germany), Maggie began to spend a lot of time in writing a diary every day. The activity of writing in her diary had become a form of counterdiscourse set up to position her more as an agentive subject who took the initiative to 'sort her [own] mind out' and who, during her half-a-year study in St Petersburg, 'finished four little books of diary'. This sense of self-empowerment motivated Maggie to spend even more time in writing her diary than learning the Russian language, although the latter activity could have helped her move out of marginalisation into more strategic social positioning in that situation (as Teri had done, mentioned previously). Regarding the linguistic medium of her diary writing practices, Maggie sometimes purposefully wrote in English with the intention of exercising her L2. Possibly because diary writing was a channel for 'mental cleansing' for Maggie and the only audience was herself, she was not worried about her expressive command of features such as connotation and collocation in English, as mentioned by Derek. Also, Maggie, as an Anglophile, was motivated to use English for the purposes of creative and spontaneous expressions.

Finally, during Maggie's university years in Germany, she co-founded a creative writing interest group. The group members, the number of which fluctuated between 5 and 10, met every two or three weeks in the evening 'at someone's place or at some local pub'. In this little creative writer community, Maggie's social relations with the other members had to be negotiated based on her selecting what work of hers should be read out in front of the group and predicting the audience's reception and her own role as a supportive member of this community.

Compared with Derek, Maggie's construction of her creative writer identity has more explicitly suggested the shaping effect of the social context on her writing practices – for example, her emotionally fluctuating period of living in metropolitan St Petersburg and her participation in this creative writing group made up of friends.

Fai and Teng

Fai and Teng, the two Chinese Malaysians, performed their short story writer identities in contrasting social circumstances, Fai nearly exclusively for educational success in his highly competitive private school in Malaysia and Teng mostly in the personal domain as a release and intellectual contrast from his stressful manual working life in Britain.

Fai

Fai commented that in his Malaysian educational context, 'the main determiner of whether you get an A or not [in a language exam] is your essay'. Thus, students who excel in such exam writings, through aligning with the values endorsed by teachers and examiners, have better prospects of educational success and future educational opportunities. In Fai's English language exam, the writing section usually offered two options: an argumentative writing task and a story writing task; and Fai always picked the latter. His reason was strategic: Fai did not see himself possessing what was required by his educational context of an argumentative writer – that is, reading newspapers extensively and regularly and being knowledgeable and analytical of ongoing national and world affairs. However, Fai perceived himself as an imaginative writer equipped with original ideas. Therefore, he paid allegiance to the story writing practices espoused within his educational context, such as integrating L2 idioms and proverbs into the stories, planting a twist in a story's ending and creating tangible images to which the audience could easily relate. Obviously, Fai's story writing practices were primarily goal-driven rather than for self-expressive or improvisational needs. One demonstration of Fai's commitment to practising L2 story writing for enhanced educational positioning is that he had been taking private tutoring in English story writing on a weekly basis since the fifth year of primary school (probably also enabled by his parents' economic status). Furthermore, since the second year of secondary school, Fai had been writing an L2 short story every week which would then be handed in to his private tutor – who was a freelance writer for a well-known Malaysian newspaper and also an experienced L2 writing teacher. In these private tutoring sessions, this tutor initiated Fai's access to a range of English idioms and tropes for descriptive writing; she also illustrated to Fai the connotations of certain words and the artistic value embedded in particular literary styles for story writing. In a word, Fai had inherited considerable symbolic capital from this knowledgeable other; and such a form of knowledge empowerment eventually transformed Fai into a successful and confident L2 student story writer.

Fai's student story writing experience tells that his story writer identity is formed by the values and practices of his educational context, e.g. the inclusion of story writing tasks into English language exams, the weight allocated to writing in the authority's assessment of students' English proficiency and the competitive culture among students in Fai's private school. Consequently, Fai's formative story writing practices had been highly exam-oriented, rule-governed and primarily conducted in English.

Teng

In stark contrast to Fai, Teng was a rebellious student who defied rules and power figures in school. Teng's story-writing practices, in either his L1 Chinese or L3 English, inside or outside the school context, were primarily performed for self-entertainment. Thus, when Teng sensed a constraint put on him by his writing classroom, he did not conform to the prevalent practices as Fai did but rather disengaged himself from them. For example, Teng, from Malaysia like Fai, similarly mentioned that one highly valued practice in his O-level context was artistic incorporation of quotations from canonical literary classics into one's own story. Teng was clearly disheartened by such a practice, which requires literary knowledge from a fairly well-read writer. Teng believed that his stories should unravel on their own rather than align to a prescribed imitative model. These self-oriented and anti-establishment beliefs underlying Teng's story writing practices became most apparent during his decade-long working life in the UK.

In the UK, Teng committed to his duties in the working places where considerable time and physical work were required of him. Although Teng understood the necessity to comply with the social practices in his working context so as to make a living, he sensed himself embracing a less powerful social membership than he would have desired. Consequently, Teng's creative writing practices served either as cathartic mediation or a stage on which to enact his imagination. His creative writing was mostly conducted in English; it ranged from the mythical/fantastical genre to the autobiographical genre, from short-story length to novel length. The suggestion is that story writing in English was employed by Teng as a form of counterdiscourse, like Maggie's engagement in diary writing, for the purposes of strengthening his sense of activated and legitimate social existence in an English-speaking country.

One illuminating instance of Teng's employing story writing in English as a counterdiscourse is that he took two years, while working in restaurants in the UK, to write a novel-length mythological story (a copy of which was given to me by Teng) with characters borrowed from Greek mythology. His creation of this story in English can be seen as a process of self-empowerment, becoming a competent ESL speaker as well as a knowledgeable and imaginative person. His story demonstrates a mixture of references to Greek mythology, particular Japanese cartoons and computer games, ancient Chinese classics and ideologies from Daoism. He thus engages in a 'dialogue' (Bakhtin, 1986) with a range of well-established discourses from different cultures. On the other hand, his creation process is also self-indulgent and untended as his manuscript continuously reveals little attention to grammar, over-heavy appropriation of the original literature classics and slightly perplexing plotlines and repetitive action scenes (my own judgement as a reader).

Nonetheless, in a striking gesture of revitalising his self-identity as an L2 individual who is able to influence his own life in the UK, Teng optimistically sent his manuscript to HarperCollins Publishers in hand-written form. When asked how the idea of sending his work to a UK publisher occurred to him, Teng said: 'I just did it, J.K. Rowling she did it.' By aligning himself with J.K. Rowling, Teng probably identified with the material power to be gained by a creative writer in making impacts on society, no matter how peripherally he/she might have been socially positioned in the first place. However, Teng's non-conformity to the practices and values established in the world of publishers and published writers (e.g. the hand-written format of his manuscript for submission and also reflected in my judgement of his work as a reader mentioned above) brought him a rejection from HarperCollins. Still, this rejection did not stop Teng from continuing practising story writing for self-actualisation and entertainment.

Teri

Teri's story writing practices in English were driven by her 'need to tell' (Teri, in-depth interview) to a Western or even global audience about Afghanistan and the immigrant experience of moving from a turbulent, underdeveloped country to more stable and developed Western countries.

As previously mentioned, Teri has had a geographically and culturally diverse life experience in Afghanistan, Russia and Britain, which greatly feeds into her story writing activities. Teri only started writing about her childhood experience as an Afghani immigrant when she settled down in Britain, a country which, in Teri's perception, allows for more freedom of speech and individuality than Afghanistan or Russia do. In this country, Teri correctly sensed that there would an audience curious to hear her stories and successfully published her first story, 'Five Leaves', with an established UK publisher whilst she was attending college in the UK. The story tells her personal journey as a young child leaving Afghanistan under the Soviet invasion of her country, immigrating to Russia and learning to adapt to the alien environment.

When Teri joined the BA course in English Literature and Creative Writing at this UK university, her Afghan roots and her immigrant identity were even more purposefully and professionally integrated with her story writer identity than ever before. Furthermore, her story writing practices became a medium to fulfil her self-perceived political and journalistic missions; namely, exposing to the world the depressing situation in Afghanistan through telling the stories of real Afghan people's lives. For example, Teri's final project for her BA course was based on her first-hand perception of the bombing that happened at the Indian Embassy in Kabul on 7 July 2008; she and her family happened to be visiting Kabul at that particular time. Teri recounted that when the bomb went off, she and her family were driving nearby but fortunately escaped uninjured. Teri and her father, driven by their investigative instinct, went to see what had happened and became objective observers. During Teri's later visits back to Afghanistan, she felt a 'sense of survivor's guilt' (Teri, in-depth interview) when she saw her relatives suffer from poverty and fear of the Taliban while she lived in comfort and received a first-class education in the UK. Motivated by such a feeling, and more importantly by her self-perception that she possessed not only the first-hand knowledge of what had been going on in Afghanistan but also a highly proficient English literary voice and a perceptive mind, Teri became devoted to writing about the Afghan people's lives to the extent of seeing it as a strong possibility of becoming her life-work and future career.

Teri's politically and journalistically oriented story writing practices are greatly facilitated by the rich social resources she possesses (the focus of the later detailed discussion on Teri). To name a few, there are: the social network Teri has established throughout her long-term immigrant experience; Teri's relatives back in Afghanistan, whom she and her family visit regularly; Teri's father – a highly experienced political journalist – with whom Teri frequently discusses journalism and current affairs in Afghanistan; her father's colleagues who work in mass media (such as the BBC); and Teri's supervisors – established creative writers – in her degree course who appreciate Teri's autobiographical and journalistic style of storytelling and who provide constructive feedback on her work.

Summary

So far, I have depicted the five focal participants' unique trajectory of achieving their individual L2 speaker identities and their creative writer identities, through 'investing them' with their own 'personality' and 'enacting them in a distinctive way' (Fairclough, 2003: 160–161). The next section, through conducting some discursive analyses on the individuals' particular interview comments, examines the focal participants' discursive identity constructions at the *textual* level and the level of *discursive* strategies. The focus is on how these five individuals idiosyncratically position themselves in the specific social milieus which seem to be indispensable for the writers' practices of L2 creative writing. As previously mentioned, such communities take conspicuous proportions of the individuals' We- and You-statement results compared to the equivalents of the other participants'.

L2 Creative Writers' Discursive Constructions of Their Social Localities in the In-Depth Interviews

The following shows how the writers' identity constructions can be inspected through an integration of content and discursive analyses. As previously explained in Chapter 3, I will discuss the focal participants' discursive identity constructions at the *textual* level and the level of *discursive* strategies.

Derek's positioning in the professional CoP: An experienced secondary-school EFL teacher

Derek's We- and You-statements which signify his positioning within the category 'Professional' take a markedly higher proportion than the equivalent of any other participant's (when it applies, see Table 6.1). This indicates that Derek has a particularly strong sense of his social role as an EFL teacher, especially when his professional identity is intertwined with his L2 creative writer identity and literature reader identity. In his recounting of his teaching experience, Derek portrayed his professional self as a versatile and resourceful EFL teacher situated in a bilingual secondary school in Argentina. His teaching was not limited to the English language, but extended to creative writing in English and teaching literature in English. Derek commented that he tried to incorporate a diversity of creative writing activities into his English language class, as shown in the following comments (both are quoted from the in-depth interview; comma indicates short pausing):

but you see this is the way this is 2007, the thing is every year I changed the syllabus because I got bored so I changed everything so this was last year, you see activity on narrative and descriptive writing and then I like doing this like dividing the units into topics you see now native American voices, at the end of the topic of death, life is a journey, *Catcher in the Rye*.

you see this is the book, *Creative Ways*, I think you can download it from the internet I think it's published by the British Council, I am not sure now, it has sections for different techniques for you to use so I have used them with my students like finishing the story off and you have the story swapping stories, so I used these activities to for creative writing.

Derek gave the above comments when showing me his course syllabus on his laptop. It can be seen that Derek had constantly put himself in the position of activated social actor, i.e. 'the one who does things and makes things happen' (Fairclough, 2003: 145). In particular, he portrayed himself as an EFL teacher in a legitimate position to carry out professional actions in his classroom based on his personal preference, e.g. 'I got bored so I changed everything' (line two, first extract), and 'I like doing this like dividing the units into topics' (line three, first extract), and also based on his own choices, e.g. his decision to use the book *Creative Ways* published by the British Council in his own language class (see second extract).

In addition, Derek fashioned himself as a self-made literature teacher, echoed strongly in his response, shown below, to my question on his own literature teachers in university (in the quotation '...' indicates some fragments of words are skipped for clarity's sake):

I have one of the teachers she used to be, like you know, a heavyweight in literature in my country but she only has a BA, like she has been studying all her life but without any formal without doing any formal courses without doing any formal degree that she has been studying and she has been reading a lot and she has been attending seminars and conferences all around the world but you know ... I don't think she is the person who needs to go back to university or like you have a degree saying proving ahh well these ... then sometimes on the other hand, you have people, I don't know, you have a MA in this and then you know your knowledge isn't deep perhaps

The discursive strategy of 'legitimation' by reference to a successful and well-known role model in his proximity in real life was employed by Derek to justify the identity of self-made yet accomplished literature teacher. This corresponds with the 'self-made' theme which also runs through Derek's story writer identity (mentioned in an earlier section when I summarised Derek's creative writing experience). Furthermore, a 'logic of difference' was constructed to demonstrate Derek's allegiance to the identity of a self-made literature teacher. He depicted two contrasting social groups and declared his affiliation with one of these two. On the one hand, his role model's self-made learning process was highlighted through a descriptive three-part list structure, i.e. 'she has been *studying* and she has been *reading* a lot and she has been attending seminars and conferences all around the world'. Derek explicitly gave his endorsement of this literary 'heavyweight's autodidactic accomplishments, e.g. 'I don't think she is the person who needs to go back to university or like you have a degree saying proving ahh well these'. In contrast, Derek's comment criticised qualification-driven learning as sometimes producing less satisfactory intellectual outcomes, e.g. 'then sometimes on the other hand, you have people, I don't know, you have an MA in this and then you know your knowledge isn't deep perhaps'.

Previously I mentioned that Derek was reluctant to perform creative writing in English as he perceived that his power to impose reception on the audience and his creative and expressive control might be compromised if he wrote in the L2. However, Derek did seem motivated to engage in L2 creative writing as entailed by his EFL teacher identity, e.g. writing an English play for his students to perform each year and occasionally composing poems in English as prompts for classroom activities. Derek was willing to invest in L2 creative writing for professional purposes because it reinforces his enactment of the versatile EFL teacher identity and also because it does not compromise his power to impose reception on the audience in this particular context. Derek's students probably possessed much less English linguistic and cultural capital and also occupied a less powerful social position than Derek did.

Identity exists at the crossroads of social forces and personal agency. So far we have seen that self-power, self-agency and initiative-taking are constantly reproduced in Derek's fashioning of his professional identity. Next, we will look at how Maggie's self-positioning in her local creative writing interest group suggests the constraints exerted by social circumstance.

Maggie's self-positioning in her local creative writing interest group

Maggie's We- and You-statements which indicate her membership in the 'Creative Writer' community take a visibly higher proportion than the counterpart of any other participant's (Table 6.1). Her sense of her immersion in this community is mainly realised through her participation in the local creative writing interest group started by her and her university friends back in Germany. The members were required to share their work with everyone regularly; and hence Maggie's social positioning in this community was visibly related to such factors as how often her work was read out, in which language it was written, implication of content and how it was received by the others. In short, the social shaping effect exerted by an audience came into play. Unlike Derek, who emphasises individuality and self-sovereignty as a published short story writer, for Maggie, socialisation with friends who share her interest in creative writing is important for her performances of creative writing. For example, she told me about some of the group's activities in the following comments in the in-depth interview (words in [ ] are my explanation):

> the first, because when we first participate in this meeting and we sort of try to give each other like an incentive like seed, OK next for next time everybody, we tried that once, we said OK next time everybody do something on [the topic of] an empty bottle of wine and just can do anything on it
>   we agree on OK everybody thinks of doing something, oh we did that we picked like three random words and said OK everybody does something and these words need to occur somewhere in the story, it was just like an adjective a noun and a verb

Both extracts illustrate the collective aspect of the knowledge practices of this localised community through the repetitive use of pronouns like 'we' and 'everybody' when indicating who designed and who performed these activities. In addition, the way that Maggie repeatedly addressed herself as part of the community in 'we' and also that 'we' were always put in the position of activated social actors seem to show that Maggie was motivated by the kind of power she was vested with to act within this community.

However on the other hand, Maggie sometimes did feel embarrassed by reading her work out to the other members, in particular to her friends, as shown in the following comment:

> I feel embarrassed because when there are close friends which know each other and I am generally shy I would say and especially when you come to do that having a group around me and not so much when I have like two or three people around yeah I was shy and, embarrassed yes, you have judgements always, people always judge you

The above extract indicates that Maggie's anticipation of the reception of her creative writing by a judgemental audience in this particular social site somehow constrained her individual agency. The I-statements included in the above extract are mostly about feelings, e.g. 'I feel embarrassed', 'I am generally shy', 'I was shy and, embarrassed', which are used to legitimise (i.e. emotions are natural and individual) the less powerful social position negotiated by Maggie (than her identity as an agentive diary writer in her private domain, as discussed earlier) in the reading-out session of this community. In addition, another kind of legitimation, i.e. legitimation by reference to common sense, was also employed by Maggie to justify her less powerful or somewhat constrained writer position, in 'when *you* come to do that having a group around me ... *you* have judgements *always, people always* judge *you*'. At the textual level, generic 'you' and the relatively vague term 'people' were used by Maggie to reinforce the notion that 'being judged' as a creative writer does not just happen to her or inside her writing group, instead it is an ordinary social phenomenon. Also, the amplifier 'always' in '*always* judge you' emphasises the pervasiveness of such a phenomenon.

Next, I will move onto Fai and Teng, presenting how creative writing practices come out of the interrelation between institutional rules and the writers' worked-at social positioning. I will illustrate how Fai positioned himself in his secondary school as a well-trained and educationally aspirant L2 student story writer whose writing practices and values were visibly shaped by his writing teachers. I will also show how Teng, who had previously survived as an immigrant restaurant worker in the UK for a decade, voluntarily conducted L2 creative writing to engage with the language in order to empower his self-esteem as a capable and natural multilingual speaker who can pick up different practices of languages and dialects at ease.

Fai's self-identity as a compliant L2 student writer

The We- and You-statement coding results in Table 6.1 suggest that Fai's L2 story writer identity is closely associated with his secondary school experience back in Malaysia where most of his story writing practices happened. Fai indicates a clear division between the powerful social group *teachers* and the less powerful and compliant social group *students*, with the former exercising perceptible control or influence on the latter's L1 and L2 writing practices, as shown in the following comment:

> but for the Malay it's more intensive *we* have to do *we* have to do homework for our novels which is literature Malay literature the novel part *we* have to do that *we* have to do an essay so these two things *we* have to hand them in in the next session which is a week later and the other one *we* have to, for English *we* have to write an essay every week and they are basically mainly short stories

In the above extract, Fai explicitly identifies himself as situated in the dutiful social group of students who is constantly referred to as 'we' (all italicised). Fai constructs a string of clauses which share the pattern of 'we have to do something'; and through deploying such a descriptive list structure with deontic modal verb 'have to', Fai set up a relation of meaning equivalence. That is, regarding the teacher-assigned Malay and English writing tasks in Fai's educational context, whichever the language, the levels of obligation and compliance expected from the students in accomplishing such writing were consistent.

In contrast to Derek, Fai positions himself as an L2 student story writer who willingly and even gratefully fell under the control of the more experienced and knowledgeable teachers. Fai did not challenge the teachers' views on his writing as Derek did; instead he strongly identified with the practices and values suggested by his teacher, as shown in the following comment (my explanation is provided in [ ] to fill in the ellipses in the comments):

> I think the only thing I can say about the effort I have put in [creative writing] is when I read the materials that my teacher <u>my tuition teacher gave me those things</u> are, <u>she gave us things</u> that we have, the push she gave us wasn't like just write and write and write, <u>she gave us things and asked us to evaluate asked us how we think</u> about this essay writing of the style and as, she really <u>she really showed me</u> what's the art of it, we looked at things like sight hearing colour temperature so in each words they tend to have different connotations and different situation so then <u>she showed us</u> how descriptive writing is by <u>giving us</u> very very short phrases from excerpts from books and that kind of like, it really <u>makes you think</u> how can you put a word into [the context]

Throughout the above extract, the teacher and the students' different ownership of authority and initiative is represented in the recurring structure of 'she (the tuition teacher) did something to us' or 'she asked us to do something' (see the underlined parts in the above extract). The tuition teacher is consistently designated as the activated social actor, and Fai and his tuition mates are the passivated social actors. Fai's above comment particularly constructs the facilitating effect played by his tuition teacher on how he gradually formulates his own L2 story writing habitus, such as the awareness of sharpening up the literary representation of his story through palpable descriptive details and subtle language.

When asked what his best story writing experience is so far, Fai remarked: 'oh the nicest part I guess is when, you get the teacher's recognition after you have improved when they say you have improved when they really think you are better'. In this comment, Fai's employment of generic 'You' and his juxtaposition of this 'You' with 'the teachers' (also referred to as 'they') seems to show that he naturally took up the <u>student</u> identity when negotiating his <u>story writer</u> identity. He explicitly situated himself in the social group of students when talking about his primary L2 story writing values (hence his best writing experience), rather than fashioning himself as an individual or idiosyncratic story writer as Derek does. The teachers' approval of Fai's story writing products, i.e. the powerful social members' recognition of Fai's alignment with the institutionally ratified practices, was central to Fai's sense of satisfaction gained from performing such writing activities.

Teng's self-positioning in the CoP of proficient L2 (or L3) speakers

As for the other Chinese Malaysian story writer, Teng, his story writing practices in English, particularly during the decade he was working in Britain, were conducted entirely for his own pleasure and fulfilment, a reason worth noticing. Neither did Teng's previous educational engagement specialise in English language or literature as Derek's and Maggie's had done nor did his writing classroom experience encourage him (a rebellious student) to work on English story writing as intensely as Fai's had done. In addition Teng's occupation had not involved creative writing in English as Derek's profession entails. In view of Teng's We- and You-statement coding result, which shows that his self-positioning in the category 'L2 Speaker' community takes a larger percentage than that of any other participant's, I would argue that Teng's commitment to writing stories in English is closely associated with his self-identity as a multilingualist and his sense of his social existence and status in the UK.

Teng is a multilingualist and also a multidialectalist. He is a native speaker of Malay, Mandarin, Cantonese and Hakka and he is also a proficient English speaker. Understandably, Teng is proud of his language ability; he remarked that (my explanations in [ ]):

> so obviously *you* just pick it [the language] up *you* just pick it up you just flip flip them [different languages] around and <u>even</u> my father my grandmother have this kind of ability since they have lived there [the multicultural Malaysian society] for so long they flip their language around

As shown above, Teng's repetitive use of generic 'You' (italicised above) demonstrates his self-perception of belonging to the social group of multilingual speakers who can naturally pick the languages up and 'flip them around'. To strengthen his self-representation as a competent and perhaps also inherent multilingual speaker, a logic of equivalence is set up. That is, Teng portrayed that his father and grandmother, despite coming from elder generations and probably equipped with less symbolic or materialistic resources as connoted by the amplifier 'even' (underlined above), can also perform such language practices with expertise and ease.

Throughout his working experience in different cities in Britain, Teng's language ability allowed him to pick up the local English through immersion, as described in his following comment:

you pick them up everywhere, daft is a Leicester word called stupid, then you know wee means small in Scotland so it is, I want a wee one means I want a small one, when I first heard about it it was a bit weird, then obviously you just pick it up then you start to learn, you just eventually you know, you'll be there you know what I'm saying you just have to pick it up then it becomes easy now I mean there was a certain age when I got to Liverpool I didn't get a clue what they talked about

When one lives in a foreign environment, it is often through producing the target language for meaningful purposes, i.e. 'intervening in and potentially changing social life' (Fairclough, 2003: 223), that the person manages to establish his/her sense of social existence or social legitimacy. For Teng, creative writing in English was an important medium for him not only to produce the target language in a written and perhaps, to a certain degree, literary form but also to exercise his power of imagination and self-agency. Thus it became a significant symbolic mediation through which Teng strengthened his sense of self-esteem and self-sovereignty regarding his socialisation in Britain. As shown in the following two extracts, Teng portrayed himself engaging in meaningful dialogues with British people in relation to his self-initiated creative writing practices in English:

the things about movement actually is is one of the things you know, you try I try to think like I say, if I if I grab a sword if I put it this way how should I say it, then obviously you have to find someone and ask and obviously not the Chinese you have to find an Englishman and say this is what I have done so what should I say, what's this movement, this movement, what's this, then you learn it from there I suppose

one of the lady [in HarperCollins] would actually remind me, you know normally they [the publisher] just send it [the manuscript] back they didn't say anything they just say we don't have time for it, one of the lady says first of all they don't do handwriting anymore you have to print it out, secondly you need an agent to introduce you in you don't just go in to publisher anymore like J.K. Rowling herself, she did as I did, she sent it out sent it out sent it out nobody wants it then she finds an agent

Such relatively knowledge-oriented, constructive and also purposeful interactions with the native speakers show Teng agentively tapping into his possibly relatively limited social capital to strengthen his sense of social legitimacy in the UK through the mediator of the L2 story writer identity. In the first extract, Teng not only depicted the power rooted in his imagination and inquisitive mind as a story writer, but also portrayed his 'capacity to truly act as a social agent' (Fairclough, 2003: 223) seeking help from 'an Englishman' so as to increase his own linguistic capital which would facilitate his L2 story writing practices. As shown in the second extract, discursively Teng set up a relation of meaning equivalence in his alignment of his own experience, and perhaps implicitly also of his economic circumstance and his creative initiative, to J.K. Rowling's when she first sent her Harry Potter manuscript to a publisher. It is worth noticing that Teng did not call attention to the evidently different L1 identities held by him and J.K. Rowling behind this similar action of posting a manuscript to a UK book publisher. His obliviousness of this identity difference, in my view, precisely reveals Teng's sense of self as a competent L2 user and also as an imaginative L2 story writer.

Finally, we will look at how Teri's story writing practices, ideationally and politically driven by her Afghan roots and her family's war experience, are set in a nexus of rich social relations which she actively tapped into.

Teri's self-positioning in various social circles which are indispensable to her story writing practices

The proportion of Teri's We- and You-statements indicating her positioning in the 'Socialising Community' category is larger than any other participant's counterpart. Teri's interview comments particularly demonstrate how the L2 creative writers' 'capital' accumulated across diverse social worlds could vitally shape their literary practices.

Teri's story writing is reality based and has a political overtone. She, with her parents and sisters, has regularly visited Afghanistan to see relatives and family friends. In such social encounters Teri witnessed the stark contrast between her relatives' life situation in Afghanistan and that of her own family in Britain. This contrast enthused Teri's story writing practices, as shown in her comments below:

> I spent a lot of time travelling this past holiday I went to three different places because we were visiting three different families and I went back home I went to Afghanistan so I was seeing people who have lived through the war and are still in the country and there is a need to tell their stories because they don't have this language and the people who need to know or the people in the West, because in Afghanistan everyone has had the same experiences but different paths to it so there's a lot of materials all the time and in fact I was sitting yesterday and I wrote three different pieces
>
> I'm currently working on the, bombings that happened on the Indian Embassy in Afghanistan in Kabul it was quite recent it was on the seventh of July and the reason that's important for me because I was there I was I was driving a emm my taxi and with my family our chauffer was driving by when the car bomb exploded and we heard it but we were sufficiently far away then we were not damaged then

obviously the first thing me and my dad do was we got out of the car and went towards it to see what was happening and so we were a part of what happened but it didn't happen to us, we weren't damaged at all so we were observers ... and that piece is going to be about guilt this sense of a survivor's guilt ... I left [Afghanistan] in 1992 just before the Taliban took over emm there *is* this mounting pressure of, there <u>is</u> this mounting pressure that can't be quite put into words and this sense of guilt when you <u>go</u> back and you <u>see</u> people your relatives other Afghans <u>really really</u> suffering and they <u>don't have</u> like basic needs and here you <u>are living</u> a life of <u>extreme</u> comfort and luxury but at the same time you <u>don't have</u> the economy to help them or the social status

In the above extracts, we can see that, in contrast to Fai who tends to fashion himself as a compliant and passivated social actor in his construction of his story writer identity, Teri often put herself in the position of, or among, activated social actor(s) who performed a series of actions and assertively articulated specific, often politically oriented, views. As shown in both extracts, in her demonstration of assertion, epistemic modality (underlined above), realised by the use of non-hedged, present (or present perfect or present continuous) tense and amplifiers, was employed by Teri to accentuate her affinity with the claims she was making.

Secondly, Teri described how, throughout her previous nearly two-decade-long immigration experience, she has gradually accumulated a rich social network of globally dispersed friends who had also left their relatively deprived motherlands and immigrated to more developed countries. Teri constructed a strong alignment between herself and this circle of friends in terms of their similar sociocultural experiences and immigrant identities. This solidarity allows Teri confident access to the life stories of other immigrants, which in turn adds to her 'capital', greatly facilitating her story-writing practices, as shown in the following comment ([ ] enclose my explanations):

60% [of the ideas for her stories] from personal experiences personal experiences not just me but people I know and obviously because of the countries that I come from Russia and Afghanistan I know a huge network of people a huge network of people who have gone through the exact same things that I have but taking different paths because I left Afghanistan when I was four I now live in England my relatives my friends they live all over the world but they have left poor countries as well and they had to immigrate and they struggled to come out of a worsened country learn new languages adapt conform and now they are trying to get on in Austria emm Spain, America

Thirdly, Teri also depicted herself actively engaging in social contacts with more powerful, professionally established or knowledgeable social agents than herself in specific CoPs in relation to story writing or journalism. More importantly, such social relations are represented by Teri as being conducted on rather equal footings, hence revealing Teri's sense of an empowered self with initiatives, cultural capital and recognised knowledge practices. Such social relations proactively negotiated by Teri with these expert members in the CoPs concerned contribute to the constant transformation of her story writing practices. Teri's comments below respectively indicate her social capital embodied in her intellectual discussions with her father's colleagues on political and journalistic issues and her dynamic one-to-one interactions with her professor from her creative writing degree course:

> I <u>know</u> people who work for the Persian BBC so I'<u>m</u> in contact with them when if they come to my house or I go to visit them emm the man who works for a particular show he and his wife used to work with my father in the same newspaper in Afghanistan so I <u>have high</u> contacts with them so when we do sit together what do you talk about so I <u>do have great</u> access to information which <u>obviously</u> feeds into the pieces that I write as a form of journalism and the short story that I end up writing
>
> I <u>trust</u> my professors <u>a lot</u> because emm especially there is one professor I don't know if I should give her name [name deleted] she is she is the translator for Orhan Pamuk who won the Nobel prize I think this year or the Booker prize, not sure, but emm she she <u>is very</u> good and her form of writing <u>is very</u> similar to mine so when I read her I <u>see a lot</u> of my writing style in her work so <u>a lot of the time</u> I will <u>immediately</u> show her or even before I've written something share my ideas with her and I bounce ideas off her so I <u>trust</u> her judgment <u>a lot</u>

In the two extracts above, again we can see that textually Teri constantly positions herself as an activated social actor. Furthermore, epistemic modality (underlined above), signified by non-hedged, present tense and accentuated by several amplifiers, threads through both extracts, announcing Teri's assertion.

In the first extract above, it is worth noticing that, although this social contact that Teri nurtured was enabled (at least in the beginning stage) by her father's professional positioning, Teri fashions herself as an independent social agent engaging in regular knowledge exchanges with a couple who worked for the Persian BBC, as shown in her almost continuous textual representations of 'I' or 'my' in opposition to 'they', 'them' or 'people' (all of which reference this couple). Teri's construction of her rather equally footed social interactions with these two journalistic professionals comes to a highpoint in 'so when we do sit together what do you talk about'. This 'we' references Teri and this couple, i.e. the particular participants of these political and journalistic discussions; and this 'you' references the wider, general community of people who are, in one way or another, engaged in journalism. This arrangement of the particular and the wider (see Fairclough, 2003: 150) shows Teri's self-perception that she and this couple are situated in the same CoP, though probably she as a novice and they as expert members.

Next, in the second extract above, Teri firstly represents her professor as a highly regarded scholar and translator. Then Teri strongly aligns her own interest, value and story-writing practice with those of her professor, thus positioning herself and her professor in the same social group of story writers. Facilitated by her negotiations of such shared memberships, Teri actively seeks out this expert member's thoughts on her own writing or ideas in a fairly free and vigorous manner; and through such social activities Teri accumulates symbolic capital for herself.

Conclusion

In this chapter, I have briefly described the individual trajectories of the five focal participants' English language learning and their creative writing experiences. Embedded in such representative sketches of the five individuals' autobiographical histories, I further examined the writers' concrete interview comments indicating the individuals' self-positioning in specific CoPs fundamental to their previous creative writing practices and self-esteem. Based on such qualitative discussions on the focal participants' sociocultural roots, the next chapter will look at the focal participants' instantiations of certain writer voices in their think-aloud writing activities. Focusing on the five focal participants' think-aloud writing processes under the present two story-writing tasks, through tangible examples, I will examine the indication, arising from the previous quantitative data analysis results, that L2 creative writers employ habitual cognitive writing activities shaped by their past life histories.

7   Five Focal Cases

The previous chapter narrated the stories of how five L2 creative writers have reproduced their L2 (or L3) identities and creative writer identities through personalising them with their primary concerns and needs in specific social circumstances. Throughout such unique socialisation trajectories, each L2 creative writer has gradually developed a certain propensity or capacity to practice particular forms of creative writing. Continuing from the last chapter's discussion, this chapter looks into the five L2 creative writers' *writer voices* as revealed in their think-aloud utterances. It demonstrates the significance of inspecting the performative constituents of the L2 writers' identity constructions as manifested by their variable selections from possible actions, values and knowledge in their cognitive writing processes. The focus is put on the individuals' characteristic writing behaviours sustained across the two different story writing tasks (i.e. the Autobiographical writing and the Story-continuation tasks).

My interest in examining the tangible details of L2 students' creative writing processes was initiated by my own experience as an EFL teacher incorporating creative writing activities into the classroom. I cannot help asking to what extent the teachers' perceptions match the students' actual reflexive projection of their identities, which are related to their decision making in the process of creative writing, particularly in terms of the purposes behind their instantiations of personal knowledge and language use. As narrated in the last chapter, the five L2 writers in the present study bring with them diverse autobiographical selves. For them, L2 creative writing activities have functioned as idiosyncratic epistemological tools, positioning the writers – who are acquiring a certain nature of knowledge, be it linguistic, ideological and/or stylistic – in personal ways and in situated contexts. In Chapter 3, I have explained the approaches underpinning my motives for looking at how identity constructions are occasioned in the writers' emergent thoughts in the writing processes.

Think-Aloud Utterances: Knowledge Construction and Writer Voice

These five creative writers' cognitive writing processes across the two task conditions have shown distinctive features, such as consistently spontaneous, or proactive, or retroactive writing processes. In the following, one by one, we will look at how features revealed in the writers' think-aloud writing processes speak of their writer voices which are connected to their autobiographical self-identities discussed in the last chapter.

Derek, a proactive writer

Writing under the Autobiographical or the fictional Story-continuation task, the proportion taken by Derek's 'Planning' activities constantly exceeds the equivalent shown in a majority of the other 14 participants' writing processes. Meanwhile, the proportion occupied by his 'Revising' activities is visibly small (Table 4.3, Chapter 4). When writing for his autobiographical story, Derek was creating the stream of consciousness – rather cynically toned – going through the mind of a fictional protagonist, i.e. a celebrated comedian, who was performing on stage in front of a large audience. The protagonist's stream of consciousness went on intermittently, interrupted by the 'tick tack' rhythm of a metaphysical clock in his head. Perhaps by this point, the reader could detect traces of an unconventional, modernist tendency in Derek's autobiographical story. To illustrate the above description, an excerpt from Derek's think-aloud utterances is provided. The 'he' and 'I' in Excerpt 1 refer to this fictional protagonist, the comedian. The underlined parts are Derek's verbalising of his concurrent writing, and the parts within [ ] are his reading of what has been written down.

As shown in Excerpt 1 above, an emerging pattern of Derek's writing behaviours is an alternation between Planning and Composing activities, interspersed with four occurrences of Monitoring activities. Derek took visible control of the initial formulation of his stories, consciously attending to Planning for the purpose of generating or setting explicit ideational or discoursal designs. One illuminating example is in Units 7–10. Derek wanted to textually represent the metaphysical ticking of a clock unreeling in the protagonist's mind, and hence he decided not to put any space between words (see Unit 8). This literary technique is, of course, associated with James Joyce, and Derek's possible appropriation and reconceptualisation of the device as revealed in this particular planning activity signals his reading of and alignment with modernist texts. In addition, Unit 10 says: 'time's arrow, which is a book he has read'. There indeed is a book called *Time's Arrow*, and Derek possibly has read this book. *Time's Arrow* is a postmodern novel written by Martin Amis who recounts in a reversed order a German Holocaust doctor's life, 'in part to evoke the progress-denying catastrophe that was the Nazi Holocaust' (Diedrick, 2004: 12). In this novel, the narrator serves as a consciousness living within this protagonist and experiencing and recounting the protagonist's life in 'reverse[d] chronological time entirely' (12). As shown in Excerpt 1, Derek recontextualised the literary technique of stream of consciousness in his story; meanwhile he also made explicit references to this postmodern novel which deploys consciousness. Derek's re-voicing of these two modernist literary references, both

Excerpt 1 Derek's think-aloud utterances from the Autobiographical writing task

Think-aloud utterances	Categorisation of writing behaviours
7. <u>tick tack</u>, <u>tick tack tick tack tick tack</u>	Composing: Verbalising one's writing
8. and now he is obsessed with it so let's put it all together	Planning: Goal-setting on local event
9. <u>tick, tack tick tack tick, tack</u>	Composing: Verbalising one's writing
10. like he wants to keep coming unstop, that's going on in his mind and he, he feels like time's arrow, which is a book he has read	Planning: Goal-setting on local event
11. <u>time's arrow, is pointing, at me</u>	Composing: Verbalising one's writing
12. let's change the perspective	Monitoring: Commenting on literary technique
13. [time's arrow is pointing at me]	Composing: Reading what has been written down
14. <u>I know all those people I know all those people, are out there</u>	Composing: Verbalising one's writing
15. well, not are out there let's see	Monitoring: Evaluating phrasing
16. [time's arrow is point at me and all those people are out there]	Composing: Reading what has been written down
17. huh dying	Composing: Tentative formulations
18. yes because he is famous	Monitoring: Commenting on vocabulary
19. <u>dying to see me</u>	Composing: Verbalising one's writing
20. like here comes the clock again	Planning: Goal-setting on local event
21. <u>tick tick</u>	Composing: Verbalising one's writing
22. and change it	Planning: Goal-setting on local event
23. <u>tack tack, tick tick tack tack tack tack tack</u>	Composing: Verbalising one's writing
24. OK so emm, I also know because he knows he knows everything from them well he thinks he does	Planning: Goal-setting on local event
25. <u>I also know, because I can see it can see it can see it that the lights are out, but the very moment I step, on stage that bloody stage that bloody stage</u>	Composing: Verbalising one's writing
26. a spot	Composing: Tentative formulations
27. I think you can spot	Monitoring: Evaluating vocabulary
28. <u>spot will light up and show my,</u>	Composing: Verbalising one's writing
29. show my what my presence, my let's say my material OK	Planning: Idea-generating of local event
30. <u>my material presence in this world presence in</u> no in this world to them I wonder	Composing: Verbalising one's writing

having something to do with narrator/protagonist's consciousness, is no coincidence. We should recall that such an experimental story writer self-representation was previously constructed in Derek's retrospective accounts of his L1 literacy experience (described in Chapter 6); that is, Derek declared the disagreement between his own somewhat 'avant-garde' practice and his writing teacher's rather mainstream interests. This disagreement marks Derek's sense of individuality and self-sovereignty which is essential to his own sense as a creative writer, as similarly represented by the manner in which he, as a published story writer, distanced himself (socially and metaphorically) from the circle of commercial creative writers when he was back in Argentina.

So far, I have illustrated that Derek's Planning activities are indexical of his discoursal knowledge and particularity. This voice is carried through to his Story-continuation task. As shown in Excerpt 2, Derek accentuated his literary voice through appropriating the Shakespearean theme 'the

Excerpt 2 Derek's think-aloud utterances from the Story-continuation task

Think-aloud utterances	Categorisation of writing behaviours
56. [I really wonder and I would drive her into the same line]	Composing: Reading what has been written down
57. of questions I wonder whether I really wonder whether she is positively aha positively positively certain of her feelings, for him	Composing: Verbalising one's writing
58. emm her ability ehh let's make him the question form	Planning: Goal-setting on local event
59. how deep no, how certain, how sure is she of her own feelings, (9 seconds), how certain is she of his, feelings for her, what what what proof, which can not, be	Composing: Verbalising one's writing
60. what	Planning: Idea-generating of local event
61. washed away by time	Composing: Verbalising one's writing
62. washed away ah like Shakespeare	Monitoring: Commenting on phrasing
63. washed away by the ravages of time, does she possess, to believe that they are bounded by love	Composing: Verbalising one's writing
64. ehh [what proof which cannot be washed]	Composing: Reading what has been written down
65. well it's just time to suit this	Monitoring: Evaluating phrasing
66. [to believe that they are that they bounded]	Composing: Reading what has been written down

ravages of time' in his story. This came up when he was creating a rather sentimental account of the thoughts of the narrator who was witnessing a wedding ceremony of her two good friends.

In Units 62–65, we can sense a trace of self-amusement in Derek for finding himself summoning up this timely Shakespearean theme to spice up his romantic tragedy (as revealed in Unit 65). This is particularly the case after the nine-second uncertainty, as shown in Unit 59, where Derek seemed to be struggling with how to proceed with his creation of the narrator's sentimental rhapsody.

Derek's accentuation of specific literary forms in his writing processes are identifiable choices made by him as declarations of his preference for and knowledge of particular literature. Such knowledge is not, in a traditional or explicit sense, associated with sociocultural heritage or personal experience. Derek's voice instantiated in the choices he had made while writing expresses and, more importantly, empowers his self-identity as a self-governed and experienced story writer.

Maggie, a spontaneous but also meticulous writer

In sharp contrast to Derek, Maggie is a more spontaneous writer, who to a great extent relies on natural surges of inspiration to pour out her stories. The coding results in Table 4.3 show that the proportions taken by Maggie's Planning activities under the two tasks are rather minimal, with her goal-setting activities next to none; meanwhile, her attention to Revising, noticeably regarding the language, stands out from the other 14 L2 creative writers. We should recall the long-term diary-writer identity taken up by Maggie since she was 13 (previously described in Chapter 6). The practice of diary writing was particularly important for Maggie when the social context disrupted the stability of her emotional state. Under both story writing tasks, Maggie tended to write down the most likely things flowing through her mind first and then later refine the language and content through extensive and repeated revising efforts. This might reflect the influence of a self-perceived judgmental audience (i.e. me, the researcher) on her cognitive writing processes. For example, after she finished the Autobiographical writing task, I asked for her reflection on this writing experience and her newly created story; she said that 'the idea that there is an audience, was more connected with being anxious'. Her voice instantiated in the present story-writing tasks, i.e. that of a sensitive and meticulous L2 creative writer striving to perfect her stories for a judicious audience, echoed the indication that her writer identities are often portrayed in the in-depth interview as being shaped (constrained or facilitated) by the social contexts. At the same time, as revealed in the previous chapter, although Maggie, as a diary keeper, valued spontaneity and authentic feelings, she had an intrinsic concern for the aesthetics of literary form, especially in English, i.e. as an admirer of the

English language and literature and also as an MA degree student studying literature in the UK. All of these could have led her to work on refining her writing.

Two excerpts from Maggie's think-aloud utterances will be explored here. These illustrate her revising effort in her autobiographical story writing processes (The double underlined parts are the revisions actually made to the written text). Compared with Derek's apparently fictional and somewhat avant-garde story of the stand-up comedian, Maggie's autobiographical story resembles the genre of 'chick-lit': social observation centring on the lives of young intellectual women. Maggie's autobiographical story concerns the protagonist's mixed feelings towards drifting away from her old, 'artless' friends upon her acquaintance with a new group of 'cool' people. In Excerpt 3 she describes the protagonist's apprehension about reconciling her two circles of friendship in an approaching birthday party.

It can be seen in this excerpt that Maggie's writing process is more retroactive than Derek's. Several times she went back to concretising further what she had written previously, gradually enlivening her story with descriptions of increasingly tangible scenes and expressive language. For example, Maggie's voice as a writer who retraces her previous text so as to give the most colourful account that she can manage is testified to in Units 96, 101 and 103. Unit 101 invigorates Unit 96's somewhat plain and vague account 'I soon found her people to be different' with 'I was utterly fascinated by her and her friends'; but Maggie did not stop there: Unit 103 again replaced the slightly ambiguous 'they dressed differently' produced in Unit 101 with 'they dressed in a conspicuous way'. A similar cycle could be seen in Units 103, 105, 107 and 109, where the indistinct 'everything' in 'they shared a passion for everything' was improved upon by the more animated description 'loved the music of the sixties, were politically serious and earnest'. Again, Maggie did not stop there; in Unit 109 she improved upon the texture of authenticity by specifying the music as 'Beat' (a 1960s rock music genre). It is not coincidental that Maggie invoked some notion of English-speaking culture in her writing, as attested by the example in Excerpt 4.

After some effort of searching for a 'stronger expression' to indicate 'mocking', Maggie assuredly (i.e. showing little sign of hesitation or self-questioning) uses the relatively uncommon (for an L2 speaker) yet highly culturally indexical vocabulary 'Beatniks' in the phrasal revision she performed. She replaced the rather common phrasing 'making fun of the other' with the more literarily buoyant 'calling the other weird beatniks'. Such a revising activity undoubtedly fashions Maggie as a discriminating and cultured L2 writer who is well-informed about the cultural history and literature of English-speaking countries.

Maggie's meticulous attention to language through revising and her recontextualisation of cultural references in her stories continues in her Story-continuation writing process, as shown in Excerpt 5.

Excerpt 3 Maggie's think-aloud utterances from the Autobiographical writing task

Think-aloud utterances	Categorisation of writing behaviours
94. I cannot remember how we became, we grew grew we grew close very soon	Composing: Verbalising one's writing
95. [we grew close very soon]	Composing: Reading what has been written down
96. and, I felt started being more and more, and I started being and I started um as I, I started going to the parties she and her, got to the parties of, her and her friends, I soon found her people people to be di different from my own circle of friends from my own friends first first of all they dressed dressed differently, no	Composing: Verbalising one's writing
97. but, [circle of friends] but my friends, whereas my friends emm	Planning: Idea-generating of local event
98. OK read the first draft whereas my friends, emm, (9 seconds) um, um first I, going over my my notes again	Planning: Reviewing one's notes
99. again time I can't look that way, (10 seconds)	Monitoring: Commenting on writing procedures
100. the group of Jeanne were being different from	Planning: Reviewing one's notes
101. I soon found I, I was fascinated, utterly fascinated by her and her friends they dressed different they dressed I liked, their way to	Composing: Verbalising one's writing
102. [I soon found her people to be different from my own friends]	Composing: Reading what has been written down
103. they dressed in a conspicuous way conspicuous way and, and shared, shared a	Composing: Verbalising one's writing
104. a very shared a shared shared a a liking for shared a	Composing: Tentative formulations
105. passion for every thing	Composing: Verbalising one's writing
106. [and shared], [in a conspicuous way]	Composing: Reading what has been written down
107. loved, loved the six loved, the, loved the music of the sixties, were political tically serious rious and earnest and	Revising: Revising content
108. emm need to change it	Monitoring: Evaluating content or ideas
109. interested in the Beat, were political seri, serious serious and earnest and earnest about al:most everything um, whereas my own fre friends never understood and even mocked my liking for books that were way way above above my, my intellectual lev level	Composing: Verbalising one's writing

Excerpt 4 Maggie's think-aloud utterances from the Autobiographical writing task

Think-aloud utterances	Categorisation of writing behaviours
322. [I enjoyed myself and felt at ease until Jeanne approached me with an alarmingly raised eyebrow] and started to, [each of the groups making fun of the other]	Composing: Reading what has been written down
323. mocking, the other looking for stronger, expression mocking, (8 seconds)	Planning: Looking for phrasing
324. with, <u>calling the,</u> <u>other weird beatniks</u>	Revising: Revising phrasing

Excerpt 5 Maggie's think-aloud utterances from the Story-continuation task

Think-aloud utterances	Categorisation of writing behaviours
41. [the bride and the groom slapped me on the back saying well done], [as if, I alone have], [as if, I alone have been, involved in, in the in the growth of]	Composing: Reading what has been written down
42. in the relation in the in the arrangement as as I have been, (8 seconds) as	Revising: Trying alternative phrasing
43. <u>as,</u> I was, as I was, <u>some sort of a match</u> <u>maker they had paid</u>	Revising: Revising phrasing

In this excerpt Maggie perhaps felt that the phrase 'involved in the growth of their relationship' sounds bland and, more importantly, fails to accentuate her intended meaning, i.e. the way in which the narrator 'I' played a critical role in the newly-weds' past relationship. In response, she tried out other options, and she eventually sharpened her sentence with the more colloquially toned and vibrant phrasing 'some sort of matchmaker they had paid'.

In Excerpt 6, Maggie's recontextualisation of an ideology from specific canonical literature to refine her story can be seen. Maggie's compositional process concerns the narrator 'I's personal narrative on her friend Lamar, a methodical and driven-to-succeed American businessman who had found his perspectives on life and marriage altered completely after he returned from his honeymoon in Europe.

It is worth noting in Excerpt 6 the fairly blatant manner in which Maggie's story suggests recourse to her own reading, drawing on her knowledge as a literature MA degree student (described in Chapter 6). Her scenario echoes that of Henry James' *The Ambassadors* (1903), where the rather puritanical and culturally impoverished American Lewis Lambert Strether has his

Excerpt 6: Maggie's think-aloud utterances from the Story-continuation task

Think-aloud utterances	Categorisation of writing behaviours
184. [but now they had been to Europe, now that they, had been to Euro Europe this image of her in, her had faded to him apparently for when I met up with Lamar very late in the very evening he went into length about how much Europe had refined him how much something had made him realise]	Composing: Reading what has been written down
185. what he needed	Revising: Revising content
186. had, opened his eyes to the needs of his life	Revising: Revising phrasing
187. [realised, and made him realise]	Composing: Reading what has been written down
188. what, it was his puritan, his puritan	Revising: Revising content
189. emm economic	Revising: Trying alternative vocabulary
190. his puritan career, was missing	Composing: Verbalising one's writing
191. [thinks about getting his marriage annulled but then he had not revealed to me]	Composing: Reading what has been written down
192. then he had not yet, told me about the, most impo portent import, tant revelation	Revising: Revising phrasing
193. about his most important	Revising: Trying alternative vocabulary
194. his most important revelation in Europe	Composing: Verbalising one's writing

horizons widened during a visit to Europe (Rosenbaum, 1994). As shown in Excerpt 6, the beginning displays that Rereading was used to stimulate the flow of writing, as Maggie earlier got stuck at 'had made him realise' and left the sentence unfinished and moved on to writing something else. After writing 'what he needed' in Unit 185 to fill in what was previously left blank, Maggie immediately rephrased 'had made him realise what he needed' into 'had opened his eyes to the needs of his life'. It is possibly a more animated phrasing; but more importantly it noticeably re-accentuates what James (1987) says of Strether in his note for *The Ambassadors*: Paris is 'the vision that opens his eyes' (141, cited in Hutchison, 2005: 41). Maggie did not stop there; she then attempted to revise 'had opened his eyes to the needs of his life' into 'what it was his puritan career was missing'. It can be seen that the latter revision equally is a re-contextualisation of James' depiction of the puritanically minded Strether. In Unit 193, Maggie immediately tested whether 'his' worked better than 'the' as the determiner to lead 'most important revelation', i.e. both are grammatically correct but send slightly different connotations. Then in Unit 194, not only did Maggie replace 'his' with 'the', she also slightly extended the content, i.e. further modifying 'revelation' with 'in Europe'.

In contrast to the purposeful, self-assured voice exuding from Derek's think-aloud utterances, Maggie's writing activities construct her as a proficient and literary L2 writer who repeatedly retraces her text so as to improve it down to the very details. Like Derek, Maggie did not conspicuously call upon her L1 (German) cultural resources or dramatic personal experience in her writing processes (though her autobiographical story does sound less fictional). Her sense of empowerment seems to reside in the testimony of her ability to take discriminating ownership of specific notions reflected in some cultural artefacts (music, literature) of English-speaking countries; her sense of empowerment is also achieved through the way she exploits her ability to construct suitable language. L2 writers like Derek and Maggie have formed a visible creative writing habitus (i.e. their characteristic story-writing processes visibly propelled by planning activities or revising activities, their implementation of specific literary techniques, language choices or ideology), which is closely related to the particular self-images they intend to construct for themselves through creative writing and accordingly their realisation of self-empowerment. The question to be asked is how teachers, in their design and execution of L2 creative writing activities in classroom, could acknowledge or respond to the idiosyncratic self-perceptions of L2 writers like Derek and Maggie, who do not necessarily fit into the stereotypes of L2 writers as often posed in existent discussions on classroom L2 creative writing activities.

Next, I move on to another two L2 creative writers – Fai and Teng, two Chinese Malaysians. Their writer voices illustrate how creative writing practices arise from an interrelation between institutionalised rules and the writers' negotiations of desired social positioning.

Fai, a strategic and duteous writer

In Chapter 6, I demonstrated that Fai's L2 story writer identity is closely associated with his positioning in his student writer community, where most of his story writing practices happened. Fai positions himself in his educational context as a well-trained L2 student story writer whose writing practices and values were visibly shaped by his writing teachers. Compared to the other 14 creative writer participants, Fai's writing processes under both story writing tasks manifest a tendency for balancing strong attention to Revising Activities with a reasonable amount of Planning effort. Fai demonstrates a retrospective writing behaviour fortified by a sense of strategic navigation. This, I would argue, reflects Fai's exam-oriented, result-driven L2 story writing practices which were intensively cultivated throughout his secondary school education in Malaysia.

First of all, some examples of Fai's think-aloud utterances in his Autobiographical writing are shown in Excerpts 7 to 10. In his Autobiographical story writing process, Fai was seeking to describe a comical scene where the boy narrator 'I' was nervously dressing up for his first date yet frustratingly found his preparations disturbed by a mouse.

In Excerpt 7, we can see that, similar to Maggie, Fai's writing activities go through a few cycles which gradually concretise the details and language, e.g. 'breathed in deeply', 'slicking my hair to the back', 'getting on my nerves'. Fai shows as strong a dedication to revising as Maggie does. His commitment to refining the language and content of his stories, like what Maggie exhibits, might be similarly related to the writer's awareness of a judgemental audience. Fai's story writing habitus had been formed under the circumstance of his regular completion of teacher-assigned story writing tasks and his L2 stories constantly falling under evaluation and scrutiny by his writing teachers or examiners. In addition, the symbolic capital Fai had garnered from his writing teacher has possibly nurtured his awareness of the need to sharpen up the literary representation of his story and also enabled his access to the language essential for his performances of such dynamic revising efforts. Some more excerpts of Fai's revising activities in his autobiographical story writing process are given in Excerpt 8, where Fai is wrestling with the most vivid way of expressing the effect of an electric shock on a victim.

Excerpts 8 and 9 show Fai's meticulous concern with detailing the sight, the sound and the temperature of the scene with rich descriptive language, e.g. 'snapped in mid-air', 'sizzling cockles', 'writhing'. Such revising activities resonate with Fai's previous comments in the in-depth interview on his tuition experience in L2 story writing: 'we looked at things like sight hearing colour temperature so in each words they tend to have different connotations', and also with Fai's statement in response to my question about what characterises good L2 creative writing: '[the] details that the audience can relate [to] easily'. Another example of Fai's engagement in revising is provided in Excerpt 10. Fai is looking for alternative phrasing to enhance his depiction of the frustrated protagonist who had caused catastrophic damage to the house after a disastrous mouse-hunt; Fai started rereading what he had previously written.

He deftly replaced 'turn' with 'blasted'. Similarly, Excerpt 10 demonstrates Fai's expertise in enhancing the vividness of the descriptive L2 phrasing.

As shown in these excerpts, Fai's revising activities reveal his identification with some commonly espoused mainstream story writing practices, such as attending to the tangible details 'that the audience can relate [to] easily' (Fai, in-depth interview) and using an unexpected choice

Excerpt 7 Fai's think-aloud utterances from the Autobiographical writing task

Think-aloud utterances	Categorisation of writing behaviours
11. [I tried to perfect, carefully slicking my hair to the back carefully slicking my hair towards the back I tried to perfect my I tried to perfect my]	Composing: Reading what has been written down
12. composure	Composing: Verbalising one's writing
13. no leaving aside emm I'm going to delete this then summarise a, oh maybe I should start it with just how, emm	Planning: Goal-setting on local event
14. I breathed in deeply I breathed in deeply	Revising: Revising content
15. yeah that's better	Monitoring: Evaluating content or ideas
16. [I breathed in deeply comma]	Composing: Reading what has been written down
17. and trying to put back the same words that I used just now, perfecting no slicking my hair	Planning: Goal-setting on local event
18. [I breathed in deeply]	Composing: Reading what has been written down
19. trying to get the perfect posture	Composing: Verbalising one's writing
20. OK no, slicking my hair to the back I can't put it as a sentence	Monitoring: Commenting on grammar
21. slicking my hair to the back [I breathed in deeply]	Revising: Revising content
22. that was that was all I could in [trying to get the perfect composure]	Revising: Revising phrasing
23. when my nerves were really	Composing: Verbalising one's writing
24. I'm trying to say that, my emm I'm trying to say that I was very nervous at that point of time so, trying to fit in the sentence of perfect posture and really deep into my nerves	Planning: Goal-setting on local event
25. [slicking my hair to the back I breathed in deeply that was all I could do in trying to get the perfect posture when my nerves were really]	Composing: Reading what has been written down
26. bothering	Composing: Verbalising one's writing
27. really emm getting on my nerves	Revising: Trying alternative phrasing

Excerpt 8 Fai's think-aloud utterances from the Autobiographical writing task

Think-aloud utterances	Categorisation of writing behaviours
241. he snapped in midst air like cockles on hot frying pan [frying pan]	Composing: Verbalising one's writing
242. like cockles jumping skipping, emm how should I say the what the cockles does on a hot pan frying pan, like cockles	Planning: Looking for vocabulary
243. emm, like sizzling cockles	Revising: Trying alternative phrasing
244. cockles hopping no not hopping jumping on the frying pan, it	Composing: Verbalising one's writing

Excerpt 9 Fai's think-aloud utterances from the Autobiographical writing task

Think-aloud utterances	Categorisation of writing behaviours
402. [like sizzling cockles]	Composing: Reading what has been written down
403. writhing [on the frying pan]	Revising: Revising vocabulary
404. on a hot frying on a hot pan	Revising: Revising phrasing
405. on a hot frying pan	Composing: Verbalising one's writing

Excerpt 10 Fai's think-aloud utterances from the Autobiographical writing task

Think-aloud utterances	Categorisation of writing behaviours
264. [out of frustration and fear of punishment I ran back to my room and smashed the door behind me then I turned on I tuned my radio to its loudest]	Composing: Reading what has been written down
265. blasted the radio to its loudest	Revising: Trying alternative phrasing

of word to create a vibrant and diversely descriptive image, e.g. Excerpts 8 and 9, where his cockles first skip, then hop, then jump and finally vividly 'writhe' on the pan.

Next, Fai's Planning activities also demonstrate his alignment with the practice of attending to identifiable details associated with story writing, as shown in Excerpts 11 to 13 from his Story-continuation think-aloud utterances, specifically the part where the writer was trying to recreate the

Excerpt 11 Fai's think-aloud utterances from the Story-continuation task

Think-aloud utterances	Categorisation of writing behaviours
69. <u>she can't be the one for him</u>, <u>not when I am around</u>	Composing: Verbalising one's writing
70. oh OK OK too much of personal comment	Monitoring: Evaluating content or ideas
71. I should think of something, I should think about, how should I write to make it sound more more sophisticated	Planning: Idea-generating of local event
72. [I will never forgive if she is going to take him as another rebound]	Composing: Reading what has been written down
73. OK I'm gonna step in another story, put them in, restaurant, bar or, there will be people, emm ahh, the restaurant then	Planning: Goal-setting on local event

Excerpt 12 Fai's think-aloud utterances from the Story-continuation task

Think-aloud utterances	Categorisation of writing behaviours
149. [depressed looking in the mirror]	Composing: Reading what has been written down
150. emm, when I say that she is, how to make her sadder make her a wuss, emm, make her a desperate person	Planning: Idea-generating of local event

Excerpt 13 Fai's think-aloud utterances from the Story-continuation task

Think-aloud utterances	Categorisation of writing behaviours
12. OK emm she is suicidal, not, she is jealous I'm gonna say, don't don't want them to get together so now then I'm trying to break them apart, emm, suicidal, next thing, know that they're, know that this girl is, too low class, wouldn't fit the guy emm, OK, I'm gonna put that down	Planning: Goal-setting on local event
13. emm they can never last	Composing: Tentative formulations
14. and, OK I'm done there	Monitoring: Evaluating content or ideas
15. [they can never last]	Composing: Reading what has been written down
16. emm I'm gonna put down an example, have to put down an example say, arguments then emm	Planning: Goal-setting on local event

female protagonist's monologue of bitterness and grudge against her rival in love.

Excerpt 11 reveals Fai's awareness of being creative and discriminating in expression rather than being over-expressive in spontaneous venting of 'personal comment'. Excerpts 11 and 13 show him trying to enliven the monologue with substantive events.

Different from Derek's or Maggie's, Fai's story writer voice does not reaccentuate modernist literary techniques or certain knowledge about the cultural history and literature of the English-speaking countries; rather, his voice is empowered through the writing processes, which invoke a structured and purposeful story writer. Fai is motivated by his self-image as a story writer who is equipped with the discoursal and linguistic skills necessary to create easily accessible humorous or dramatic content. We shall remember that, as discussed in Chapter 6, the teachers' approval of Fai's story writing products, i.e. the powerful community members' recognition of Fai's alignment with the institutionally ratified practices, was central to Fai's sense of satisfaction gained from performing such types of writing activities and, more importantly, vital to his educational achievement in his secondary school.

In stark contrast to Fai, Teng – the other L2 story writer from Malaysia – is a rebellious individual who paid little heed to rules in school back in Malaysia. His L2 creative writing practices were mostly voluntarily conducted during his stressful manual working life in Britain, mostly in restaurants, as an immigrant. We shall look at some of Teng's think-aloud utterances next.

Teng, a spontaneous and expressive writer

Under the present two story writing tasks, the proportions taken by Teng's spontaneous Composing activities are substantial. Meanwhile, his Planning activities are extremely minimal, and his Revising activities, though slightly above the average in proportion among the 15 L2 creative writers, show noticeable attention to grammatical issues. Teng habitually relies on the natural flow of inspiration to formulate his stories. Such spontaneous writing behaviours correspond to his former emotion- or imagination-driven L2 story writing experience. Furthermore, the content of his verbalisations of his concurrent writing across the two story-writing tasks is fairly expressive, personal and, to some extent, cathartic, perhaps resonating with his sometimes materialistic philosophies, as shown in the following examples. Teng's Autobiographical story is epitomised by its title 'The Book of Life'. In his fictional Story-continuation writing, Teng was declaring, through the narrator 'I', what it means for a man, who is struggling in a 'cruel and cold' 'business world', to have a prudent and understanding wife. This somehow reminds me of Fai's own stressful experience of surviving in Britain in the hospitality and catering industry for a decade. Under both writing tasks, regarding Teng's indisputably central writing activity, Composing, the proportions respectively taken by his 'Verbalising one's writing' and 'Reading what has been written down' surpass the equivalents of most of the other participants' (Table 4.3). Teng's performances of 'Verbalising one's writing' are highly instantaneous as they are preceded by very little planning effort, as shown in Excerpts 14 and 15.

The interlacing between Teng's verbalising his concurrent writing and his reading what has been previously written down is evident. Thus, Rereading was employed by Teng as a 'springboard' to stimulate his creational flow, a more improvisational idea-generation approach compared to Derek or Fai's proactive and purposeful planning shown earlier.

Teng's rereading activities also brought him to revising. In particular, during his rereadings, the grammar-checker function of Word (which was turned on on my computer) prodded Teng to revise his grammatical mistakes promptly. Teng also conducted revising activities at a phrasal level; however, the phrasal possibilities are less literary, dramatic or diversely descriptive than those demonstrated by Maggie or Fai, as shown in the Excerpts 16, 17 and 18.

Excerpts 16 and 17 respectively show that Teng added and deleted some single adverbs; and Excerpt 18 shows that he slightly extended the phrasing, which, however, effects little transformation of the aesthetic or literary effect.

Excerpt 14 Teng's think-aloud utterances from the Autobiographical writing task

Think-aloud utterances	Categorisation of writing behaviours
52. it's gonna make us it's apostrophe it's [is it because] it's going to make us better I'm sure it is apostrophe I'm sure it is but but thinking of having a bigger house a bigger house more money more money and become more famous, M O U S famous, then one's also apostrophe one's place cannot C A N N O T cannot be cannot	Composing: Verbalising one's writing
53. [then one's place cannot be]	Composing: Reading what has been written down
54. threatened R E A T E H T E N	Composing: Verbalising one's writing
55. [cannot be threatened]	Composing: Reading what has been written down
56. man don't man don't, don't think as logic as animals as animals, animals animals animals take and work for what they need, they don't, apostrophe they don't save, they don't save	Composing: Verbalising one's writing

Excerpt 15 Teng's think-aloud utterances from the Story-continuation task

Think-aloud utterances	Categorisation of writing behaviours
28. <u>when he was</u> when he, when he <u>was frustrated</u>	Composing: Verbalising one's writing
29. [when he was frustrated]	Composing: Reading what has been written down
30. <u>by his work the business world where the business business world could be could be</u>	Composing: Verbalising one's writing
31. [where the business world could be]	Composing: Reading what has been written down
32. <u>cruel and cold cruel and cold a wife a wife like Cherylle Cherylle Cherylle R Y</u>	Composing: Verbalising one's writing
33. [a wife like Cherylle]	Composing: Reading what has been written down
34. <u>is definitely the right candidate candidate candidate I do not understand why they could have have gone together in the first place in the first place and I do feel I do feel sorry for myself for myself that I might have made a mistake to introduce introduce and create and create this disaster this disaster the thing I really didn't want to see is is</u>	Composing: Verbalising one's writing

Excerpt 16 Teng's think-aloud utterances from the Autobiographical writing task

Think-aloud utterances	Categorisation of writing behaviours
84. [anybody to be better than us it is because]	Composing: Reading what has been written down
85. even even here we are <u>even it's even it's</u>	Revising: Revising phrasing
86. [even it's because, it's because it's going to, even it's because it's going to make to make]	Composing: Reading what has been written down

Excerpt 17 Teng's think-aloud utterances from the Autobiographical writing task

Think-aloud utterances	Categorisation of writing behaviours
185. [but that doesn't mean you have, you have to just waste]	Composing: Reading what has been written down
186. <u>you have to waste</u> no 'just'	Revising: Revising phrasing

Excerpt 18 Teng's think-aloud utterances from the Story-continuation task

Think-aloud utterances	Categorisation of writing behaviours
152. [I always said the more the merrier and I never think that either one of them would be interested]	Composing: Reading what has been written down
153. and be together	Revising: Revising phrasing

Clark and Ivanič (1997) state that writers' 'different experiences and encounters [in their life histories] lead to differential access to discourse types' (140). Teng had far less formal opportunity to encounter literary discourses in English than Derek, Maggie or Fai, but he had been exposed to informal native-speaker English in the spoken medium much more intensely than the other three had experienced. More importantly, these four writers in their respective writing histories practiced L2 creative writing to fulfil different combinations of self-identities. Teng, who was fulfilling his self-identities as an experienced and capable multilingualist and multiculturalist pronouncing his social existence in the UK, engages extensively in spur-of-the-moment writing behaviours in a discourse of spoken English. L2 story writing, in this case, explicitly puts a premium on Teng's personal knowledge and insights into life – in particular, his emotion – all of which channel into his sense of an authorial identity.

Regarding writers' sense of self-worth – an important aspect of writers' affect – Clark and Ivanič (1997) state that 'people's life-histories also shape the sense of self-esteem and status with which they approach all aspects of social life, including writing' (141). Writers' sense of self-esteem and status is related to their own evaluation of how much, and what varieties of, 'capital' they have gained throughout their life histories and accordingly of their power to impose reception on the audience. This self-evaluation results in specific feelings generated in writers, e.g. Derek's confidence or relaxedness, Maggie's anxiety, Fai's directedness or Teng's sentimentality, when engaging in a present writing activity. Writers' affect, implied in Clark and Ivanič's (1997) framework, influences the length writers would go to in order to establish a particular intensity of self-representation and authorial stance in their texts, e.g. Derek's instantiations of unconventional, modernist literary techniques, Maggie's painstaking efforts in refining the language of her story, Fai's care directed to some mainstream story-writing conventions and Teng's highly spontaneous and expressivist writing style. An emergent issue for L2 teachers and writing instructors to consider is that, despite the campaign to encourage students to engage in creative writing activities for language acquisition or voice enhancement purposes, students' 'life-histories' will have naturally led some to 'feel relatively authoritative and powerful as authors; others less so' (Clark & Ivanič, 1997: 141).

Consequently, it might not be realistic to expect the students to universally play with the second language or their imagination enthusiastically, or function as cultural informants emancipated by writing about emotional, dramatic personal experiences.

In the next section, we will look at the final case: Teri, the Afghan immigrant with asylum seeking experience in Russia and Britain, a journalist's daughter, a creative writing degree student who perceives her story writing on Afghan people's lives as part of a political mission and possibly a career.

Teri, an ideationally attentive writer

Teri is another proactive writer among the participants, whose Planning and Monitoring activities together serve as the pillar propping up her writing processes. Her engagement in the above two types of writing activities demonstrates her strong awareness of the ideological and literary possibilities for representing her stories in precisely the way she had intended.

Firstly, Teri's proactive writing behaviour is conveyed in her ideological and literary intentions underlying her planning activities, as shown in Excerpt 19. In her Autobiographical writing, Teri was contemplating writing about her life experience back in Afghanistan. In her fictional Story-continuation writing, Teri was seeking to describe a wedding scene through the main characters' eyes.

In Excerpt 19, Unit 3 shows that, to generate ideas, Teri freely questioned herself about several possibilities for the content to follow which have different ideological implications. For example, childhood experience suggests innocence and the indelibleness of memory; the experience of going back to Afghanistan as a teenager or adult suggests cultural perceptions and self-awareness; and her most recent thoughts on her Afghan home are more politically oriented. The other Planning activities shown in Excerpt 19 particularly demonstrate Teri's deliberation in relation to some recognised literary criticism, e.g. engaging beginning and reliable narrator (Unit 10), management of multiple characters and perspectives (Unit 20), the idiosyncrasy of the first-person narrator (Unit 315), the balance between realistic and dramatic representations (Unit 383) and the theatrical effect expressed through juxtaposing action scene with stillness (Unit 449). Such writing behaviours, I would argue, respond to Teri's two-year-long disciplinary practices in her English Literature and Creative Writing degree course and accordingly the 'voice' she had formed in that particular social circumstance.

Next, Teri's Monitoring activities more often than not correspond to the ideologies brought up in her Planning activities, which function to evaluate if particular literary representations have been properly implemented, as shown in Excerpt 20. Teri's writing activities recurrently reaccentuate two

Excerpt 19 Examples of Teri's Planning activities in the Autobiographical and Story-continuation tasks

---

3. so do I want to write about my experiences about when I was a child there do I want to write about how I felt going back or should I write something then that I've been thinking of recently which are political issues

(Idea-generating of global event, Autobiographical writing)

---

10. oh err an interesting beginning something to draw people in err I want them to realise that it's a memory when I was a child I'm going back to it after so many years so maybe I should just be honest in how yes I'm going to make my the well it's about me so I'm going to make my narrator really reliable, I hope, OK

(Goal-setting on literary technique, Autobiographical writing)

---

20. before we had Cherylle's story I don't want to start with Cherylle's story I want to start with a bit of the author himself then I'm going to give Cherylle's side so the author the narrator tells his own side first own side first then describes a bit from Cherylle's point of view then from Lamar's and then we go back to him mentioning the doom of the relationship but with hope that he is in fact wrong

(Goal-setting on global event, Story-continuation)

---

315. yeah well I don't want it to be rather shy I want to be able to think, what I saw

(Goal-setting on local event, Autobiographical writing)

---

383. I don't wanna make this too sick I wanna write it as exactly what happens

(Goal-setting on local event, Autobiographical writing)

---

449. OK I wanna I wanna speak of a sudden calmness, the calmness after something scary happened that everyone just goes quiet

(Goal-setting on local event, Autobiographical writing)

---

major practices associated with short story writing, i.e. the balance between drama and reality and the perspectives of different characters.

In Excerpt 20, Units 14, 298 and 111 show that, under the Autobiographical task, Teri more than once monitored the balance in her story between the rather personal and faithful illustration of the event and the literary and dramatic portrayal of it. Units 115 and 155 show Teri's concern with controlling the points of view, from which the story unfolded, when juggling multiple characters and also her concern with maintaining a consistent representation of the texture of the narrator. Teri's story writing practices are fairly ideationally or ideologically driven, rather than linguistically focused as Fai's or Maggie's are. The indication is that as a story writer Teri's sense of agency rests upon her carefully transforming ideas and raw materials into meaningful stories which fulfil her 'need to tell' (Teri, in-depth interview). In her personal case, she feels a political mission to tell a Western or even global audience about real Afghan people's lives and the immigrant experience of moving from a turbulent, underdeveloped country to more stable and developed Western countries. Given her previous

Excerpt 20 Examples of Teri's Monitoring activities

---

14. OK this automatically says that I don't actually remember everything, so how reliable well I'm not saying that I want the memory to be reliable or fact I want the narrator to be reliable and that's why I'm going to honestly say what I don't remember what had been told to me and how this memory has been constructed because everybody knows that eye witness testimonies aren't always true

(Evaluating content or ideas, Autobiographical writing)

---

298. the next, that's going too far in the personal description

(Evaluating content or ideas, Autobiographical writing)

---

111. ah shall I go into speech I think I should go into a speech because that makes it more of a story, the story so, yeah if I don't go into a speech it's pretty boring to just read, err how a person's memory is put exactly on paper as the story

(Evaluating literary technique, Autobiographical writing)

---

115. I don't wanna overly describe how this character felt I just want to see how the author sees the two characters

(Evaluating content or ideas, Story-continuation)

---

155. emm no I don't want to talk about the guest list because if this is a male narrator he and he has this sense of I don't care really, he wouldn't be writing about the guest list he doesn't care

(Evaluating content or ideas, Story-continuation)

---

life experience and her privileged access into rich social networking, Teri agentively exploits the content and ideology of her stories.

Conclusion: Creative Writers' Identities Enacted in Decision-Making Moments

This chapter exhibits that the five L2 creative writers' enactments and deployments of particular mediational means for self-representations in the present writing activities are closely associated with their past cultural-linguistic experiences. In reinforcement of the previous chapters' across-the-board quantitative analyses, this chapter's selective and highly descriptive qualitative interpretations illuminate how L2 creative writers' voices are distinctively expressed in their ongoing struggles to choose among multiple possibilities for the applications of knowledge and resources. In their story creation processes the five L2 creative writers engaged in specific language play, adopted particular discourses and ideologies and demonstrated characteristic writing procedures. All of these actually express the writers' ever-evolving 'personalities'. Firstly, such 'personalities' are autobiographical and socioculturally sedimented. They entail individual perspectives held by the L2 creative writers regarding how significantly their language and creative writing practices figure in their identity negotiations and social interactions. Secondly, such 'personalities' are also emergent, revealed throughout the L2 creative writers' psychological activities while creating stories. Indeed, such 'personalities' allow the individual writers to manage a sort of ontological security among their multiple identities and positioning in an intricate web of social relations.

Hence, this chapter argues that, to understand L2 creative writers' writing behaviours, an active consideration of the ideological and dialogic meaning of the writers' linguistic and literary engagements is needed. The key concept is that identity is performed. Throughout the actual writing process, the L2 creative writers sensed the opportunities for conducting certain images or characters that they intended to associate with themselves and accordingly made decisions to situate the 'self' as part of certain social groups through performing their ideologies and practices. Such voluntary acts of writing practices (e.g. Maggie's attention to the aesthetics of language in her story writing processes) lead to identity reproductions or transformations (e.g. an Anglophile who is motivated to use English for the purposes of creative and spontaneous expressions).

This and the previous chapters have told the stories of five idiosyncratic L2 creative writers. The pedagogical implication is that L2 teachers and writing instructors need to consider how creative writing is *personally* employed by L2 individuals as a meaning-making and hence self-empowering tool which enables the writers to develop as confident, empowered and autonomous individuals in cross-cultural contexts.

8 Conclusion

In this final chapter, I will first briefly review the objectives of this research and the findings and conclusions emerging in the previous chapters. Next, I will discuss how the present research may have made some contribution to two fields of L2 studies, i.e. L2 creative writing research and L2 writer identity research. Third, I will reflect on this inquiry's identity-centred relational methodology; that is, this inquiry, to some extent, manages to tackle one frequently addressed methodological problem associated with writer identity studies. The issue is: how can the identity researcher avoid essentialist reasoning and the obscuration of individual history when carrying out across-the-board examinations on a reasonable sample size? Meanwhile, how can the researcher also avoid the pitfall of anecdotal story-telling or relying on the evidence of only a few detailed individual cases on which to predicate the analysis and generalisations of the identity phenomenon under investigation? Next, the limitations of this inquiry will be reflected upon. The final section of this chapter ventures forth into a future direction implied by the findings of this inquiry for another genre of L2 writing: creative pedagogical approaches to L2 disciplinary writing.

The Findings

Let us first review the three research questions. This research investigates (a) the 15 L2 creative writers' autobiographical identities negotiated in retrospective accounts of their life histories, (b) their task-situated writers' voices constructed in their cognitive writing processes and (c) the interrelationship between these two types of identities. Chapters 4 to 7 have demonstrated two parallel data analyses: the quantitative examination targeting the entire 15 L2 creative writers, and the qualitative discussion concentrating on five selected focal participants. I believe these four chapters have demonstrated that there is a visible linkage between the L2 creative writers' self-representations of their past experiences and the writers' cognitive story-writing processes which signify particular trajectories of decision-making and knowledge enactment endeavours. I also hope that by this point the reader has seen how I have intended the present research to be an organic integration of two fields of L2 studies – the often socioculturalist L2 identity studies and the often cognitivist process-oriented L2 writing research.

Regarding the quantitative examination, first of all, I-statement analysis was used to uncover the 15 L2 creative writers' discursive movements of self-positioning when recounting their linguistic, literacy, educational and professional experiences; and second, think-aloud protocol analysis was employed to record the writers' emergent thoughts while writing under the present two story-writing tasks. Based on such quantitative analyses, Chapter 4 established a discernible pattern in the category-by-category comparison of (what I have termed) the 'Proactive Voice Writers' and the 'Retroactive Voice Writers' I-statement coding results. I concluded that, to fashion their autobiographical identities, the Proactive Voice Writers employ more assertive, socially constituted and self-assured I-statement approaches, whilst the Retroactive Voice Writers employ more implicit, expressive, idiosyncratic and self-critical I-statement approaches. In addition, such discursive tendencies for their autobiographical selves are also connected with how the Proactive Voice Writers and the Retroactive Voice Writers react to changes made to the symbolic mediations (i.e. Autobiographical writing, or fictional Story-continuation writing) embedded in the immediate task context. The Proactive Voice Writers, when asked to create a partially pre-determined fictional story, decisively and conclusively accentuate their writer voices as proactive and spontaneous creative writers and distance themselves from the projection of retroactive, evaluative and meticulous writers even further; in contrast, the Retroactive Voice Writers exhibit a less definite image of the task influence exercised on their writer voices. The quantitative data analysis displayed in Chapters 4 and 5 confirms that 'the here-and-now is an improvisational achievement, but it does not stand alone: it is socially structured' (Prior, 2006: 56).

However, it is the qualitative examination of the five focal participants' concrete interview comments and their specific think-aloud utterances which demonstrates that each L2 creative writer has a distinctive 'personality'. Firstly, such 'personalities' reside in how individual L2 creative writers justify and represent their life stories, entailing the writers' distinctive perspectives regarding how significantly their language and creative writing practices constitute, and meanwhile are constituted, in their identity negotiations and social interactions in different situations and contexts. Secondly, such 'personalities' are performative, revealed throughout the L2 creative writers' emergent thoughts while writing, especially their idiosyncratic ongoing struggles to choose among previous ideologies or discourses for self-representation. Perceptible connections are discovered between these two types of 'personalities' regarding each focal participant, thus further reinforcing the indication emerging from the previous quantitative analysis.

The above quantitative and qualitative findings suggest certain directions for theory development in L2 creative writing research as well as in L2 writer identity research. Firstly, regarding L2 creative writing research, we need to improve our understandings of how creative writing is employed by L2 learners, not only for language or literacy acquisition purposes but also as a self-empowering tool to achieve particular social positioning. Secondly, concerning L2 writer identity research, more research needs to be done regarding this micro and dynamic view of writer identity which resides in the *movements* of the writers' emerging *thoughts* situated in and mediated by an immediate creative writing context. In the following section, I will elaborate on these two points.

Implications for L2 Creative Writing Research and L2 Writer Identity Research

Implications for L2 creative writing research

Firstly, when we look at creative writing studies and projects conducted in EFL and ESL contexts, a pedagogical goal (as opposed to, for example, sociopolitical goals) and instrumental motive is often evident, such as motivating L2 students to write for authentic and aesthetic purposes, and ultimately to promote language learning, writing development or classroom cohesiveness. Investigating the pedagogical possibilities offered by creative writing is certainly worthwhile for the various audiences of L2 teacher practitioners and educators. However, the findings of this inquiry targeting 15 practised L2 creative writers who simultaneously are ESL speakers suggest that directions in L2 creative writing research can be extended and developed. L2 creative writing research might delve beneath the students' manifestations of language or writing developments and innovations or displays of positive emotional states or individualistic perspectives (as tend to be heightened by the Expressivists) and investigate the underlying identity issues behind such linguistic, literacy and emotional manifestations. By doing so, L2 teacher researchers could develop an increasing understanding of students' L2 creative writing practices so as to create and support the writing contexts which are likely to foster the students' meaningful L2 practices.

For example, the five focal participants' demonstration of distinctive 'voices' throughout their cognitive performances under the present two story-writing tasks particularly supports the socioculturalist claim that 'students may be engaged in the same task, but they may not necessarily be engaged in the same activity or dwelling in one context' (Maguire & Graves, 2001: 589). The five focal participants, in their cognitive writing processes, employed self-indicative problem-solving means, be it linguistic (e.g. Maggie and Fai's exertion on aesthetic phrasing), discoursal (e.g. Derek and Fai's deployments of specific literary knowledge) or ideational (e.g. Teri's ideological concern with her autobiographical story on Afghanistan). In particular, the five focal participants' voices are revealed in how they engaged in 'dialogues' (Bakhtin, 1981, 1986) with existent ideologies and discourses, e.g. Maggie's re-accentuation of the ideology underlying Henry

James's *The Ambassadors* in her Story-continuation writing process and her reference to 'Beat' and 'beatnik' in her Autobiographical writing, and Derek's recontextualisation of 'stream of consciousness' in his Autobiographical writing. The five L2 creative writers' voices are also revealed in how they align themselves with particular story writing values, e.g. Fai's commitment to particular mainstream story writing practice and Seng's identification with the values of expressive and personal writing style. The above findings indicate that the L2 creative writers' enactments and deployments of particular mediational means for self-representations in a particular context are closely associated with the individuals' *interpretation* of their previous cultural-linguistic experiences.

Language is commonly seen by L2 sociolinguists as 'playing the central role in both interpreting and proclaiming identity' (Joseph, 2004, cited in Omoniyi & White, 2006: 2). Similarly, L2 (or even L3) creative writing practices could also play a central role in proclaiming identity for the L2 (or L3) individuals who 'invest' in such literacy practices and play a central role in interpreting identity for the interested and empathetic audience, including those L2 teacher practitioners who introduce creative writing activities to their classrooms. Examination of the five focal participants also shows evidence of creative writing practices being an important medium through which the L2 writers' various identities intersect (e.g. Derek's identity as an EFL teacher, a published L1 story writer, a keen literature reader and an advanced ESL speaker). Thus, if we extrapolate from such findings to the ESL/EFL classroom, it might be enlightening if L2 creative writing were treated as a social practice of achieving 'ontological security' (Block, 2006a: 35) among a student's multiple identities and positioning in an intricate web of social relations. In future ESL/EFL creative writing research, some productive questions which might be asked are: why an L2 creative writer uses certain vocabulary, takes on a particular discourse, adopts specific ideology or exhibits certain writing procedures in the creation process – in short, what his/her 'voice' is; in addition what intentions such a 'voice' serves in the writer's constant reformulations of his/her positioning in particular contexts.

In Chapter 1, I mentioned a body of creative writing studies which indeed approach creative writing practices as meaningful social actions and situated activities. However, such studies, embracing a sociohistorical or/ and a poststructuralist perspective, often target distinctive social groups: socially marginalised native English-speaking writers, published native English-speaking writers (e.g. Clark & Ivanič, 1997: Chapters 4 and 5), published immigrant L2 writers from particular sociohistorical periods (e.g. Pavlenko & Lantolf, 2000; Pavlenko, 2004; Ros i Solé, 2004) or immigrant children living and studying in an English-speaking context (e.g. Maguire & Graves, 2001; Yi, 2007, 2010). I would hope that as a supplement to the above sociocultural array of creative writing research, the present research provides a somewhat novel perspective on investigating L2 creative literacy practices. Firstly, the present research shifts attention to contemporary and relatively mainstream ESL speakers/writers studying in universities who may be more representative of ESL university student writers around us who have had reasonable experience of L2 creative writing practices than the targets of previous research. Secondly, the present research shifts attention to the L2 creative writers' cognitive writing processes in contrast to the usual focus on the writers' sociocultural interactions and creative literacy products. This leads to my next section on the contribution this present research might offer to L2 writer identity research.

Implications for L2 writer identity research

Findings from the present research indicate that L2 creative writers' cognitive writing processes speak palpably of their writer voices. This is an area which has not been sufficiently looked into in L2 writer identity studies. The present research strengthens my hypothesis that writer's voice is not simply a product, a static mark left in written texts for linguists, literature scholars or historians to scrutinise; rather, writer's voice permeates through everything involved in creating a piece of work, an important part of which is the dynamic writing process.

My perusal of existing L2 writer identity studies sometimes made me sense a hidden fear among their authors that examination of the cognitive behaviours of L2 writers might negatively affect the sociocultural or poststructuralist agenda of the research. In Chapter 2, I pointed out that the Cognitivist *process* approach has undergone vehement criticism from some L2 writing scholars for its excessive concern with psychological matters and for exerting a normative influence in investigating writing issues. The present study shows that examining the L2 writers' cognitive writing activities does not automatically turn L2 writing research into a mentalistic study, oblivious to the notion of writing as a social act. In fact, what matters is what role such psychological investigation plays in interpreting the particular L2 writing phenomenon under study. Through examining L2 writers' 'voices' embodied in their cognitive writing processes, L2 writer identity research has the potential of facilitating (a) L2 teacher practitioners' implementation of L2 creative writing activities in the classroom and (b) various audiences' understanding of L2 creative writers as a social group.

In the L2 classroom, insights gained from investigating L2 creative writers' cognitive writing processes could increase L2 teachers' critical insight into the task procedures of particular creative writing activities in their classrooms. For example, it is not uncommon to see classroom-based L2 creative writing projects in which teachers/researchers adopt a *process* approach, e.g. brainstorming session, recursive writing and group revising activities, in an effort to build a cohesive classroom atmosphere and navigate students' creative writing processes (e.g. Elgar, 2002; Ensslin, 2006). In relation to such L2 creative writing projects, findings of the present research suggest that L2 creative writers have distinctive 'voices' enacted in their cognitive writing processes: some demonstrating proactive and relatively focused and structured writing behaviours, and some demonstrating retroactive tendencies or highly spontaneous writing behaviours. Such different strands of 'voices' are shown as relating to the L2 creative writers' self-identities formed through their previous sociocultural experiences. In addition, the Proactive Voice writers and the Retroactive Voice writers tuned their 'voices' differently in reaction to the changing of tasks from the Autobiographical writing to the Story-continuation writing. Therefore, an emergent issue is that L2 teachers/writing instructors might reflect on the manner in which they regulate the classroom creative writing processes. When we implement a particular creative writing activity (e.g. story writing or poetry writing) in the classroom, we need to expect and acknowledge different creation processes and thus self-representational measures exhibited by the students, e.g. engagement in structured planning or improvisation.

Outside the classroom context, a further implication for L2 writer identity research is that examining the cognitive writing processes of individual L2 creative writers can promote various audiences' (not limited to L2 scholars') understanding of the 'stream of consciousness' of this particular social group. The broad community of L2 creative writers, such as the growing group of fanfiction writers, has not been sufficiently studied as a legitimate and meaningful community of practice. Thus, compared to the macro community of ESL/EFL speakers, or various academic discourse communities, the social group of L2 creative writers, as I perceive, remains veiled by a stereotypically romantic perception held by the general public. However, this inquiry shows that L2 creative writers' self-perceptions and their cognitive writing activities could be examined in a systematic and sensitive manner by taking an identity-centred relational stance, which will be reflected on below. Perhaps everything comes with a price. There are limitations of this research for choosing particular data collection and analysis approaches, which are also discussed in the following.

An Identity-Centred Relational Methodology and the Limitations of This Research

This inquiry addressed the reflexive constitution of *individuals'* identity constructions. That is to say, themes conveyed in the interview transcripts regarding writer experiences and patterns of cognitive writing processes observed in the think-aloud protocols are *not* primarily sought out for the purpose of acquiring the knowledge of some 'superior', 'valid' or 'expert' trends or phenomena, but of acquiring the knowledge of individual's socially shaped mind. Regarding both the quantitative and the qualitative analyses, I adopted a hermeneutic, explanatory and inductive model to tease out the identities of individual writers. Such a decision was made based on the present research's perception of each participant as a unique human with a complicated yet essential sociocultural experience.

The hermeneutic and explanatory model of analysis is particularly demonstrated in the I-statement analysis and think-aloud protocol analysis. The development of these two coding systems progressed simultaneously with my recursive and repetitive interpretations and examinations of the interview transcripts and the think-aloud protocols over a period of eight months (on top of transcribing all the recordings). Such hermeneutic data analysis processes crucially rely on the researcher's own conceptualisation and interpretation of how identities – which are results of the interrelationship between social influence and the writer's self-consciousness – are constructed in the L2 creative writers' verbalisations (interview or think-aloud). I believe the effort has proved worthwhile.

I-statement analysis proves to be a particularly powerful and sensitive discourse analysis method which attends to the individuals' self-fashioning in their vivid, retrospective accounts of life experiences. In addition, it has also enabled me to make comparisons across the entire 15 participants. Think-aloud protocol analysis provides a robust, voice-centred relational method of interpreting L2 creative writers' cognitive writing activities. Think-aloud protocol is generally perceived as a key influential data collection method in Cognitivist research. Meanwhile, 'identity' is naturally seen as a sociocultural, sociopolitical concept. The present research shows that these two entities, which seem to come from different theoretical domains and research paradigms, can be organically integrated.

This inquiry certainly has its limitations. In terms of data collection, the present research did not investigate the L2 creative writers' sociocultural experiences in a longitudinal manner, neither did it examine the participants' cognitive writing behaviours in their self-perceived natural, socially meaningful circumstances. Thus, the identity-centred relational stance and ontology represented in understanding the writers' autobiographical and emergent identities through an emic view is, to a certain extent, limited. When designing this inquiry, I considered the balance between the depth and the scope of the investigation; and also after experiencing the practical exigencies of participant recruitment, I settled on a total of 15 participants. Out of practical concerns (i.e. data analysis load), with each participant I conducted only one in-depth interview and implemented two think-aloud story writing sessions with definitive time-limits, topic definitions and my constant presence. Such conditions might be deemed 'unnatural' by some readers, but I perceive them as necessary. As the investigation of the connection between the L2 creative writers' autobiographical identities and their emergent identities, enacted in their cognitive writing processes, is an unprecedented one (at least to my knowledge), I considered it essential to investigate trends among the 15 participants through making across-the-board comparisons. Thus longitudinal interview studies or think-aloud verbalisations conducted in the L2 creative writers' natural writing situations were not taken. Future L2 creative writing research could, to a higher degree, adopt an emic stance to study the L2 individuals' sociocultural lives. Longitudinal interview studies of the L2 creative writers' on-going transformations of self-positioning in broad and intimate social contexts are required. In addition, investigations into writers' autobiographical identities could also be prompted through researchers' direct observations of the L2 creative writers' participation in particular CoP(s), virtual or physical. In the present research, using think-aloud writing to capture the L2 creative writers' emergent and highly situated enactments of specific 'voices' provides powerful examples of taking 'voice' as an epistemological stance from which to observe L2 creative writers' improvisational applications of various spheres of knowledge throughout the cognitive writing process. Future research may also examine L2 creative writers' think-aloud writing processes in the socially meaningful contexts in which the writers find themselves.

Secondly, the recruitment of participants does not strictly conform to criteria sampling; the 15 participants were recruited under two major criteria: (a) they are advanced ESL speakers, and (b) they have reasonable experiences of particular forms of creative writing. My reason for not employing strict criteria sampling is twofold: (a) L2 creative writers, as social agents, naturally bring with them diverse sociocultural experiences and identities; and (b) the present study, with its exploratory nature and embracement of an identity-centred relational method rather than looking for definite cause–effect relationships, welcomes the possibilities of having L2 creative writers coming from diverse sociocultural and educational backgrounds and of different ages – as young as 18 and as old as 30. However, such a data-sampling decision limits the possibility of examining how the L2 creative writers, in a particular shared context, display different behaviours of self-positioning and reconciliation of multiple social identities. Future research might study the L2 creative writers' self-positioning in a specifically shared CoP (e.g. a CoP like participant Maggie's creative writing interest group) where each of its members brings with him/her a unique array of social identities. How each member embarks and proceeds upon a distinctive trajectory in negotiating his/her positioning in this CoP in particular situations will be worth looking into.

Thirdly, again, concerning the issue of balancing the size of the participant pool with the depth and length of investigation undertaken with each participant, one limitation lies in the extent of the triangulation of data collection techniques. Given the large amount of accurate verbatim transcriptions and the necessity that all the data analysis must be done manually so as to achieve a consistently hermeneutic and 'accurate' explanatory model of the identities, it was not possible for me to conduct 'member checks'. It was problematic to maintain contact with participants because by the time all the analysis was completed, many of them had already finished their studies and left the UK.

Future Directions Implied by This Research for a Creative Approach to L2 Disciplinary Writing

The variations in the participants' cognitive writing behaviours arising from the change of the story-writing task type suggest that L2 creative writing activities could reinforce students' identity needs and self-esteem as articulate L2 writers who embrace distinctive ideologies and practices. Translingual writers such as Conrad, Beckett and Ha Jin have discussed the 'emancipatory detachment' inherent in composing in a second language. I would suggest that there perhaps is another layer of 'emancipatory detachment' which resides in composing through creative forms of writing. These days, globalisation has made English a lingua franca, highlighting bilingualism as a significant phenomenon to be studied. Analogically, creative forms of writing (and especially L2 creative forms of writing which is the concern of this inquiry) might also become a lingua franca of knowledge construction for people coming from diverse disciplinary communities and academic discourses. Innovative and fruitful efforts have been witnessed in mixing scientists and mathematicians with literary professionals through carefully organised creative writing workshops. The published collections of their stories, poems, drama and nonfiction effectively reflect 'mathematical and scientific themes and sensibilities' (Davis et al., 2008). The power is attested that creative writing allows for an ingenious shape which could embody specific content and intellectual creativity for the academics, yet also present as sensible and engaging reading to a layman audience.

In many senses, all good writing is creative. When some Warwick University (UK) tutors from several disciplines were asked what they valued in student writing, rather surprisingly, the top place went to 'originality and creativity' (Nesi & Gardner, 2005). It seems, therefore, that helping L2 students to find an original and creative voice is not just a matter of entertainment and self-indulgence, but an instrumentally valid objective. 'Creative writing across the curriculum' is beginning to receive some recognition in higher education (Gordy & Peary, 2005; Peary, 2013), yet it is still 'rare' (Davis et al., 2008: ix) in either L1 or L2 contexts. L2 pedagogy can certainly promote and harness this hybridisation of creative knowledge construction through literary forms at all levels of L2 disciplinary writing.

At the end of this book, with reference to my previous English-for-Specific-Purposes class (in the UK), I intend to illustrate how, with academic subjects, L2 students' conceptualisations could be effectively and enthusiastically constructed through a creative form of writing. This ESL class consists of intermediate and upper-intermediate L2 learners in a foundation programme for pre-masters international students in the UK. Other than English, the students also had subject courses, mostly in Business or Engineering. Many of the students would like to perceive themselves as capable adults negotiating their entry into L2 academic communities. Accordingly, I designed the creative writing tasks with the intention of integrating creative writing elements with some ESP elements. In one such activity:

(1) I identified a relevant business-related topic, namely, 'Business Ethics', and located a relatively light and accessible article – Carr's (1968) *Is Business Bluffing Ethical?* I selected some interesting and controversial parts from the article, put them together and adapted the language where necessary.

(2) The students were asked to read my edited version of the article in class. I explicitly instructed them to find at least one idea from the text which they did not quite agree with (hence practising critical thinking skills). The students were able to discuss and exchange their ideas with each other in pairs/groups.

(3) The students were then asked to dramatise their critical interpretations and opinions through creating a short story of 300–400 words. They were encouraged to adopt basic narrative elements, such as scene setting, introducing main characters and developing conflict, climax and resolution. The activity provided a medium for them to express their understanding of the ethical issues involved in a creative and personal way. Moreover, the necessity of adopting a narrative stance and tracing characters' thoughts encouraged the creative writers to consider multiple points of view and develop a sense of empathy for the characters in their writing.

(4) The above was done as homework. The reason is I also asked the students to document their writing processes. This was achieved through L2 think-aloud writing, which can be considered to be not only a research instrument but also a learning tool. The students were given demonstrations of think-aloud procedure and practice sessions in the classroom. Subsequently, in their own space and privacy, they were asked to think-aloud in English as much and as continuously as they could throughout their story-creation process within a time limit of 1 hour. Recordings of the sessions were required to be handed in along with their stories.

(5) The think-aloud recordings proved particularly useful when I needed to find out the reasons and processes behind a student's adoption of a certain discourse, language or idea. Locating such thought processes of

the L2 student helped me to ascertain this individual's self-perceptions and goals (e.g. a proficient L2 learner, or a keen business apprentice, or, perhaps, a reluctant writer who copied from the internet). Such knowledge is critical for me to understand and appreciate the L2 students' writer voices and design future writing tasks.

Ultimately, future investigations into the rich range of identities, cognitive activities and literary texts associated with creative forms of writing in an L2 will develop our currently fairly weak understanding of the relationship between why and how L2 writers engage with creative thinking and writing in particular social or academic circumstances.

Appendix A: Question List for the In-Depth Interview

Demographic background

(1) Age range: 20–30, 30–40 or above 40?
(2) Nationality and L1?
(3) How long have you stayed in the UK?

Educational experience

(1) What education degree are you studying for now?
(2) What did you study previously?

Professional experience

(1) Apart from study, did you (or do you) have any full-time or part-time working experience?
(2) If so, what did you do and for how long? Could you describe your job experience to me?

Language-related experience

(1) Other than your L1(s) and English, do you speak any other language?
(2) When and where did you begin to learn English?
(3) How would you assess your English proficiency compared to other international students around you? Have you taken any English proficiency test before?
(4) Is learning English of personal importance to you, especially for your future career (to get a good job)? In what way?

Writing experiences

About writing in your L1

(1) What kinds of L1 writing have you done in school, as far as you can remember? For example, what kinds of L1 writing did you often do in primary school, in secondary school, and in university respectively?

(2) Generally speaking, what do you think are your **strengths** and **weaknesses** when writing in your L1? And what are your feelings about writing in your L1 in general, e.g. tedious, sentimental, or challenging?

(3) How much effort did you put into practicing your L1 writing, can you give me a few examples? What were your readers' responses (e.g. teachers' feedback) to your L1 writing like? How do you feel about their views?

(4) Do you think you are a good writer in your mother tongue?

About writing in English:

(1) When did you first start writing in English? For example, what kinds of L2 writing activities did you often do in primary school (if this applicable), in secondary school and in university respectively?

(2) Among the types of English writing you have just mentioned, which do you most frequently do now?

(3) As you are currently studying in the UK, does academic writing take a large proportion of your total amount of English writing? Could you describe your writing assignments for your current course to me? What's your typical writing process like?

(4) In your opinion, how much effort have you put into improving your L2 writing skills (very much, average, not so much, none at all)? Can you give me a few examples? How would you rate your own L2 writing performance?

(5) How difficult is it for you to write something for *academic purposes* in English? Where do the main difficulties lie? On the other hand, what do you think are your *strengths* when writing for academic purposes in English?

(6) How have What are your readers (such as teachers) responded to your L2 academic writing and other types of L2 writing? How do you feel about their views?

(7) Generally speaking, what are your feelings about writing in English? And do you think you are a good writer in English?

Reading experience

(1) How often do you read literature (stories, poems, drama etc.) in your L1? How much time do you spend on it approximately? What types of L1 literature do you read most often? What is your favourite topic and genre and why is that?

(2) How often do you read literature in English? (If the interviewee mentions *reading literary work in English*) Then could you tell me for what purposes (e.g. coursework or leisure)? Do you have any favourite topic, style or writer?

Creative writing experience

(1) What are your *experiences* of L1 and L2 creative writing like? How did they start? Have you ever received any training in creative writing? Were you ever a member of any creative-writing interest group? Have you ever published any work (especially in L2)?

(2) Do you practice creative writing in your L1 regularly? Why?

(3) Do you practice creative writing in your L2 regularly? Why?

(4) Compared with academic writing, what do you think is special or essential to a satisfying piece of creative writing work, with an eye to your own experience?

(5) What do you think are your main *strengths* and *weaknesses* as a creative writer? What's the main challenge of doing creative writing in your L1 or English?

(6) When you were doing a piece of creative writing in your L1 or L2, did you consider showing your work to others afterwards? Did you ever let others read your work? Have you received any feedback? Or did you just write for yourself and keep it to yourself?

(7) Do you often have ideas for stories? If so, do you usually carry out your thoughts?

(8) Usually, how do you generate ideas for your story?

(9) Do you think creative writing in English helps you learn the English language? If so, can you describe how it helps?

(10) Can you compare doing creative writing in your L1 with that in your L2? Which language do you most often write in now? Also, is there any difference for you between doing English creative writing in your home country previously and now in the UK (if applicable)?

(11) Do you think you would carry on creative writing in English in the future, would it contradict or help with your professional or life goals?

Appendix B: An Illustration of the 19 Communities Established through Coding the Participants' We- and You-Statements

Below, within ( ), are the adjacent clauses which are provided to illustrate the contexts; within < > are my explanations to fill in the ellipses; and '...' indicates some comments are omitted. In addition, in the { } following each example, the participant who uttered the We- and You-statement is indicated.

(1) Professional identity
perhaps you know <u>you</u> really learn (when <u>you</u> teach) {Derek}
(perhaps you know you really learn) when <u>you</u> teach {Derek}

(2) Educational community
in two years <u>you</u> get your A-grades (and then we all work for that) {Sebastian}
(in two years you get your A-grades) and then <u>we</u> all work for that {Sebastian}

(3) Community of L2 speakers
<u>we</u> learned three languages concurrently {Ho}
(when I was at school at primary school) <u>we</u> started learning French {Jingjing}

(4) Student writer group in a particular context
ahh because it's just boring as <u>you</u> have to write about economics {Yi}
(when I was doing a Conformity Psychology assignment) it depends on the research <u>you</u> can get out from it {Teng}

(5) Community of L1 student writers
Malay it's usually factual but <u>we</u> have been given emm materials about that article (so you have to read them up and you sort of translated it into your essay) {Fai}
so <u>you</u> have to read them <the articles> up {Fai}
and <u>you</u> sort of translated it into your essay {Fai}

(6) Community of L2 (or L3) student writers

just to make <u>us</u> write in English (to practise the language) {Eliza}

(just to make us write in English) <in order for <u>us</u>> to practise the language {Eliza}

(7) Community of bilingual (or multilingual) student writers

<u>you</u> have to do a Malay essay exam as well as the Mandarin and the English {Seng}

(and I find) them those <writing styles> taught <u>you</u> can use in Malay and English as well {Fai}

(8) Community of creative writers

if <u>you</u> can give them a punch in a short story {Teri}

<u>you</u> cannot show if it's too personal and too private {Yi}

(9) Member of a particular nationality

because in Malaysia <u>we</u> produce petrol {Ho}

(Bor Hit have you ever heard Bor Hit, he is, I think, like the best writer) <u>we</u> have in Argentina well old time, 90 years ago 100 years ago {Derek}

(10) Member of a particular ethnicity

(we or maybe Asian Asian have the same characteristic as well I think Chinese also have the same), <u>we</u> try to learn everything {Ho}

(because you know Chinese family like mine in Malaysia they grow up), you use <u>you</u> use your mother tongue {Teng}

(11) Member of a socialising community

a former student of mine, now <u>we</u> are close friends {Derek}

(I started writing a lot during classes with another friend of mine) because <u>we</u> were absolutely bored {Marjorie}

(12) Community of readers

so in the class sometimes <u>we</u> were distributed with books (I mean short quick version of Shakespeare simplified version of Romeo and Juliet things like that) {Ho}

(but I liked him <Jingjing's literature teacher> because he actually encouraged us to try to be unique to learn literature) because for example <u>we</u> were reading a poem {Jingjing}

(13) Individuals with a particular skill

it's when when <u>you</u> write from right to left (and you have to put the text in a mirror in order to read it)

(it's when when you write from right to left) and <u>you</u> have to put the text in a mirror (in order to read it)

(14) Individuals with insight
(I was vomiting when I had the exam … that was really horrible), but sometimes when <u>you look back</u> your life (it might not be a bad thing) {Ho}
but it's like you <u>you realise</u> (they they <pigeons> look so delicate and look so smart but in a way they are so fragile, again it's beauty and death) {Dong}

(15) Member of immigrants
(and how it's difficult to learn a new language) or <u>you</u> feel alien {Teri}

(16) Member of computer game players
there are cards so <u>you can summon</u> {Yi}
<u>you can create</u> creature to fight people {Yi}

(17) Member of experienced internet users
<u>you</u> just put on things to sell on internet {Yi}
because like almost <u>everyone</u> is speaking English (if you are on the Internet) {Yi}
(because like almost everyone is speaking English) if <u>you</u> are on the Internet {Yi}

(18) Member of British society
(some of the language I used over there <in Malaysia> doesn't match) what <u>we</u> use over here <in Britain> {Teng}

(19) Gender identity
<u>you</u>'re supposed to be feminine {Ankita}
<u>you</u>'re supposed to be gentle {Ankita}

References

Abdi, R. (2002) Interpersonal metadiscourse: An indicator of interaction and identity. *Discourse Studies* 4 (2), 139–145.

Alhaisoni, E. (2012) A think-aloud protocols investigation of Saudi English major students' writing revision strategies in L1 (Arabic) and L2 (English). *English Language Teaching* 5 (9), 144–154.

Antaki, C. and Widdicombe, S. (eds) (1998) *Identities in Talk*. London: Sage Publications.

Atkinson, D. (1999) TESOL and culture. *TESOL Quarterly* 33 (4), 625–654.

Atkinson, D. (2001) Reflections and refractions on the JSLW special issue on voice. *Journal of Second Language Writing* 10, 107–124.

Atkinson, D. (2002) Toward a sociocognitive approach to second language acquisition. *Modern Language Journal* 86, 525–545.

Atkinson, D. (2003) L2 writing in the post-process era: Introduction. *Journal of Second Language Writing* 12, 3–15

Ayçiçeği, A. and Harris, C.L. (2004) Brief report: Bilingual's recall and recognition of emotion words. *Cognition and Emotion* 18 (7), 977–987.

Bakhtin, M.M. (1981) *The Dialogic Imagination: Four Essays by M. M.Bakhtin* (M. Holquist, ed.; C. Emerson and M. Holquist, trans.). Austin: University of Texas Press.

Bakhtin, M. M. (1986) *Speech Genres and Other Late Essays* (C. Emerson and M. Holquist, eds; Y. McGee, trans.). Austin: University of Texas Press.

Baldwin, T. (1944) *William Shakespeare's Small Latin and Less Greek*. Illinois: University of Illinois Press.

Bartholomae, D. (1985) Inventing the university. In M. Rose (ed.) *When a Writer Can't Write* (pp. 134–165). New York: Guilford.

Bate, J. (2008) *Soul of the Age: The Life, Mind and World of William Shakespeare*. London: Viking Press.

Bazerman, C. and Russell, D. (eds) (2003) *Writing Selves/Writing Societies: Research from Activity Perspectives*. Fort Collins, CO: The WAC Clearinghouse and Mind, Culture, and Activity. See http://wac.colostate.edu/books/selves_societies (accessed 27 November 2012).

Belz, J.A. (2002) Second language play as a representation of the multicompetent self in foreign language study. *Journal of Language, Identity, and Education* 1 (1), 13–39.

Belcher, D. (1994) The apprenticeship approach to advanced academic literacy: Graduate students and their mentors. *English for Specific Purposes* 1 (3), 23–34.

Belcher, D. (2014) What we need and don't need intercultural rhetoric for: A retrospective and prospective look at an evolving research area. *Journal of Second Language Writing* 25, 59–67.

Beretta, A. (1991) Theory construction in SLA: Complementarity and opposition. *Studies in Second Language Acquisition* 13, 493–511.

Besemeres, M. (2002) *Translating One's Self: Language and Selfhood in Cross-cultural Autobiography*. Bern: Peter Lang.

Black, R.W. (2005) Access and affiliation: The literacy and composition practices of English-language learners in an online fanfiction community. *Journal of Adolescent and Adult Literacy* 49 (2), 118–128.

Block, D. (1996) Not so fast: Some thoughts on theory culling, relativism, accepted findings and the heart and soul of SLA. *Applied Linguistics* 17, 63–83.

Block, D. (2006a) Identity in applied linguistics. In T. Omoniyi and G. White (eds) *Sociolinguistics of Identity* (pp. 34–49). London: Continuum.

Block, D. (2006b) *Multilingual Identities in a Global City: London Stories*. London: Palgrave.

Block, D. (2007) *Second Language Identities*. London: Continuum.

Boswell, J. (1791) *The Life of Samuel Johnson, LL.D.* London: Penguin English Library.

Bourdieu, P. (1977) The economics of linguistic exchanges. *Social Science Information* 16, 645–668.

Bourdieu, P. (1991) *Language and Symbolic Power*. (J.B. Thompson, ed.; G. Raymond and M. Adamson, trans.). Cambridge: Polity Press.

Bourdieu, P. and Passeron J. (1977) *Reproduction in Education, Society, and Culture*. Beverley Hills, CA: Sage Publications.

Bowden, D. (1999) *The Mythology of Voice*. Portsmouth, NH: Boyton/Cook Heinemann.

Boyd, W. (2008) Love Hurts. In *The Dream Lover* (pp. 157–168). London: Bloomsbury.

Boyd, W. (2008) *The Dream Lover*. London: Bloomsbury.

Brown, J.D. and Rogers, T.S. (2002) *Doing Second Language Research*. Oxford: Oxford University Press.

Bruffee, K. A. (1986) Social construction, language, and the authority of knowledge: A bibliographical essay. *College English* 48, 773–790.

Burck, C. (2005) *Multilingual Living: Explorations of Language and Subjectivity*. Houndmills: Palgrave Macmillan

Burkhalter, N. and Pisciotta, S.W. (1999) Language and identity: A reading-to-write unit for advanced ESL students. *Teaching English in the Two Year College* 27 (2), 203–208.

Burroway, J. and Stuckey-French, E. (2007) *Writing Fiction: A Guide to Narrative Craft*. New York: Pearson Longman.

Burton, J. and Carroll, M. (eds) (2001) *Journal Writing*. Alexandria, VA: TESOL.

Canale, M. and Swain, M. (1980) Theoretical bases of communicative approaches to second language teaching and testing. *Applied Linguistics* 1, 1–47.

Carr, A. (1968) Is business bluffing ethical? *Harvard Business Review* 46, 143–153.

Cenoz, J., Hufeisen, B. and Jessner, U. (eds) (2003) *The Multilingual Lexicon*. London: Kluwer Academic Publishers.

Chamcharatsri, P. (2009) Negotiating identity from auto-ethnography: Second language writers' perspectives. *Asian EFL Journal* 38, 3–19.

Chen, J.F., Warden, C.A. and Chang, H. (2005) Motivators that do not motivate: The case of Chinese EFL learners and the influence of culture on motivation. *TESOL Quarterly* 39(4), 609–633.

Clachar, A. (1999) It's not just cognition: The effect of emotion on multiple-level discourse processing in second-language writing. *Language Sciences* 21, 31–60.

Clark, R. and Ivanič, R. (1997) *The Politics of Writing*. London: Routledge.

Connor, U., Nagelhout, E. and Rozycki, W. (eds) (2008) *Contrastive Rhetoric: Reaching to Intercultural Rhetoric*. Amsterdam: John Benjamins Publishing.

Cook, G. (1997) Language play, language learning. *ELT Journal* 51 (3), 224–231.

Cook, G (2000) *Language Play, Language Learning*. Oxford: Oxford University Press

Cox, M., Jordan, J., Ortmeier-Hooper, C. and Schwartz, G.G. (eds) (2010) *Reinventing Identities in Second Language Writing*. Urbana: NCTE Press.

Creative Writing (n.d.) *Foreign Language Teaching Methods: Writing*. Austin: The University of Texas at Austin. See http://coerll.utexas.edu/methods/modules/writing/03/ (accessed 3 September 2011).

Creme, P. and Hunt, C. (2002) Creative participation in the essay writing process. *Arts and Humanities in Higher Education* 1 (2), 145–166.

Cumming, A. (1989) Writing expertise and second language proficiency. *Language Learning* 39, 81–141.

Cumming, A. (1990) Metalinguistic and ideational thinking in second language composing. *Written Communication* 7 (4), 482–511.

Danziger, K. (1990) *Constructing the Subject: Historical Origins of Psychological Research.* Cambridge: Cambridge University Press.

Davis, C., Senechal, M.W. and Zwicky, J. (eds) (2008) *The Shape of Content.* Wellesley, MA: A K Peters.

Day, S.X. (2002) 'Make It Uglier. Make It Hurt. Make It Real': Narrative construction of the creative writer's identity. *Creativity Research Journal* 14 (1), 127–136.

Dickinson, L. (1995) Autonomy and motivation: A literature review. *System* 23 (2), 165–174.

Diedrick, J. (2004) *Understanding Martin Amis.* South Carolina: University of South Carolina Press.

DiPardo, A. (1990) Narrative knowers, expository knowledge: Discourse as a dialectic. *Written Communication* 7 (1), 59–95.

Dörnyei, Z. (1994) Motivation and motivating in the foreign language classroom. *Modern Language Journal* 78, 273–284.

Dörnyei, Z. (1996) Moving language leaning motivation to a larger platform for theory and practice. In R.L. Oxford (ed.) *Language Learning Motivation: Pathways to the New Century* (pp. 71–80). Honolulu: University of Hawaii, Second Language Teaching and Curriculum Centre.

Dörnyei, Z. (1998) Motivation in second and foreign language learning. *Language Teaching* 31, 117–135

Dörnyei, Z. (2002) The motivational basis of language learning tasks. In P. Robinson (ed.) *Individual Differences and Instructed Language Learning* (pp. 137–158). Amsterdam: John Benjamins.

Dörnyei, Z. (2005) *The Psychology of the Language Learner: Individual Differences in Second Language Acquisition.* London: Lawrence Erlbaum Associates.

Dörnyei, Z. (2009) The L2 motivational self system. In Z. Dörnyei and E. Ushioda (eds) *Motivation, Language Identity and the L2 Self* (pp. 9–42). Bristol: Multilingual Matters.

Dörnyei, Z., Csizér, K. and Németh, N. (2006) *Motivational Dynamics, Language Attitudes and Language Globalisation: A Hungarian Perspective.* Clevedon: Multilingual Matters.

Dörnyei, Z. and Ushioda, E. (2009) Motivation, language identities and the L2 Self: Future research directions. In Z. Dörnyei and E. Ushioda (eds) *Motivation, Language Identity and the L2 Self* (pp. 350–356). Bristol: Multilingual Matters.

Doyle, C.L. (1998) The writer tells: The creative process in the writing of literary fiction. *Creativity Research Journal* 1 (1), 29–37.

Duff, A. and Maley, A. (2007) *Literature.* Oxford: Oxford University Press.

Eckert, P. and McConnell-Ginet, S. (1999) New generalizations and explanations in language and gender research. *Language in Society* 28 (2), 185–202.

Elgar, A.G. (2002) Student playwriting for language development. *ELT Journal* 56 (1), 22–28.

Ellis, R. and Yuan, F. (2004) The effects of planning on fluency, complexity, and accuracy in second language narrative writing. *Studies in Second Language Acquisition* 26 (1), 59–84.

Englander, K. (2009) Transformation of the identities of nonnative English-speaking scientists as a consequence of the social construction of revision. *Journal of Language, Identity, and Education* 8, 35–53.

Englert, C.S., Mariage, T.V. and Dunsmore, K. (2006) Tenets of sociocultural theory in writing instruction research. In C.A. Macarthur, S. Graham and J. Fitzgerald (eds) *Handbook of Writing Research* (pp. 208–221). New York: The Guilford Press.

Ensslin, A. (2006) Literary hypertext in the foreign language classroom: A case study report. *Language Learning Journal* 33, 13–21.

Ericsson, K.A. and Simon, H.A. (1993) *Protocol Analysis.* Cambridge, MA: Bradford/MIT Press.

Faigley, L. (1986) Competing theories of process: A critique and proposal. *College English* 48, 527–542.

Fairclough, N. (2003) *Analysing Discourse*. London: Routledge.

Fang, X. and Warschauer, M. (2004) Technology and curricular reform in China: A case study. *TESOL Quarterly* 38 (2), 301–323.

Fellows, O.E. and. Milliken, S.F. (1972) *Buffon*. New York: Twayne.

Firmat, G.P. (2003) *Tongue Ties: Logo-eroticism in Anglo-Hispanic Literature*. New York: Palgrave Macmillan.

Flower, L.S. and Hayes, J.R. (1980) The dynamics of composing: Making plans and juggling constraints. In L. Gregg and E. Steinberg (eds) *Cognitive Processes in Writing* (pp. 31–50). Hillsdale, NJ: Lawrence Erlbaum Associates.

Flower, L. and Hayes, J.R. (1981) A cognitive process theory of writing. *College Composition and Communication* 32 (4), 365–387.

Flowerdew, J. (2000) Discourse community, legitimate peripheral participation, and the non-English speaking scholar. *TESOL Quarterly* 34 (1), 127–150.

Fussell, S. (ed.) (2002) *The Verbal Communication of Emotions: Interdisciplinary Perspectives*. Mahwah, NJ: Lawrence Erlbaum Associates.

Gardner, R.C. (1985) *Social Psychology and Language Learning: The Role of Attitudes and Motivation*. London: Edward Arnold.

Gardner, R.C. (2000) Correlation, causation, motivation, and second language acquisition. *Canadian Psychology* 41, 10–24.

Gardner, R.C. (2001) Integrative motivation: Past, present and future. See http://publish. uwo.ca/~gardner/docs/GardnerPublicLecture1.pdf (accessed 14 September 2009).

Gardner, R.C. and Lambert, W. (1959) Motivational variables in second language acquisition. *Canadian Journal of Psychology* 13, 266–272.

Gardner, R.C. and Lambert, W. (1972) *Attitudes and Motivation in Second-Language Learning*. Rowley, MA: Newbury House.

Gardner, R.C. and MacIntyre, P.D. (1991) An instrumental motivation in language study: Who says it isn't effective? *Studies in Second Language Acquisition* 13, 57–72.

Gardner, R.C., Tremblay, P.F. and Masgoret, A.M. (1997) Toward a full model of second language learning: An empirical investigation. *Modern Language Journal* 81, 344–362.

Gardner, R.C., Masgoret, A.M., Tennant, J. and Mihic, L. (2004) Integrative motivation: Changes during a year-long intermediate-level language course. *Language learning* 54 (1), 1–34.

Gardner, S. and Fulwiler, T. (eds) (1999) *The Journal Book: For Teachers in Technical and Professional Programs*. Portsmouth: NH: Boynton/Cook.

Gee, J.P. (1999) *An Introduction to Discourse Analysis: Theory and Method*. London: Routledge.

Gee, J.P. (2005) *An Introduction to Discourse Analysis: Theory and Method*, 2nd edition. New York and London: Routledge.

Giddens, A. (1991) *Modernity and Self-Identity: Self and Society in the Late Modern Age*. Cambridge: Polity.

Gillaerts, P. and Van de Velde, F. (2010) Interactional metadiscourse in research article abstracts. *Journal of English for Academic Purposes* 9 (2), 128–139.

Gordy, L.L., and Peary, A. (2005) Bringing creativity into the classroom: Using sociology to write first-person fiction. *Teaching Sociology* 33 (4), 396–402.

Grant, L. and Ginther, A. (2000) Using computer-tagged linguistic features to describe L2 differences. *Journal of Second Language Writing* 9 (2), 125–145.

Grosse, C.U., Tuman, W.V. and Critz, M.A. (1998) The economic utility of foreign language study. *The Modern Language Journal* 82 (4), 457–472.

Gu, M. (2009) College English learners' discursive motivation construction in China. *System* 37, 300–312.

Gu, M. (2010) Identities constructed in difference: English language learners in China. *Journal of Pragmatics* 42 (1), 139–152.

de Guerrero, M.C.M. (2005) *Inner speech – L2 thinking words in a second language*. New York: Springer.

Halliday, M.A.K. and Hasan, R. (1985) *Language, Context and Text: Aspects of Language in a Social-semiotic Perspective*. Victoria: Deakin University Press.

Hanaoka, O. (2007) Output, noticing, and learning: An investigation into the role of spontaneous attention to form in a four-stage writing task. *Language Teaching Research* 11 (4), 459–479.

Hanauer, D.I. (2010) *Poetry as Research: Exploring Second Language Poetry Writing*. Amsterdam: John Benjamins Publishing Cooperation.

Haneda, M. (1997) Second language learning in a 'community of practice': A case study of adult Japanese learners. *The Canadian Modern Language Review* 54, 11–27.

Haneda, M. (2005) Investigating in foreign-language writing: A study of two multicultural learners. *Journal of Language, Identity, and Education* 4 (4), 269–290.

Harklau, L. (2002) The role of writing in classroom second language acquisition. *Journal of Second Language Writing* 11, 329–350.

Hayes, J.R. (2012) Modeling and remodeling writing. *Written Communication* 29 (3), 369–388.

Hidi, S. and Boscolo, P. (2006) Motivation and writing. In C.A. Macarthur, S. Graham and J. Fitzgerald (eds) *Handbook of Writing Research* (pp. 144–157). New York: The Guilford Press.

Higgins, E.T. (1987) Self-discrepancy: A theory relating self and affect. *Psychological Review* 94, 319–340.

Hinkel, E. (2002) Adverbial markers and tone in L1 and L2 writing. *Journal of Pragmatics* 35, 1049–1068.

Hirvela, A. and Belcher, D. (2001) Coming back to voice: The multiple voices and identities of mature multilingual writers. *Journal of Second Language Writing* 10, 83–106.

Hull, G.A. and Katz, M. (2006) Crafting an agentive self: Case studies of digital storytelling. *Research in the Teaching of English* 41 (1), 43–81.

Hull, G. and Rose, M. (1989) Rethinking remediation: Toward a socio-cognitive understanding of problematic reading and writing. *Written Communication* 6, 139–154.

Humphreys, G. and Spratt, M. (2008) Many languages, many motivations: A study of Hong Kong students' motivation to learn different target languages. *System* 36, 313–335.

Hutchison, H. (2005) James's spectacles: Distorted vision in *The Ambassadors*. *The Henry James Review* 26 (1), 39–51.

Hyland, K. (2003) Genre-based pedagogies: A social response to process. *Journal of Second Language Writing* 12, 17–29.

Hyland, K. (2004) Disciplinary interactions: Metadiscourse in L2 postgraduate writing. *Journal of Second Language Writing* 13 (2), 133–151.

Hyland, K. (2005a) Stance and engagement: A model of interaction in academic discourse. *Discourse Studies* 7 (2), 173–192.

Hyland, K. (2005b) *Metadiscourse: Exploring Interaction in Writing*. London: Continuum.

Hyland, K. (2005c) Representing readers in writing: Student and expert practices. *Linguistics and Education* 16, 363–377.

Hyland, K. and Tse, P. (2004) Metadiscourse in academic writing: A reappraisal. *Applied Linguistics* 25 (2), 156–177.

Ivanič, R. (1998) *Writing and Identity: The Discoursal Construction of Identity in Academic Writing*. Philadelphia: Benjamins.

Ivanič, R. and Camps, D. (2001) I am how I sound: Voice as self-representation in L2 writing. *Journal of Second Language Writing* 10, 3–33.

Jackson, C.N. and Dussias, P.E. (2009) Cross-linguistic differences and their impact on L2 sentence processing. *Bilingualism: Language and Cognition* 12 (1), 65–82.

Jacobs, C.L. (2008) Long-term English learners writing their stories. *English Journal* 97 (6), 87–91.

James, H. (1903) *The Ambassadors*. New York: Harper and Brothers.

James, H. (1987) *The Complete Notebooks of Henry James* (L. Edel and L.H. Powers, eds). Oxford: Oxford University Press.

Johns, A.M. (1990) L1 composition theories: Implications for developing theories of L2 composition. In B. Kroll (ed.) *Second Language Writing: Research Insight for the Classroom* (pp. 24–36). Cambridge: Cambridge University Press.

Joseph, J. (2004) *Language and Identity: National, Ethnic, Religious*. Basingstoke: Palgrave Macmillan.

Joyce, J. (1939) *Finnegans Wake*. London: Faber and Faber.

Kang, J.Y. (2005) Written narratives as an index of L2 competence in Korean EFL learners. *Journal of Second Language Writing* 14, 259–279.

Kinginger, C. (2004) Alice doesn't live here anymore: Foreign language learning and identity reconstruction. In A. Pavlenko and A. Blackledge (eds) *Negotiation of Identities in Multilingual Contexts* (pp. 219–242). Clevedon: Multilingual Matters.

Kubota, R. and Lehner, A. (2004) Toward critical contrastive rhetoric. *Journal of Second Language Writing* 13, 7–27.

Kumaravadivelu, B. (2003) Critical language pedagogy: A postmethod perspective on English language teaching. *World Englishes* 22 (4), 539–550.

Lamb, M. (2002) Explaining successful language learning in difficult circumstances. *Prospect* 17 (2), 35–52.

Lamb, M. (2004) Integrative motivation in a globalizing world. *System* 32, 3–19.

Lamb, M. (2007) The impact of school on EFL learning motivation: An Indonesian case study. *TESOL Quarterly* 41 (4), 757–780.

Lamb, M. (2009) Situating the L2 self: Two Indonesian school learners of English. In Z. Dörnyei and E. Ushioda (eds) *Motivation, Language Identity and the L2 Self* (pp. 229–247). Bristol: Multilingual Matters.

Lantolf, J.P. (ed.) (2000) *Sociocultural Theory and Second Language Learning*. Oxford: Oxford University Press.

Lantolf, J.P. and Thorne, S.L. (2006) *Sociocultural Theory and the Genesis of Second Language Development*. Oxford: Oxford University Press.

Latif, M.M.A. (2009) Toward a new process-based indicator for measuring writing fluency: Evidence from L2 writers' think-aloud protocols. *The Canadian Modern Language Review* 65 (4), 531–558.

Lave, J. and Wenger, E. (1991) *Situated Learning: Legitimate Peripheral Participation*. Cambridge: University of Cambridge Press.

Le Ha, P. (2009) Strategic, passionate, but academic: Am I allowed in my writing? *Journal of English for Academic Purposes* 8 (2), 134–146.

Leki, I. (2001) 'A narrow thinking system': Nonnative-English-speaking students in group projects across the curriculum. *TESOL Quarterly* 35 (1), 39–67.

Li, T. and Wharton, S. (2012) Metadiscourse repertoire of L1 Mandarin undergraduates writing in English: A cross-contextual, cross-disciplinary study. *Journal of English for Academic Purposes* 11, 345–356.

Light, G. (2002) From the personal to the public: Conceptions of creative writing in higher education. *Higher Education* 43, 257–276.

Littlewood, W. (1996) Academic writing in intercultural contexts: Integrating conventions and personal voice. *Hong Kong Journal of Applied Linguistics* 1, 1–18.

Lyons, Z. (2009) Imagined identity and the L2 self in the French foreign legion. In Z. Dörnyei and E. Ushioda (eds) *Motivation, Language Identity and the L2 Self* (pp. 248–273). Bristol: Multilingual Matters.

MacIntyre, P.D., Mackinnon, S.P. and Clément, R. (2009) The baby, the bathwater, and the future of language learning motivation research. In Z. Dörnyei and E. Ushioda (eds) *Motivation, Language Identity and the L2 Self* (pp. 43–65). Bristol: Multilingual Matters.

Maguire, M.H. and Graves, B. (2001) Speaking personalities in primary school children's L2 writing. *TESOL Quarterly* 35 (4), 561–593.

Maley, A. (2009) Creative writing for language learners (and teachers). *Teaching English*. British Council. See http://www.teachingenglish.org.uk/articles/creative-writing-language-learners-teachers (accessed 3 September 2011).

Maley, A. (2012) Creative writing for students and teachers. *Humanising Language Teaching* 14 (3). See http://www.hltmag.co.uk/jun12/mart01.htm (accessed 10 January 2013).

Maley, A. and Duff, A. (1994) *The Inward Ear: Poetry in the Language Classroom*. Cambridge: Cambridge University Press.

Maley, A. and Duff, A. (2005) *Drama Techniques: A Resource Book of Communication Activities for Language Teachers*. Cambridge: Cambridge University Press.

Maley, A. and Moulding. S. (1985) *Poem into Poem*. Cambridge: Cambridge University Press.

Maley, A. and Mukundan, J. (eds) (2011a) *Asian Short Stories for Young Readers*. Petaling Jaya: Pearson Malaysia.

Maley, A. and Mukundan, J. (eds) (2011b) *Asian Poems for Young Readers*. Petaling Jaya: Pearson Malaysia.

Mason, D. (2010) Review of the book *Poetry as Research: Exploring Second Language Poetry Writing* by D.I. Hanauer. *System* 38 (4), 645–647.

Matsuda, P.K. (2001) Voice in Japanese written discourse: Implication for second language writing. *Journal of Second Language Writing* 10, 35–53.

Matsuda, P.K. (2003) Process and post-process: A discursive history. *Journal of Second Language Writing, 12*, 65-83.

Matsuda, P.K., Canagarajah, A.S., Harklau, L., Hyland, K. and Warschauer, M. (2003) Changing currents in second language writing research: A colloquium. *Journal of Second Language Writing* 12, 151–179.

McCaslin, M. (2009) Co-regulation of student motivation and emergent identity. *Educational Psychologist* 44 (2), 137–146.

Mckinlay, A. and Dunnett, A. (1998) How gun-owners accomplish being deadly average. In C. Antaki and S. Widdicombe (eds) *Identities in Talk* (pp. 34–51). London: Sage Publications.

McRae, J. (1991) *literature with a Small 'l'*. London: Macmillan.

Menard-Warwick, J. (2006) 'The thing about work': Gendered narratives of a transnational, trilingual Mexicano. *The International Journal of Bilingual Education and Bilingualism* 9 (3), 359–373.

de Milliano, I., van Gelderen, A. and Sleegers, P. (2012) Patterns of cognitive self-regulation of adolescent struggling writers. *Written Communication* 29 (3), 303–325.

Moore, J.N. (2002) The landscape of divorce: When worlds collide (review of the book *Waiting*, H. Jin). *English Journal* 92 (2), 124–127.

Mori, S. and Gobel, P. (2006) Motivation and gender in the Japanese EFL classroom. *System* 34, 194–210.

Morita, N. (2004) Negotiating participation and identity in second language academic communities. *TESOL Quarterly* 38 (4), 573–603.

Morley, D. (2007) *The Cambridge Introduction to Creative Writing*. Cambridge: Cambridge University Press.

Morley, D. (2012) Serious play: Creative writing and science. Cambridge: Cambridge University Press. In D. Morley and P. Neilsen (eds) *The Cambridge Companion to Creative Writing* (pp. 153–170). London: Sage Publications.

Mukundan, J. (ed.) (2006) *Creative Writing in EFL/ESL Classrooms II*. Petaling Jaya: Pearson Longman Malaysia.

Nesi, H. and Gardner, S. (2005) Variation in disciplinary culture: university tutors' views on assessed writing tasks. In P. Rea-Dickens, H. Woodfield, G. Clibbon and R. Kiely (eds) *Language, Culture and Identity in Applied Linguistics: Selected Papers from the Annual Meeting of the British Association for Applied Linguistics* (pp. 99–118). Sheffield: Equinox.

Norton, B. (1995) Social identity, investment, and language learning. *TESOL Quarterly* 29 (1), 9–31.

Norton, B. (1997) Language, identity, and the ownership of English. *TESOL Quarterly* 31 (3), 409–429.

Norton, B. (2000) *Identity and Language Learning: Gender, Ethnicity, and Educational Change*. Essex: Longman.

Norton, B. (2001) Non-participation, imagined communities and the language classroom. In M.P. Breen (ed.) *Learner Contributions to Language Learning: New Directions in Research* (pp. 159–171). Harlow: Longman.

Norton, B. and Toohey, K. (2001) Changing perspectives on good language learners. *TESOL Quarterly* 35 (2), 307–322.

Norton, B. and Gao, Y.H. (2008) Identity, investment, and Chinese learners of English. *Journal of Asia Pacific Communication* 19, 1–8.

Okamura, A. and Shaw, P. (2000) Lexical phrases, culture, and subculture in transactional letter writing. *English for Specific Purposes* 19 (1), 1–15.

Omoniyi, T. (2006) Hierarchy of identities. In T. Omoniyi and G. White (eds) *Sociolinguistics of Identity* (pp. 11–33). London: Continuum.

Omoniyi, T. (2010) Writing in Englishes. In A. Kirkpatrick (ed.) *Routledge Handbook of World Englishes*. London: Routledge.

Omoniyi, T. and White, G. (2006) Introduction. In T. Omoniyi and G. White (eds), *Sociolinguistics of Identity* (pp. 1–8). London: Continuum.

Ouellette, M.A. (2008) Weaving strands of writer identity: Self as author and the NNES 'plagiarist'. *Journal of Second Language Writing* 17, 255–273.

Pavlenko, A. (2004) 'The making of an American': Negotiation of identities at the turn of the Twentieth Century. In A. Pavlenko and A. Blackledge (eds) *Negotiation of Identities in Multilingual Contexts* (pp. 34–67) Clevedon: Multilingual Matters.

Pavlenko, A. (2006) *Emotions and Multilingualism*. Cambridge: Cambridge University Press.

Pavlenko, A. (2008) Emotion and emotion-laden words in the bilingual lexicon. *Bilingualism: Language and Cognition* 11 (2), 147–164.

Pavlenko, A. (2008) Bilingual bliss, bilingual blues: Reflections by and about bilingual writers. (Review of the books *Translating One's Self: Language and Selfhood in Cross-Cultural Autobiography* by M. Besemerse; *Tongue Ties: Logo-Eroticism in Anglo-Hispanic Literature* by G.P. Firmat; *Bilingual Games: Some Literary Investigations* ed. D. Sommer; *Exile, Language, and Identity* ed. M. Stroińska and V. Cecchetto; *Lives in Translation: Bilingual Writers on Identity and Creativity* ed. I. De Courtivron; *Switching Languages: Translingual Writers Reflect on their Craft* ed. S. Kellman; and *The Genius of language: Fifteen Writers Reflect on their Mother Tongue*s ed. W. Lesser.) *International Journal of Bilingual Education and Bilingualism* 8 (4), 345–352.

Pavlenko, A. (ed.) (2011) *Thinking and Speaking in Two Languages*. Bristol: Multilingual Matters.

Pavlenko, A. and Blackledge, A. (eds) (2004) *Negotiation of Identities in Multilingual Contexts*. Clevedon: Multilingual Matters.

Pavlenko, A. and Blackledge, A. (2004) Introduction: New theoretical approaches to the study of negotiation of identities in multilingual contexts. In A. Pavlenko and

A. Blackledge (eds) *Negotiation of Identities in Multilingual Contexts* (pp. 1–33). Clevedon: Multilingual Matters.

Pavlenko, A. and Lantolf, J.P. (2000) Second language learning as participation and the (re)construction of selves. In J.P. Lantolf (ed.) *Sociocultural Theory and Second Language Learning* (pp.155–177). Oxford: Oxford University Press.

Peary, A. (2013) Spectators at their own future: Creative writing assignments in the disciplines and the fostering of critical thinking. *The WAC Journal* 23, 65–81.

Peyton, J.K. and Reed, L. (1990) *Dialogue Journal Writing with Nonnative English Speakers: A Handbook for Teachers*. Alexandria, VA: TESOL.

Piller, I. (2002) *Bilingual Couples Talk: The Discursive Construction of Hybridity*. Amsterdam: Benjamins.

Pousada, A. (1994) The multilingualism of Joseph Conrad. *English Studies* 75 (4), 335–349.

Prior, P. (2001) Voices in text, mind, and society: Sociohistoric accounts of discourse acquisition and use. *Journal of Second Language Writing* 10, 55–81.

Prior, P. (2006) A sociocultural theory of writing. In C.A. Macarthur, S. Graham and J. Fitzgerald (eds) *Handbook of Writing Research* (pp. 54–66). New York: The Guilford Press.

Quinlan, T., Loncke, M., Leijten, M. and Waes, L.V. (2012) Coordinating the cognitive processes of writing: The role of the monitor. *Written Communication* 29 (3), 345–368.

Reay, D. (2004) 'It's all becoming a habitus': Beyond the habitual use of habitus in educational research. *British Journal of Sociology of Education* 25 (4), 431–444.

Rijlaarsdam, G. and van den Bergh, H. (2006) Writing process theory: A functional dynamic approach. In C.A. Macarthur, S. Graham and J. Fitzgerald (eds) *Handbook of Writing Research* (pp. 41–53). New York: The Guilford Press.

Roca de Larios, J., Murphy, L. and Manchón, R.M. (1999) The use of restructuring strategies in EFL writing: A study of Spanish learners of English as a foreign language. *Journal of Second Language Writing*, 8 (1), 13–44.

Roebuck, R. (2000) Subjects speak out: How learners position themselves in a psycholinguistic task. In J.P. Lantolf (ed.) *Sociocultural Theory and Second Language Learning* (pp. 79–95). Oxford: Oxford University Press.

Rosenbaum, S.P. (ed.) (1994) *The Ambassadors: An Authoritative Text, The Author on the Novel, Criticism*. New York: W.W. Norton and Company.

Ros i Solé, C. (2004) Autobiographical accounts of L2 identity construction in Chicano literature. *Language and Intercultural Communication* 4 (4), 229–241.

Rubio, F. (ed.) (2007) *Self-Esteem and Foreign Language Learning*. Newcastle: Cambridge Scholars Publishing.

Santos, T. (1992) Ideology in composition: L1 and ESL. *Journal of Second Language Writing* 1 (1), 1–15.

Sasaki, M. (2000) Toward an empirical model of EFL writing processes: An exploratory study. *Journal of Second Language Writing* 9 (3), 259–291.

Sasaki, M. (2004) A multiple-data analysis of the 3.5-year development of EFL student writers. *Language Learning* 54 (3), 525–582.

Schultz, K. (2006) Qualitative research on writing. In C.A. Macarthur, S. Graham and J. Fitzgerald (eds) *Handbook of Writing Research* (pp. 357–373). New York: The Guilford Press.

Scollon, R., Tsang, W.K., Li, D., Yung, V. and Jones, R. (1998) Voice, appropriation and discourse representation in a student writing task. *Linguistics and Education* 9 (3), 227–250.

Severino, C., Gilchrist, M. and Rainey, E. (2010) Second language writers reinventing identities through creative work and performance. In M. Cox, J. Jordan, C.

Ortmeier-HooperandG.G.Schwartz(eds)*ReinventingIdentitiesinSecondLanguageWriting* (pp. 174–194). Urbana: NCTE Press.

Sharon, M. (2013) Investigating the reading-to-write processes and source use of L2 post-graduate students in real-life academic tasks: An exploratory study. *Journal of English for Academic Purposes* 12 (2), 136–147.

Shedivy, S.L. (2004) Factors that lead some students to continue the study of foreign language past the usual 2 years in high school. *System* 32, 103–119.

Sheldon, E. (2011) Rhetorical differences in RA introductions written by English L1 and L2 and Castilian Spanish L1 writers. *Journal of English for Academic Purposes* 10, 238–251.

Sherry, N. (1972) *Conrad and His World.* London: Routledge.

Skinner, E.N. and Hagood, M.C. (2008) Developing literate identities with English language learners through digital storytelling. *Reading Matrix* 8 (2), 12–38.

Smagorinsky, P. (1994) Think-aloud protocol analysis: Beyond the black box. In P. Smagorinsky (ed.) *Speaking about Writing: Reflections on Research Methodology.* London: Sage Publications.

Sommer, D. (ed.) (2003) *Bilingual Games: Some Literary Investigations.* New York: Palgrave Macmillan.

Spinks, L. (2009) *James Joyce: A Critical Guide.* Edinburgh: Edinburgh University Press.

Stapleton, P. (2002) Critiquing voice as a viable pedagogical tool in L2 writing: Returning the spotlight to ideas. *Journal of Second Language Writing* 11, 179–190.

Starks, D. (2006) The changing roles of language and identity in the New Zealand Niuean community: Findings from the Pasifika languages of Manukau Project. *International Journal of Bilingual Education and Bilingualism* 9 (3), 374–391.

Swain, M. and Lapkin, S. (1995) Problems in output and the cognitive processes they generate: A step towards second language learning. *Applied Linguistics* 16 (3), 371–391.

Taguchi, T., Magid, M. and Papi, M. (2009) The L2 Motivational Self System among Japanese, Chinese and Iranian learners of English: A comparative study. In Z. Dörnyei and E. Ushioda (eds) *Motivation, Language Identity and the L2 Self* (pp. 66–97). Bristol: Multilingual Matters.

Tannen, D. (1984) Spoken and written narrative in English and Greek. In D. Tannen (ed.) *Coherence in Spoken and Written Discourse* (pp. 21–41). Norwood, NJ: Ablex Publishing Corporation.

Tang, R., and John, S. (1999) The 'I' in identity: Exploring writer identity in student academic writing through the first person pronoun. *English for Specific Purposes* 18, 23–39.

Tarnopolsky, O. (2005) Creative EFL writing as a means of intensifying English writing skill acquisition: A Ukrainian experience. *TESL Canada Journal* 23 (1), 76–88.

Taylor, S.J., and Bogdan, R. (1998) *Introduction to Qualitative Research Methods.* New York: John Wiley.

Teaching English – British Council and BBC. The British Council, BBC World Service. See http://www.teachingenglish.org.uk/ (accessed 10 April 2013).

Tickoo, A. (2001) How to create a crisis: Empowering the ESL writer with lessons from narrative art. *International Journal of Applied Linguistics* 11 (1), 21–36.

Tin, T.B. (ed.) (2004) *Creative Writing in EFL/ESL Classrooms.* Serdang: Universiti Putura Malaysia Press.

Tin. T.B. (2007) A report on a collaborative creative writing endeavour: Spreading the spirit of creativity through creative writing workshops in the Asia-Pacific region. *Humanising Language Teaching* 9 (2). See http://www.hltmag.co.uk/mar07/mart05.htm (accessed 10 January 2013).

Tin, T.B. (2011) Language creativity and co-emergence of form and meaning in creative writing tasks. *Applied Linguistics* 32 (2), 215–235.

Tin, T.B. (2012) Freedom, constraints and creativity in language learning tasks: New task features. *Journal of Innovation in Language Learning and Teaching* 6 (2), 177–186.

Toohey, K. (1996) Learning English as a second language in kindergarten: A community of practice perspective. *The Canadian Modern Language Review* 52, 549–576.

Toohey, K. (1998) 'Breaking them up, taking them away': Constructing ESL students in Grade 1. *TESOL Quarterly* 32, 61–84.

Toohey, K. (2000) *Learning English at School: Identity, Social Relations and Classroom Practice.* Clevedon: Multilingual Matters.

Tsou, W., Wang, W. and Tzeng, Y. (2006) Applying a multimedia storytelling website in foreign language learning. *Computers and Education* 47 (1), 17–28.

Urciuoli, B. (1995) The indexical structure of visibility. In B. Farnell (ed.) *Human Action Signs in Cultural Context: The Visible and the Invisible in Movement and Dance* (pp. 189–215). Metuchen, NJ: The Scarecrow Press.

Ushioda, E. (2006) Language motivation in a reconfigured Europe: Access, identity, autonomy. *Journal of Multilingual and Multicultural Development* 27 (2), 148–161.

Ushioda, E. (2008) Using I-statement analysis to explore autonomy and change. See http://echinauk.org/cases2/cute2/researcha.htm (accessed 27 November 2009).

Ushioda, E. (2009) A person-in-context relational view of emergent motivation, self and identity. In Z. Dörnyei and E. Ushioda (eds) *Motivation, Language Identity and the L2 Self* (pp. 215–228). Bristol: Multilingual Matters.

Uzawa, K. (1996) Second language learners' processes of L1 writing, L2 writing and translation from L1 to L2. *Journal of Second Language Writing* 5 (3), 271–294.

Vanett, L. and Jurich, D. (1990) The missing link: Connecting journal writing to academic writing. In J.K. Peyton (ed.) *Students and Teachers Writing Together: Perspectives on Journal Writing* (pp. 21–33). Alexandria, VA: TESOL.

Vasudevan, L., Schultz, K. and Bateman, J. (2010) Rethinking composing in a digital age: Authoring literate identities through multimodal storytelling. *Written Communication* 27 (4), 442–468.

Wang, L. (2003) Switching to first language among writers with differing second-language proficiency. *Journal of Second Language Writing* 12, 347–375.

Wang, W. and Wen, Q. (2002) L1 use in the L2 composing process: An exploratory study of 16 Chinese EFL writers. *Journal of Second Language Writing* 11, 225–246.

Warden, C.A. and Lin, H.J. (2000) Existence of integrative motivation in an Asian EFL setting. *Foreign Language Annals* 33 (5), 535–547.

Weedon, C. (1987) *Feminist Practice and Poststructuralist Theory.* London: Blackwell.

Wei, Y.C. (2011) *Understanding Students' Learner Autonomy through Practitioner Research.* Unpublished PhD thesis, CAL, University of Warwick.

Wenger, E. (1998) *Communities of Practice: Learning, Meaning, and Identity.* Cambridge: Cambridge University Press.

Wertsch, J.V. (1995) Sociocultural research in the copyright age. *Culture and Psychology* I, 81–102.

Widdicombe, S. (1998) Identity as an Analysts' and a Participants' Resource. In C. Antaki and S. Widdicombe (eds) *Identities in Talk* (pp. 191–217). London: Sage Publications.

Williams, M. and Burden, R. (1997) *Psychology for Language Teachers.* Cambridge: Cambridge University Press.

Williams-Whitney, D., Mio, J.S. and Whitney, P. (1992) Metaphor production in creative writing. *Journal of Psycholinguistic Research* 21 (6), 497–509.

Witte, S.P. (1987) Pre-text and composing. *College Composition and Communication* 38, 397–425.

Wolf, A.J.E. (2006) *Subjectivity in a Second Language: Conveying the Expression of Self.* Bern: Peter Lang.

Yang, A. and Lau, L. (2003) Student attitudes to the learning of English at the secondary and tertiary level. *System* 31, 107–123.

Yi, Y. (2007) Engaging literary: A biliterate student's composing practices beyond school. *Journal of Second Language Writing* 16, 23–39.

Yi, Y. (2010) Adolescent multilingual writers' transitions across in- and out-of-school writing contexts. *Journal of Second Language Writing* 19 (1), 17–32.

Zhao, Y. (2006) Total freedom or a certain control? The effect of different stimuli on the processes and products of three advanced L2 learners' short story writing experience. Unpublished MA dissertation, CAL (formerly CELTE), University of Warwick.

Zuengler, J. and Miller, E.R. (2006) Cognitive and sociocultural perspectives: Two parallel SLA worlds? *TESOL Quarterly* 40 (1), 35–58.

Index